Every effort has been made to produce this book sustainably.
The text and images have been printed on FSC-certified paper stocks using soy-based inks.
For further information on FSC Australia, please visit: www.fscaustralia.org

Australia's Best Eco-friendly Holidays

EXPLORE AUSTRALIA

Australia's Best Eco-friendly Holidays

Ken Eastwood

Contents

Photographic
Safari

Map of Australia

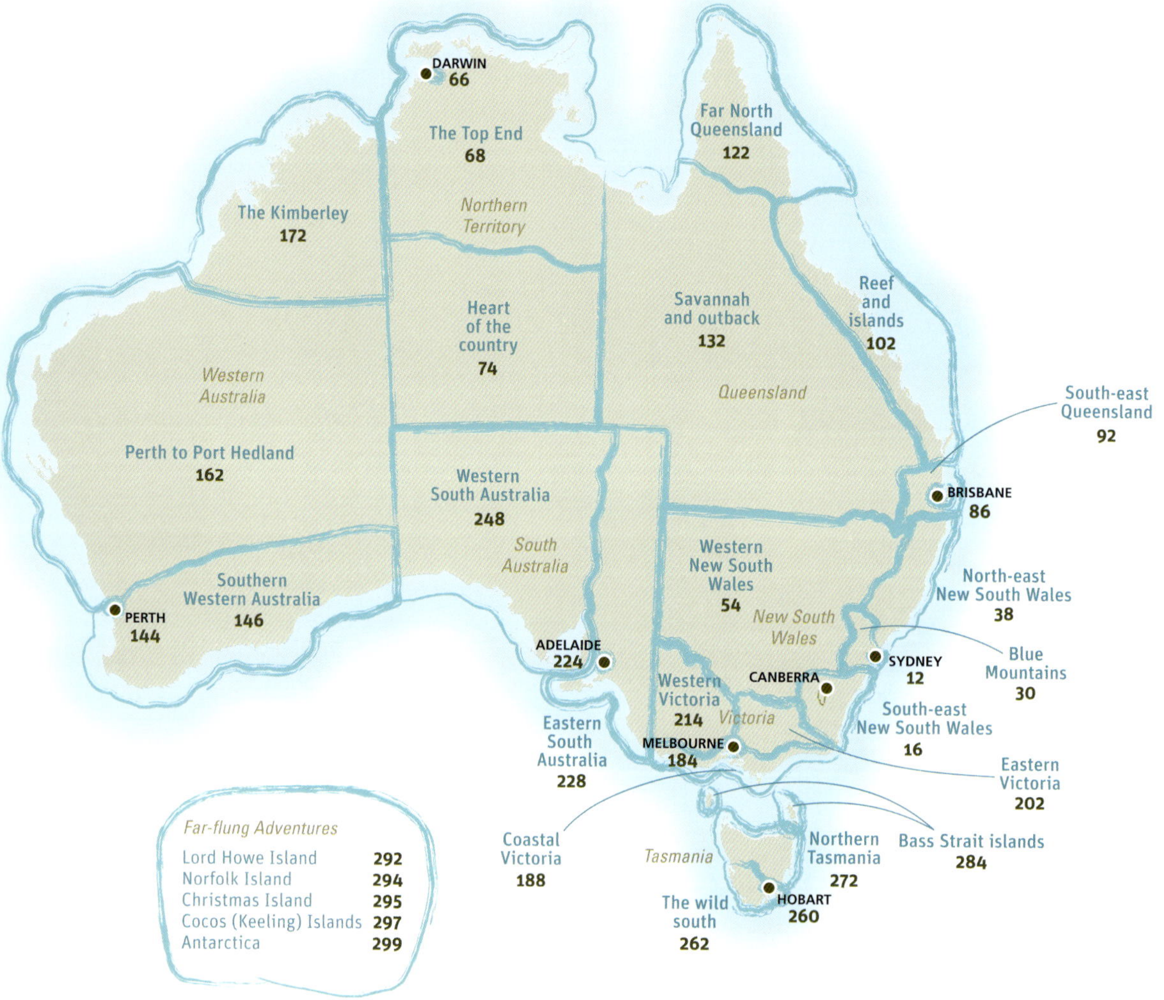

Close encounter with a sea-lion in Jurien Bay Marine Park north of Perth, Western Australia

Boardwalk in Cradle Mountain–Lake St Clair National Park, Tasmania

GREEN MEANS GO!

While our increasingly frantic world shows signs of panic as social and environmental problems escalate, a growing movement has been faithfully taking us back to the experiences that renew, replenish and revitalise: intimate encounters with wildlife, tranquil moments in the bush, and connections with our nation's rich Indigenous heritage. And it is doing it in a way that leaves the lightest possible touch on the landscape so that those who come after us will barely know where we have been.

Modern ecotourism promises escape from the artificial existence of concrete structures and crushing commitments, to a world where the trees whisper solace to your soul, snow-fed mountain streams wash away the stain of city living, the stars seem brighter and the food tastes real again. It is where broken bonds are healed and mended – those with our environment, our partners and our very selves.

Ecotourism – in all its varied forms – offers a break from the everyday, and an encounter to cherish. It can change who we are, and shape who we will be in the future. And it reminds us, once again, of our love for this land and its fragile beauty.

This is ecotourism at its best.

For the sceptics

'There's no such thing as ecotourism. It's all just marketing', was the first of many negative comments I encountered when I embarked on researching this guidebook to ecotourism in Australia. The word 'eco' has been hijacked and tortured so much that it is now the equivalent of the overused food-speak 'lite'.

Confusion reigns. 'Eco' is used by some just to indicate they are in a nice place – a so-called 'eco lodge' might be located on a beach or in a rainforest, but may not be directly contributing to conservation in any way. A morning cruise might call itself 'eco' if it has a reasonable chance of seeing wildlife, such as dolphins, whether or not there are any efforts to minimise the environmental impact of the tourists on board. Some hotels and motels describe themselves as 'eco' because they recycle their garbage and put out a card advising people to reuse their towels.

It is no wonder then that there is now wide cynicism about ecotourism. And that is a huge shame because this book is packed with hundreds of tourism operators across Australia who are serious about conserving the environment they work in and operating with minimal impact, while providing tourists with some of the most exceptional experiences in the country. These are operators who, like the small creatures they protect, nestle snuggly into the Australian soil and deserve to be cherished and supported.

We cannot deny that wherever humans are introduced to an environment, they have an impact. Even something as seemingly benign as bushwalking has far-reaching repercussions: tracks have to be maintained – often by crews in trucks or flown in by helicopter – and the effect of hundreds of walkers leads to erosion, weed invasion and changed water flow. However, interactions with our natural world restore our sanity and put our crazed modern lives into perspective: it is through breathing in the Tasmanian forests that we really understand their importance as a carbon sink and our need to cut down use of precious resources; it is through rescuing turtles ensnared by fishing nets that we increase our passion for promoting sustainable fishing practices; and it is simply through watching the rich birdlife in the local national park on a picnic that we make the real connection with putting in a frog pond or planting appropriate native shrubs and trees in our own gardens.

Tourism, done well, can be a great thing for the environment. The Great Barrier Reef generates more than a billion dollars every year from tourism, in a far more sustainable way than if we chose to mine it or fish it out (although both these practices have been done to some extent). Tourism can help communities see the financial value of their local natural environment, thereby encouraging them to set about nurturing and supporting it. In remote rural and Indigenous communities, in particular, tourism can provide some much needed cash.

Within the pages of this book you will find tourism experiences where you can have a direct positive impact on the environment, just by going there. Some operators have primarily set about conserving and preserving their area, using sustainable tourism to help pay for the conservation work. In other places you will be encouraged to contribute to conservation schemes, with time, money or planting a tree before you leave.

It would be extremely naive to suggest this is a book of 'perfect' tourism operators. None of them are. Most readily admit that they could do more for the environment, and many have plans to improve their sustainability. Instead, this is a book about options. It is the most comprehensive compendium ever compiled on this topic, with hundreds of entries. But it does not have absolutely everything. Apart from the rapidly growing nature of ecotourism in Australia, it would be physically impossible to list absolutely every ecotourism option – a description of national parks alone would be a large volume in itself. Instead, it is a tool to provide you with the best ecotourism options in a range of areas – for consideration when dreaming about or planning and embarking on your next holiday. And hopefully it will inspire you to find more options as you explore the myriad possibilities.

What is ecotourism?

Smelly composting toilets, dark dingy bunk accommodation and cold showers. That is the impression some people have of ecotourism. Yet ecotourism in Australia today comes in a spectacular variety of forms, from ultra-luxurious, $2000-a-night places with massages, spas and top-quality wine, through to free camping sites by isolated beaches. Whatever your budget, you can now find sensational ecotourism experiences in this country.

So if it is not being shown around a forest by a hippy in hemp sandals, what exactly is ecotourism? Mexican environmentalist Héctor Ceballos-Lascuráin was probably the first person to have used the term, in 1983. He defined it as:

> ... that tourism that involves travelling to relatively undisturbed natural areas with the specific object of studying, admiring and enjoying the scenery and its wild plants and animals, as well as any existing cultural aspects (both past and present) found in these areas. Ecotourism implies a scientific, aesthetic or philosophical approach, although the 'ecotourist' is not required to be a professional scientist, artist or philosopher. The main point is that the person who practises ecotourism has the opportunity of immersing him or herself in nature in a way that most people cannot enjoy in their routine, urban existences. This person will eventually acquire an awareness and knowledge of the natural environment, together with its cultural aspects, that will convert him into somebody keenly involved in conservation issues.

More than ten years later, this definition was refined and adopted by the World Conservation Union:

> Ecotourism is environmentally responsible travel and visitation to relatively undisturbed natural areas, in order to enjoy, study and appreciate nature (and any accompanying cultural features – both past and present), that promotes conservation, has low negative visitor impact, and provides for beneficially active socio-economic involvement of local populations.

The Australian non-profit organisation Ecotourism Australia defines ecotourism as 'ecologically sustainable tourism with a primary focus on experiencing natural areas that fosters environmental and cultural understanding, appreciation and conservation'.

All the definitions have common themes and, from these, we can tease apart ecotourism's essence:

- it usually, but not always, involves appreciation and increased understanding of the environment
- it has minimal impact on the environment, particularly compared to alternatives
- it has respect for, and sometimes involvement of, Indigenous peoples.

With these three threads, it becomes easier to weave the picture of ecotourism in Australia today. For example, downhill skiing may involve appreciation of the natural environment, and be great fun to boot, but the large infrastructure and power requirements mean that cross-country skiing is the favoured ecotourism option. A carbon-neutral art gallery might have minimum impact, but would only be considered as ecotourism if its art focused on the environment.

Other notable absences from this definition include fishing and tours on domesticated animals (for example, horse- and camel-riding). Anglers may well argue that fishing can be done in a sustainable manner, but the wildlife carers who spend their days untangling pelicans, turtles and other animals from fishing lines and hooks would disagree that it is the best option.

Hard-core environmentalists might question why some 4WD tour operators are included in this book, as they usually burn fossil fuels, so even if their education about the environment through which they are travelling is superb, and they pick up other people's rubbish along the way, they still have a negative impact. However, try comparing a low-impact, educative tour in a 4WD-only area versus someone who drives around a city all year in their large 4WD, just so that once a year (maybe!) they can take a two-week, four-wheel-driving holiday. It is easy to see which is the better alternative for the environment.

Ecotourism also does not have to involve great effort or expense – it may be as simple as going for a picnic, bike ride or bushwalk in a local park. The simple things are often the best.

Avoid greenwashing

In recent years, almost 70 per cent of international visitors to Australia – some 3.5 million people each year – have participated in 'nature' activities, such as visiting a national park. At the same time, Australians have annually taken nearly 16 million overnight trips that included a nature activity. The World Tourism Organisation and the International Ecotourism Society report that ecotourism is growing at about three times the rate of tourism as a whole. Yet ecotourism is still counted by tourism authorities as a niche market. It is predominantly filled by small, low-impact operators, rather than big players. For example, most accommodation listed in this book is with small operators – those with no more than a handful of cabins or similar.

However, a few larger ecotourism operators have stood the test of time, introducing thousands of visitors to wild beautiful places. Some of these were at the cutting edge of low-impact practices when they were built decades ago, but unfortunately they have not kept up with the best practice in these changing times. As a result, newer places often have far better environmental credentials. As one operator said to me, 'The difficulty of remaining eco and remaining current is that yesterday's initiative is tomorrow's norm'.

This is one of the difficulties in compiling any list of environmental best practice. It would be all too easy to dismiss those operators that have not kept up, even though some set the benchmark for what came later. In many cases, retro-fitting to become more environmentally sustainable is much more expensive than building something from scratch. And it is not necessarily better for the environment to knock something down or throw something away in order to get the 'latest, greatest thing'; usually it is a far better use of resources to continue using what you have until it needs to be replaced.

That is one reason why I am excited by moves on old sheep stations to open up shearer's quarters for tourism. Often it comes from an owner's realisation that the stock numbers previously grazed were unsustainable, and they therefore need to supplement their income by opening up their lands for tourism. By supporting such moves we encourage our hard-working farmers to manage their land in a more appropriate way than overstocking, and it gives us a chance to see part of the country that would otherwise be inaccessible. Sure, shearer's quarters in the scrub are unlikely to be as environmentally friendly as the latest whizz-bang cabins on the South Coast of New South Wales, but in context, they can be a great option for us, and for the environment.

At the opposite end of the spectrum, I think we need to question some of the new ventures that claim to be the latest in 'ecotourism'. For example, does Australia really need another massive treetop walk? And are we comfortable in locking some wild places up totally, and not even allowing tourists in?

One of the methods that can help us determine the authenticity of a tourism operator's 'eco' claims is checking their accreditation and environmental awards. There are more than 180 'eco' accreditation schemes around the world, and a few are used in Australia. The main ones are:

- Ecotourism Australia's 'eco-certification' (www.ecotourism.org.au)
- Green Globe 21 (www.ec3global.com)
- AAA Tourism's 'green star' (www.aaatourism.com.au)
- the relatively new Climate Action Certification (www.sustainabletourismaustralia.com).

Then there are state ecotourism and environmental awards, such as the New South Wales Caravan and Camping Association's Gumnut Awards (www.gumnutawards.com.au).

Once again, none of these schemes is perfect, and there are plenty of great environmentally aware tourism operators in Australia who are not accredited under any scheme and others with dubious credentials who have been accredited. Some small operators used to be accredited, but found the yearly fees too much to justify or the criteria ruled them out. However, accreditation provides a great starting point when comparing tourism operators, as it can show an organisation's commitment to environmental principles.

Responsibletravel.com suggests in the article 'Greenwashing or genuine eco-lodge? 10 ways to tell the difference' that if an organisation does not have its environmental policy written down and publicly available then it probably is not serious about it. It is certainly worth asking an operator whether they have an environmental policy, or questioning them specifically about how they treat water use, power use, the local environment and their waste.

Ecotourism hotspots

While researching this book it became clear that there are certain parts of the country that are 'hotspots' for ecotourism – areas where there is such a focus on the natural environment and the need to protect it that many tourism operators can be considered 'green'. These include Tasmania, Kangaroo Island in South Australia, the Ningaloo Reef coast in Western Australia, the Blue Mountains in New South Wales, the wider Cairns region in Queensland, the High Country in Victoria, and northern New South Wales/southern Queensland. Often such places are intimately connected with World Heritage areas, and they attract people passionate about experiencing, protecting and showing off their treasured region to others.

Ecotourism in these hotspots is generally of a very high standard, and as a result I have been more selective in which operators in these areas I included in this guidebook. If travelling in those regions, you will certainly find other operators with green credentials, and hopefully they will continue to improve.

In other regions – particularly in outback Australia – ecotourism operators are harder to come by, and observant readers will note I have been far more lenient in including operators and activities in those areas. I firmly believe it is important to promote and encourage those operators who are making even a small effort in these places, even if it is not up to the high standards elsewhere in the country. If successful, these forerunners may hopefully spark more ecotourism in their regions.

Tips for sustainable travel

One of the best tips for more sustainable travelling – and hence for ecotourism – is slowing down. Plan longer holidays, with more time at a destination, rather than racing madly between places.

This goes against our recent penchant for 'short-break' holidays, where tourists fly into a location for two or three days, then back to their busy lives. But the modern ecotourist has to take into account the energy and the greenhouse gases that are released every time they travel. Research by

Professor David Simmons at the Sustainable Tourism Cooperative Research Centre (STCRC) has shown that, on average, ecotourists use more transport than other tourists, as they are focused on getting to the next spot, rather than just sitting around a resort pool.

We certainly should not consider this lightly. According to a STCRC paper 'The carbon footprint of Australian tourism', direct carbon emissions from all tourism industries in Australia are estimated at about 10.5 million tonnes each year, 57 per cent of which are from domestic aviation. In addition, private use of motor vehicles for tourism generates an additional 11.1 million tonnes of carbon emissions. International aviation adds an estimated 7.9 million tonnes and indirect emissions for tourism, such as use of electricity, add up to an extra 32 million tonnes. It is a staggering amount of a carbon debt.

To make the most from this negative impact, spend more time on the ground when you get somewhere. Plan to spend a week or more at a location. This has added bonuses: you will feel more relaxed and will absorb much more of the environment you are in, seeing its different moods and discovering more about it. Use local, knowledgeable guides who will teach you something about the area. Eat locally produced food and drink the local wine: it will cut down dramatically on your carbon footprint if you source as much of your food as possible from the region. All the better if you can identify which farmers are carrying out sustainable practices.

Consider your methods of getting to your holiday destination, and how you will get around when you are there. If you are going to a capital city, can you get around on public transport, or by walking or cycling? Travelling in Melbourne by tram, or in Brisbane or Sydney by ferry, may be the best way to see the city. Can you plan to spend at least a few days of any holiday not using a car at all? Have you considered getting to your destination by train? Or going on one of the great train journeys?

If you are travelling by plane, take the extra minute or so to carbon-offset your flights. It usually only costs a few dollars. Bear in mind that when compulsory carbon trading comes in, Australia's carbon-offsetting schemes will change dramatically, but even if offsetting is incorporated into the price of a plane ticket, you can still voluntarily choose to do more.

Car travellers should bear in mind all the usual fuel-saving measures: take the roof racks and the extra weight off the car when you reach your destination. Accelerate slowly, keep your tyre pressures up, and flow with the traffic. Simple measures like these have been shown to increase fuel efficiency by up to a third. The *Green Vehicle Guide* (www.greenvehicleguide.gov.au) has more driving tips.

When hiring a rental car, get the smallest one that can do the job. Rental companies still proudly offer free 'upgrades' to bigger cars, but if you accept and do not need a larger car, both you and the environment end up paying for it at the bowser. Several car-rental companies now have fleets of hybrid vehicles. Avis (13 6333; www.avis.com.au) has them at major airports and capital cities. And if you are going four-wheel driving, check whether you really need the 4WD vehicle for the whole trip. If renting a campervan, get the smallest one suitable, and if possible, one of the newer models with solar power, such as from KEA Campers (1800 252 555; www.keacampers.com).

Plenty of carbon-offsetting company websites will help calculate all your carbon emissions from a trip, including car travel, food, electricity and so on. The price to do so is quite variable, but will still only be a minor expense on your holiday.

Try these carbon offsetters:

- Climate Friendly uses money from carbon offsets to build new renewable energy plants around the world, and supports the World Wildlife Fund; (02) 9356 3600 or 1300 254 628; https://climatefriendly.com
- The Carbon Reduction Institute is involved in renewable energy projects and tree planting; 1300 307 652; http://noco2.rtrk.com.au
- Carbon Neutral undertakes tree planting; 1300 851 211; www.carbonneutral.com.au
- Carbon Zero is a well-respected New Zealand offset company and has an excellent emissions calculator; 64 3 321 9831; www.carbonzero.co.nz

Voluntourism

Finally, one of the biggest ways in which you can contribute directly to the environment while on holiday is by volunteering or doing conservation work. A whole new niche segment of the market, called voluntourism, has sprung up in recent years. Tourists not only come away from a unique experience, but they get to see places that regular tourists do not, and leave knowing they have achieved something positive during their holiday.

- Conservation Volunteers Australia has one of the best Australian programs, with a huge range of trips on offer: weeding remote beaches, planting forests, mammal trapping and penguin monitoring; 1800 032 501; www.conservationvolunteers.com.au
- The non-profit Earthwatch Institute also has some superb expeditions, where you can work alongside scientists monitoring and conserving particular species or habitats; www.earthwatch.org/australia
- In Western Australia, Landscope Expeditions works with the Department of Environment and Conservation in conjunction with the University of Western Australia, to offer a small number of research expeditions. You can take part in wildlife recovery programs, botanical research and animal trapping. The trips are often to remote areas such as the Tanami Desert, Montebello Islands or the Canning Stock Route; (08) 6488 2433; www.dec.wa.gov.au
- Willing Workers on Organic Farms, or woofers, usually stay on one of 1200 organic farms across the country, exchanging their labour for free food and accommodation. In the process they learn about sustainable farming practices such as permaculture; (03) 5155 0218; www.wwoof.com.au

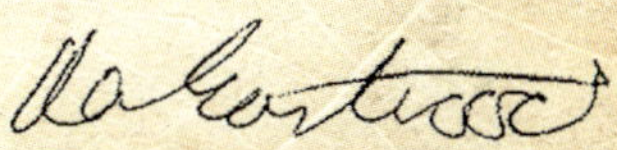

Ken Eastwood

New South Wales

New South Wales and the Australian Capital Territory contain a stunning variety of natural wonders and opportunities for ecotourists. Do not let the spread of the metropolises fool you into thinking that there are no environmentally friendly activities within cooee of Sydney, Wollongong, Newcastle or Canberra – each of these cities has a range of surprising and delightful activities just a stone's throw away, or even within the heart of the cities themselves.

Further afield, from the wild rivers in the north to the mainland's highest mountains in the south, from a coastline of sea cliffs and stunning beaches, over the Great Dividing Range encompassing the World Heritage–listed Blue Mountains and sub-tropical rainforests of the north-east, to an interior with wide open plains, there are caves and canyons to explore, rivers to raft and mountains to climb.

BLUE MOUNTAINS is an ecotourism hotspot. An area of more than 10000 square kilometres in seven national parks has been included on the World Heritage Register, and there are plenty of ways to fill an eco-friendly holiday among the region's plunging cliffs and vast forests.

NORTH-EAST NEW SOUTH WALES includes such iconic coastal areas as the Central Coast, Coffs Coast and Byron Bay. Waterfalls tumble down from the Great Dividing Range and from the beautiful highlands of New England, through rainforested gullies and volcanic formations in the far north of the state.

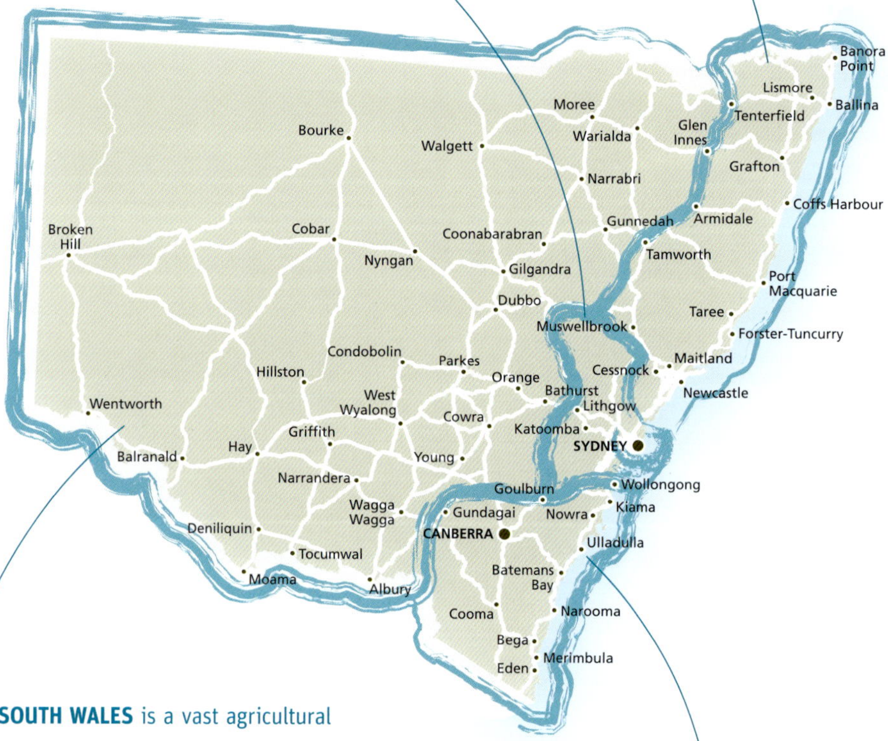

WESTERN NEW SOUTH WALES is a vast agricultural region with unusual eco-friendly holiday options. There are organic farms and produce to enjoy, ancient cultures to grapple with at places such as Mungo National Park, and wild, far-flung natural features in places such as Sturt National Park and the Warrumbungles.

SOUTH-EAST NEW SOUTH WALES contains most of Australia's alpine region, as well as dramatic gorges, peaceful rainforests and isolated coastal spots with excellent diving and snorkelling.

Sydney Visitor centres: 106 George St, The Rocks, Sydney; (02) 9240 8788; Palm Grove, Darling Harbour, (02) 9240 8788; www.sydneyvisitorcentre.com

National Parks and Wildlife Service (NPWS): (02) 9995 5550 or 1300 361 967; www.environment.nsw.gov.au/NationalParks/

Department of Environment and Climate Change (DECC): 59–61 Goulburn St, Sydney; (02) 9995 5000 or 13 1555; environment information (02) 9995 5555; www.environment.nsw.gov.au

TOP TEN

1 Play alongside seals at Montague Island, either snorkelling or scuba diving, then spend the night in the Head Keeper's Quarters and participate in conservation work

2 Go adventure-caving in Jenolan Caves

3 Sleep among the world's animals, while contributing to their conservation, in Western Plains Zoo at Dubbo

4 Admire one of the country's richest rock-art galleries in Mutawintji National Park

5 Dive with the seahorses of Nelson Bay while dolphins pass by

6 Observe nocturnal animals with night-vision goggles on a Vision Walks tour in Nightcap National Park

7 Camp beside the waves and eastern grey kangaroos at Pebbly Beach

8 Explore the wet rainforests of Barrington Tops National Park

9 Don snowshoes and walk from Charlotte Pass to Blue Lake

10 Luxuriate at Emerald Valley Villa in the Byron Bay hinterland

GREEN TRAVEL TIP Many New South Wales national parks are gated and require a day or year pass. If you are likely to visit several national parks in a year, you are best to get the yearly pass. If you are not intending to go to the Snowy Mountains, buy a pass that excludes Kosciuszko National Park, as it will be much cheaper. Many New South Wales national parks hold discovery tours and activities, particularly on weekends and holidays. Details are available at visitor centres, on information boards and on the website (see details opposite page).

Sydney

Despite its population of 4 million, and urban sprawl, Sydney still has extensive intact bushland and a wide variety of wildlife. Possums, frogs, snakes and bandicoots regularly pop into gardens on the urban fringes, and wallabies, echidnas and eastern long-necked turtles are not hard to find deeper in the bush. The city's biggest environmental success story in the past few decades is the cleaning up of its waterways and harbour. There are now excellent options for kayaking, diving and snorkelling within the harbour and along the beaches and beside headlands. Surfing and swimming remain popular year-round activities, although late-winter water temperatures can be as low as 16°C.

WHERE TO STAY

Cockatoo Island

This amazing spot, in the middle of Sydney Harbour, only opened up for public camping in 2008. For around the cost of lunch in one of the nearby expensive hotels, you can enjoy a peaceful spot on the harbour and wake to see the sun rise behind the Harbour Bridge. You can bring all your own camping gear or hire a tent, mattress, chairs and a lantern when you book. There are coin-operated barbecues on which to cook and solar-heated showers. To get there, catch a ferry from Wharf Five at Circular Quay or water taxi. Guided tours of the historic island take place on Sundays.

Camping: (02) 8898 9774; www.cockatooisland.gov.au

Ferry timetable: 13 1500

Tour bookings: (02) 8969 2100

Lane Cove River Tourist Park

Wake to kookaburras, cockatoos and a stroll along the misty Lane Cove River in this eco-certified camping and caravan park tucked into a national park. It is a quiet oasis only

Narrow-leaf drumsticks (Isopogon anethifolius) in Ku-ring-gai Chase National Park

Children enjoying the sights at Lane Cove National Park

Swimmers and surfers at Manly Beach

10 kilometres from the CBD, and offers safe cycling through the park and canoeing and rowing on the river. As well as tent and caravan sites, there is a range of cabins and a pool. The park uses only green power and all profits go back into water harvesting, solar power and bushland regeneration.

Plassey Rd, North Ryde; (02) 9888 9133 or 1300 729 133; www.lanecoverivertouristpark.com.au

WHERE TO EAT

Billy Kwong

This up-market restaurant in Surry Hills claims to have been the first restaurant in New South Wales that chose to become carbon neutral. Owned and run by passionate advocate of sustainability and ethical eating Kylie Kwong, it uses only organic and biodynamic fruit and vegetables, poultry, meat and noodles, and serves fair trade tea, coffee and chocolate. It does not take bookings (except for one table) and there are often queues to be seated.

3/355 Crown St, Surry Hills; (02) 9332 3300; www.kyliekwong.org

Green Gourmet

These totally vegan restaurants have fascinating dishes including mock fish, made from taro, mushroom steaks and desserts such as green tea moon cake.

Green Gourmet: 115-117 King St, Newtown; (02) 9519 7646; and 538 Pacific Hwy, St Leonards; (02) 9439 6533; www.greengourmet.com.au

ACTIVITIES

Bushwalking

Surprisingly, Sydney does offer some superb bushwalking through secluded bushland. Aboriginal engraving and art sites are quite common, and many are not publicised,

Learning to surf at Bondi Beach

simply leaving you to discover them, appreciate them, and leave them alone. In the north of the city, Ku-ring-gai Chase National Park is a must – particularly the river walk from Apple Tree Bay along Cowan Creek, or any of the steep tracks down to the water from West Head Road. In the south, Royal National Park's Coast Track is a 26-kilometre overnight classic, with dramatic cliffs, isolated beaches and pockets of rainforest. Alternatively, for an informative guided day walk and tour of the sights in this park, using public transport from Sydney or a carbon-positive bus ride, try Understand Down Under, which has an admirable environmental policy.

One of the newest long-distance walks in Sydney is the 100-kilometre Great Coastal Walk, from Barrenjoey Headland, at the end of Palm Beach in the north, right through to Cronulla, crossing the Harbour Bridge along the way. It is anticipated that most people would take about seven days to complete the walk, and there is a wide range of accommodation available. The website has maps and plenty of information, including where to buy food and drink.

National parks: www.environment.nsw.gov.au

Understand Down Under: 0448 388 687; www.udu.com.au

Great Coastal Walk: www.walkingcoastalsydney.com.au

Kayaking

Surprisingly, this activity has only taken off in Sydney in the past few years. With a city centred on such great waterways, there is plenty to explore, whether just for an hour or two, or a whole week. Sydney Harbour Kayaks at the Spit Bridge runs a four-hour guided kayak tour through parts of Garigal National Park every Saturday and Sunday morning, and will also hire gear and recommend other great paddles. Bundeena Kayaks at the other end of Sydney, offers tours into Royal National Park, including an unusual Night Owl Kayak Tour, which starts among jumping fish about an hour before sunset.

Sydney Harbour Kayaks: The Spit Bridge, Mosman; (02) 9960 4389; www.sydneyharbourkayaks.com.au

Bundeena Kayaks: Bonnie Vale, Bundeena; (02) 9544 5294 or 0419 254 981; www.bundeenakayaks.com.au

Learn to surf

With mother nature supplying the power, surfing is a great way to experience eco-friendly thrills and spills, and Sydney has plenty of people keen to help you get on your feet. Try Let's Go Surfing, on world-famous Bondi Beach, or the Manly Surf School at various beachside locations (Manly, Collaroy Beach, Long Reef Beach and Palm Beach).

Manly Surf School: (02) 9977 6977; www.manlysurfschool.com

Let's Go Surfing: 128 Ramsgate Ave, North Bondi; (02) 9365 1800; www.letsgosurfing.com.au

Snorkelling and diving

A growing number of Sydneysiders and visitors are discovering the joys of snorkelling in and around the harbour city. There are marine reserves to explore and an ever-changing aquarium of sea creatures. Some of the larger fish that are easy to find include friendly blue groper and the unusual wobbegong sharks and Port Jackson sharks, but seahorses and weedy sea dragons are also surprisingly common in some locations.

Great, safe spots to try snorkelling include the Long Reef Aquatic Reserve, along the swimming nets at Manly Cove and in the narrow Clovelly Bay. On a clear summer's day, another great option is to make a day of the 10-kilometre Spit to Manly walk by carrying a mask and snorkel, and diving in for a swim or two at any of the sheltered coves along the way.

Diving shops abound in Sydney, and all will offer advice and boat-based dives nearly every weekend. Easy shore dives include Gordons Bay, Clifton Gardens and the very popular Cabbage Tree Bay off Shelly Beach. Recommended dive shops include Deep 6 Diving.

Deep 6 Diving: 355 Clovelly Rd, Clovelly; (02) 9665 7427; and 1057 Victoria Rd, West Ryde; (02) 9858 4299; www.deep6diving.com.au

Taronga Zoo

One of the world's best zoos, Taronga is involved in a wide variety of threatened species recovery operations, wildlife rehabilitation and animal research work. As well as having a great day by Sydney Harbour, among a menagerie of animals from Australia and around the world, zoo-goers are encouraged to contribute directly to wildlife programs. You can also stay overnight in luxury tents as part of the Roar & Snore experience.

Bradleys Head Rd, Mosman; (02) 9969 2777; www.zoo.nsw.gov.au

Whale-watching

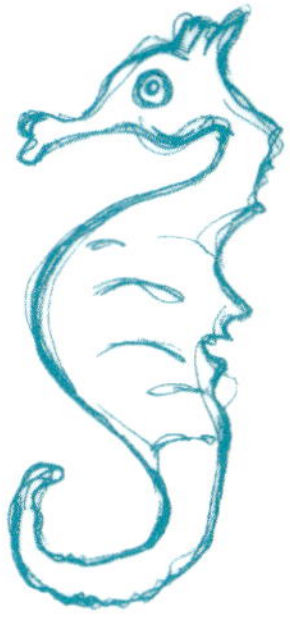

Many Sydneysiders used to travel elsewhere to do their whale-watching, not realising that between May and November, hundreds of the mammals were passing them by. Some now even enter the harbour to pose by the Opera House. You do not need to get in a boat to see them – just keep an eye out from any of the headlands from Palm Beach to Cronulla – but several companies run trips of a few hours from the city. Sydney Eco Whale Watching operates a yacht with small groups of only 20 passengers.

Yacht cruise: (02) 9878 0300 or 0409 125 186; www.austspiritsailingco.com.au

Kayaking near The Spit on Sydney Harbour

South-east New South Wales

This is a region of contrasting landscapes. From the granite boulders on top of the Australian mainland's highest point, the 2228-metre Mount Kosciuszko, mountains seem to roll to the horizon in every direction. In summer, the yellow billy-buttons and white paper daisies pepper the hillsides and persistent drifts of snow glisten in the sun. Kosciuszko, with its rounded form, is not the most dramatic mountain around, but it is still fairly special. Away to the east, over dense tracts of forests in Wadbilliga and Deua national parks, you know the coast is there somewhere, its quiet coves and beaches offering refuges for migrating whales and superb spots for swimming, snorkelling and diving. To the north, there is the little-travelled Brindabella Ranges and linked bike tracks in the Australian Capital Territory.

Swimming at Whiting Beach in Booderee National Park

GREEN TRAVEL TIP Why add to the estimated 400 million disposable cups being thrown out in Australia each year, just because you are on holidays? Cafe owners are usually happy to make you a takeaway coffee in your own mug. It does not take much extra space to throw one or two in the car, and nearly every vehicle has at least a couple of cup-holders.

← *Alpine sunrays* (*Leucochrysum albicans*) *in the Snowy Mountains*

Murrays Beach in Booderee National Park →

Wollongong and surrounds

ACTIVITIES

Birdwatching trip by boat

Being out on a heaving sea all day with a flock of keen birdwatchers could be some people's worst nightmare, but any nature lover should enjoy the experience – at least once anyway. There is the chance to spot a whole range of seabirds that rarely set foot on Australian soil, including the most spectacular giants of them all, the albatrosses. On voyages out to the edge of the continental shelf, 20 nautical miles east of Wollongong, you are also likely to see little penguins swimming past and a marine mammal or two. The Wollongong contingent of the Southern Ocean Seabird Study Association puts volunteer guides on these trips, who will help you spot some birds you have never seen before. The trips are not recommended for children or those prone to seasickness.

(02) 4271 6004; www.sossa-international.org

Safari-tent accommodation at Paperbark Camp

Bushwalking

One of the easiest and most popular walks in the area is the 1.6-kilometre raised boardwalk through the Minnamurra Rainforest in Budderoo National Park, but there are many other more challenging options for keen bushwalkers. Try the 3-kilometre Mount Kembla Summit Walk for great views.

(02) 4887 7270; www.environment.nsw.gov.au

Futureworld Eco-Technology Centre

This smallish museum in Miller Street is definitely worth a look for those interested in the future of sustainable transport, power, water use and other conundrums of modern living. There are hands-on displays.

(02) 4226 9147; www.futureworld.org.au

Kiama to Ulladulla

WHERE TO STAY

Greenpatch Camping Ground

Although it is particularly full in summer school holidays, Greenpatch in Booderee National Park is a top spot, with a beach of dazzling white sand, rockpools to explore, abundant wildlife and great snorkelling.

(02) 4443 0977; www.environment.nsw.gov.au

Paperbark Camp, Huskisson

The 12 luxury safari tents in this eco-certified resort certainly make for a relaxing and pleasant stay. They have solar-powered lighting and the ethos is one of caring for the beautiful surroundings and understanding the local Indigenous culture.

(02) 4441 6066 or 1300 668 167;
www.paperbarkcamp.com.au

ACTIVITIES

Bushwalking

From meanders along isolated beaches and around heath-covered headlands, to long hikes up rugged mountains in Budawang, Morton or Deua national parks, the South Coast provides limitless possibilities for great bushwalking. For an adventurous half-day walk with a great view, scale the cliffs and ladders to the top of the 719-metre Pigeon House Mountain in Budawang National Park. Experienced walkers will find plenty of other great hikes in this area, including the unrelenting ascent of The Castle in Morton National Park, a track that rises 400 metres in just 1 kilometre and finishes with some heart-in-mouth scrambling.

NPWS Morton (and Budawang): (02) 4887 7270
NPWS Narooma (Deua): (02) 4476 0800
www.environment.nsw.gov.au

Cycling

For a pleasant family cycle with young children, hop on the safe and gentle cycling path that winds around Jervis Bay at Huskisson and Vincentia, beside beautiful coastline and some fun playgrounds. A longer bike path heads out to St Georges Basin. Bikes can be rented from Deep 6 Diving at Huskisson.

(02) 4441 5255 or 0413 360 600;
www.deep6divingjervisbay.com.au

Kayaking

Combine the vision of snorkelling with the ease of kayaking in see-through kayaks from Huskisson, on Jervis Bay. Easy to paddle and position over schools of fish, the completely clear kayaks are a novel way for non-swimmers to observe the wildlife in the water below them.

A second operator, the Jervis Bay Kayak Company, as well as hiring sea kayaks for an hour or two, encourages you to kayak to a secluded beach or campsite and stay the night there. You will need your own camping gear, but they will provide everything else, including training if you need it.

Clear kayaks: (02) 4441 8932 or 0418 345 451;
www.canoewithaview.com.au
Kayaking/camping: (02) 4441 7157 or 0418 649 082;
www.jervisbaykayaks.com

Sailing

Imagine. No engines. Just the flapping of a sail and the splash of the waves. The South Coast's tranquil lakes and inlets are ideal for sailing. Jervis Bay Sailing Charters is one of several operators who will take you out.

(02) 4441 8777 or 0402 443 478;
www.jervisbaysailingcharters.com.au

Kayaking at Murrays Beach in Booderee National Park

Snorkelling and diving

There are plenty of places where you can dive or snorkel straight off the beach, seeing a beautiful array of creatures including weedy sea dragons, octopuses, rays and myriad other fish. The many dive shops in the area will be glad to point you in the right direction, offering gear for hire or sale and also a changing program of half- or full-day snorkelling and diving boat trips. Murrays Beach in Booderee National Park at the south end of Jervis Bay is recommended for snorkelling, and Summercloud Bay in the same area offers a shallow shore dive with the chance to see eastern blue devils, cuttlefish and red indianfish.

Whale- and dolphin-watching

Many seaside towns on the South Coast have rightfully decided to champion the passing parade of marine mammals. From May to November there are more two-to-three-hour, whale- and dolphin-watching cruises than you can wave a fin at, with sightings of humpbacks and southern right whales common, and occasional sightings of minkes, orcas, pilots and blue whales. Nearly all cruises operate under strict guidelines to protect the animals, and unethical operators are very rare. At the time of publication, the only fully certified operator with EcoTourism Australia was Dolphin Watch Cruises at Huskisson.

(02) 4441 6311; www.dolphinwatch.com.au

*A resident pod of bottlenose dolphins (*Tursiops truncatus*) in Jervis Bay, sighted from the Dolphin Watch Cruises' boat* Tekin III

Kangaroo Valley

WHERE TO STAY

There are plenty of wildlife-friendly places in the valley, many of which have echidnas, goannas and kangaroos walking past your door. Two that have made special efforts to be more environmentally friendly include Cloud Song and Crystal Creek Meadows. The latter grows citrus trees with all the wastewater, including the sewage, and encourages you to plant a tree on the 6-hectare property to offset your carbon emissions in getting there. They will even pick you up from the train station at Berry or Bowral, so you can leave the car at home.

Cloud Song: (02) 4465 1194;
www.cloudsonginkangaroovalley.com.au
Crystal Creek Meadows: (02) 4465 1406;
www.country-accommodation.com.au

ACTIVITIES

Bushwalking

There are plenty of great walks in and around Kangaroo Valley, from easy strolls to strenuous hikes. Morton National Park with its spectacular Fitzroy Falls is only a short drive away.

Fitzroy Falls Visitor Centre: (02) 4887 7270;
www.environment.nsw.gov.au

Breakfast provisions at Crystal Creek Meadows, Kangaroo Valley

Canoeing and kayaking

One of the best ways to experience this special place is paddling along the Kangaroo and Shoalhaven rivers. You can hire a canoe for an hour or two, or go on an overnight, self-guided paddle downriver. Kangaroo Valley Safaris will help set you up, provide a briefing and maps, camping equipment if you need it, and pick you up at the end of your adventure.

(02) 4465 1502; www.kangaroovalleycanoes.com.au

The Kangaroo Valley Tourist Association is very progressive in developing an eco-friendly tourism climate. This peaceful valley has taken initiatives such as endeavouring to become a carbon-neutral tourist destination, and banned the use of plastic bags. It is a secluded spot for a paddle down the river or a quiet weekend away from the hustle and bustle of the city.

www.kangaroovalleytourist.asn.au

Ulladulla to Eden

WHERE TO STAY

Camping

Throw up a tent beside beaches where kangaroos come to graze, and sleep to the sound of the waves hitting the shore. Great camping is not hard to find in this area, but make sure you include Murramarang National Park's Pretty and Pebbly beaches on your list of possibilities.

www.environment.nsw.gov.au

Lakesea Park, South Durras

This multi-award winning, 6-hectare caravan park holds a Gold Gumnut Award for its environmental stance, particularly in terms of its water usage and wildlife protection.

(02) 4478 6122; www.lakesea.com.au

Montague Island

By far one of the most interesting and intimate wildlife experiences you can have in this region is on and around this 82-hectare island off Narooma. Whales drift past, Australian and

Country-style accommodation at Cloud Song, Kangaroo Valley

Lightstation and Head Keeper's Quarters on Montague Island

New Zealand fur-seals play in the waters, and little penguins and terns nest on the island. You can dive or snorkel with the inquisitive seals, who will often swim right up to you and look you in the mask. Do a barrel roll or a somersault and watch them copy you.

One of the best ways to experience all the island has to offer is on the multi-award-winning Conservation Tours with Conservation Volunteers Australia. One- or two-night tours include staying in the restored Head Keeper's Quarters. As a volunteer, you can choose to participate for a few hours in current projects on the island. This may include penguin monitoring, revegetation work, or getting rid of noxious weeds. Half-day tours and self-guided stays on the island are also available.

Head Keeper's Quarters: 1800 032 501;
info@conservationvolunteers.com.au
Narooma Visitor Centre: 1800 240 003;
www.montagueisland.com.au

ACTIVITIES

Bushwalking

Do not leave your covered shoes at home, because this is another superb bushwalking area. One of the best coastal day walks is from Pretty Beach to the top of the 285-metre Durras Mountain with its 360-degree views. Take your bathers and enjoy a swim or two on the way back. There are plenty of other splendid walks in Ben Boyd and South East Forests national parks, and in Wadbilliga National Park a 2-kilometre stroll leads from the Cascades to a lookout over Tuross Falls.

Cycling

Back Pedal Cycle Tours is an eco-certified tour company that offers a great range of supported, safe and family-friendly cycle tours, from single-day excursions in the Bega Valley, through to the three-day 'Border Freewheel', which goes from Bombala to Orbost in Victoria. Everything is provided, from the bike to the food, and the security and safety of a support vehicle.

(02) 6492 1981; www.backpedaltours.com.au

Indigenous tours

Go on a guided 4WD or walking tour to sacred sites, learning about local Yuin culture, bush tucker and Dreamtime stories associated with the landscape. Umbarra Cultural Centre, near Wallaga Lake (just north of Bermagui), is also home to a museum and visitors are sometimes invited to take part in boomerang- and spear-throwing demonstrations.

(02) 4473 7232; www.umbarra.com.au

Sailing

Batemans Bay Sailing Charters is eco-certified and offers sailing trips out of Batemans Bay on a 12.5-metre catamaran, from a three-hour cruise around the bay to overnight excursions.

(02) 4471 7903; www.baysail.com.au

Snorkelling and diving

It is fairly hard to jump in the water in this region with a mask and not have a great time.

Sailing on the Wandera *with Batemans Bay Sailing Charters*

The many dive shops in the area can point you to the best local spots and also offer boat-based excursions. One of the most surprising and easy dives in the area is around Tathra wharf, where seahorses, blue groper and octopuses hover amid the old pylons. Just look out for the fishing hooks!

Australian Capital Territory

ACTIVITIES

Cycling

The national capital, Canberra, is almost certainly the Australian city best set up for a cycling holiday and there are plenty of well-thought-out bike tracks perfect for winding those pedals and unwinding the mind. In the city itself, there are some 400 kilometres of dedicated bike paths, and the terrain is usually fairly flat. Buses between suburbs and town centres have bike racks, and bike riders can travel on them for free. One of the easiest and most enjoyable family rides is around Lake Burley Griffin. The full ride is about 35 kilometres.

Canberra is also surrounded by pine forests with fire trails through parks, many of which allow or actively encourage mountain-biking. You can hire bikes from about a dozen shops in Canberra, and rates can be dramatically discounted if hiring for more than a few days. The company Row 'n' Ride is one family-friendly hirer that also offers free drop-off and pick-up of bikes from your accommodation.

www.pedalpower.org.au

Bus timetables: www.action.act.gov.au

Row 'n' Ride: (02) 6228 1264 or 0410 547 838; www.realfun.com.au

Hiking and bushwalking

Namadgi National Park covers an area of more than 1000 square kilometres and offers some great hiking in subalpine forests and other areas. A short walk to Yankee Hat is popular and includes several of the park's Aboriginal art sites.

Those used to carrying a pack and craving a different sort of adventure should consider embarking on the 650-kilometre Australian Alps Walking Track. Allow about eight to ten weeks for this route that travels over many of the country's highest peaks before getting to Walhalla in Victoria. Although some sections are well travelled, others are so quiet you will feel that you are the only one who has been there. The route avoids towns, but Thredbo and Hotham Heights are only a few kilometres off the track if you need to re-stock on supplies. Of course, you can plan walks that take in bite-sized sections of this classic.

www.australianalps.deh.gov.au

*A darter (*Anhinga melanogaster*) drying its wings in Tidbinbilla Nature Reserve*

Picnicking

There are many great places to unpack a picnic in the Australian Capital Territory, from the copious native areas in the Australian National Botanic Gardens, to the bird mecca of Jerrabomberra Wetlands on the Molonglo River and the snow-capped peaks of Namadgi National Park.

Tidbinbilla Nature Reserve

Families should not miss this extraordinary reserve, just 40 minutes drive from the centre of Canberra. As well as a great place for a picnic among birds and other wildlife, it contains an innovative playground, 18 bushwalks ranging from 15 minutes to six hours in duration, and a wheelchair-accessible wildlife sanctuary around a wetland. Every weekend the rangers conduct tours where you can see specific wildlife, such as koalas and platypus, and the visitor centre contains a corroboree frog display that gives you your best chance of seeing this extremely endangered little amphibian.

(02) 6205 1233; www.tams.act.gov.au

Snowy Mountains

WHERE TO STAY

Alpine Habitats, near Jindabyne

Opened in 2007, these 18 cleverly designed two-bedroom buildings are linked underground by massive worm farms that digest all the compostable waste on the site. Set amid gnarled black sallees and other snow gums, the buildings have towering floor-to-ceiling windows on the north side as part of their passive heating and cooling systems, but they also have clean-burning fireplaces that run on ethanol or methylated spirits. Rainwater is stored in large tanks, and all power is from renewable sources.

(02) 6457 2228; www.alpinehabitats.com.au

Camping

At Kosciuszko National Park there are plenty of great camping areas inside and around the park, but you will need to be prepared for cold weather at any time of year – it can snow even in summer. Recommended sites include Geehi Flats, with its stunning views of the mountains, flame robins and river gurgling by; and Sawpit Creek for its abundant eastern grey kangaroos and accessibility to the national park.

Snowy Region Visitor Centre: (02) 6450 5600; www.environment.nsw.gov.au

ACTIVITIES

Canoeing

It is certainly not the best spot in the country for canoeing and kayaking, but peaceful days can be had enjoying these activities on Lake Jindabyne, or more exciting adventures are possible on overnight excursions down the Snowy. As with rafting, trips will depend on the amount of water in the rivers.

Mountain Adventure Centre, Jindabyne: 1800 623 459; www.mountainadventurecentre.com.au

Caving

As well as the intricate limestone features of Yarrangobilly Caves, which have both self-guided and guided cave tours suitable for families, there is a beautiful thermal pool where the temperature remains at about 27°C year-round. Watch out for the mosquitoes though when you get out.

The more adventurous with a speleological bent might hike with a torch out to Blue Waterholes to investigate, carefully, some of the sinkholes and caves there.

Cross-country skiing

A delightful winter pastime, cross-country skiing is a mix of walking, gliding and skiing, and the basics are much easier to pick up than those of downhill skiing or snowboarding. You can undertake the activity at virtually any level, from gentle groomed trails through flat terrain, to multi-day overnight trips that lead up and down steep and remote mountains. You can have the thrill of downhill skiing, but without the queues to get on energy-using chairlifts, and the peace of being in the snow away from the crowds. And best of all, both rental of equipment and payment for use of the groomed trails is considerably cheaper than downhill skiing. Take a backpack with some hot soup and tasty treats and head out for a delightful picnic in the snow.

It is best to start with a guide or a lesson or two, and then progress to the well-marked tracks leading out from the resorts. Most resorts offer equipment hire and lessons and Perisher Blue has a well-developed series of groomed cross-country loops that wind through the colourful snow gums. More experienced cross-country skiers head out from Charlotte Pass and Thredbo, and can easily reach Mount Kosciuszko and back in a day. Guided trips will also take you there. Another popular route is catching the oversnow transport to Charlotte Pass from Perisher then skiing back via a cross-country trail.

Environmentally friendly accommodation at Alpine Habitats

Recently, the resurgence of alpine touring bindings has encouraged more exploration of back-country areas by downhill skiers. These bindings act like those on cross-country skis, with a heel-release option allowing you to 'walk' your feet with a locked-in toe and raised heel, but then can be fully locked down, like a downhill ski, for swift, exciting descents of fresh terrain. As back-country navigation and conditions can be difficult and dangerous, any exploration of such areas without a guide should only be done if you are self-sufficient and extremely competent.

The Mountain Adventure Centre near the Snowline Caravan Park at Jindabyne runs guided cross-country ski trips in different areas, including near Adaminaby. A multi-day course based at Charlotte Pass teaches skills for the alpine environment, including cross-country skiing, navigation and camping. The centre also offers back-country snowboarding trips. Wilderness Sports at Jindabyne and Perisher runs back-country trips and cross-country lessons, including to the top of Mount Kosciuszko. Thredbo and Charlotte Pass both offer guided trips to the back country and Selwyn Snowfields has more than 45 kilometres of marked trails nearby.

Perisher Blue: www.perisherblue.com.au
Charlotte Pass: (02) 6457 5245 or 1800 026 369; www.charlottepass.com.au
Thredbo: (02) 6459 4044; www.thredbo.com.au
Mountain Adventure Centre: (02) 6456 2922 or 1800 623 459; www.mountainadventurecentre.com.au
Wilderness Sports: (02) 6456 2966 or (02) 6457 5966; www.wildernesssports.com.au
Selwyn Snowfields: (02) 6454 9488; www.selwynsnow.com.au

Cycling and mountain-biking

The easiest, family-friendly cycling to be had is the 3.5-kilometre concrete path around Lake Jindabyne. Bikes can be hired at several places in Jindabyne, including Sacred Ride. The concrete path links up with 18 kilometres of fire trails and more challenging single-track paths suitable for experienced riders.

As well as hiring bikes, some operators, such as Mountain Adventure Centre, will drop off and pick up mountain bikes at various tracks so you do not have to worry about transporting them. One of the most popular tracks is the 16-kilometre-return fire trail from Charlotte Pass to the foot of Mount Kosciuszko, a fun and relatively easy ride, although if you are going to climb the last 1.3 kilometres to the summit, it is recommended you take a lock, as you must leave your bike at the foot of the mountain. Guided rides, such as along the Snowy River, are also available.

The Tumut State Forest Recreational Trail is another good option for mountain-biking.

If you are looking for a great extended ride, consider a seven-day, fully supported ride from

A snow gum shows off its myriad colours

Cross-country skiing in the Snowy Mountains

Mountain-biking near Thredbo

Mount Kosciuszko down to the sea at Marlo in Victoria, with Back Pedal Tours. It is generally downhill all the way! This eco-certified tour company also provides a range of shorter multi-day rides in the Snowy Mountains.

Sacred Ride: (02) 6456 1988 or 1300 736 581; www.sacredride.com.au

Mountain Adventure Centre: 1800 623 459; www.mountainadventurecentre.com.au

Back Pedal Tours: (02) 6492 1981; www.backpedaltours.com.au

Guided walks

These are often a great way to get to know the area and its natural treasures and dark moods. Guides are generally informative and helpful, and are trained to deal with emergencies and difficult situations if they arise. In winter, particularly, it is advisable to be accompanied by a guide if you are new to hiking above the snowline. Navigation can be difficult as tracks disappear under snow, and a sudden blizzard or whiteout can be disorienting and dangerous.

Guided walks here include everything from snowshoeing excursions in winter, to night-spotlighting strolls among the wallabies, brumbies and wombats around Lake Crackenback.

Kosciuszko Alpine Walks offers a range of guided walks, including an overnight hike to Kosciuszko and through the High Country, where all you take is your day pack. The overnight camping equipment and food is brought in by mountain bike.

Kosciuszko Alpine Walks: (02) 6451 3000 or 1800 020 524; www.lakecrackenback.com.au/walks

Hiking and bushwalking

There is almost no end to the hiking that can be done in the Snowy Mountains. There are hundreds of kilometres of hiking tracks, and infinite ways to wander through the hills. The most popular walks are to the top of Mount Kosciuszko from either Charlotte Pass (18 kilometres return) or Thredbo (13 kilometres return from the top of the chairlift, which is open all year). The Thredbo track is a steel mesh walkway for most of its length to prevent erosion and protect the alpine plants. It makes the path ugly, but the walking easy enough for children. (However, a lot of steps rules out strollers.)

NATURE WATCH Common wombats are exactly that – common – and are found throughout the Snowy Mountains and the south-east. They have the unusual habit of putting their cubic scats, or dung, on as high a point as their bottoms can reach, such as on top of a log or a rock. The scats are a means of communication with other wombats – individuals maintain separate feeding areas – and, placed off the ground, the 'messages' are more likely to remain undisturbed by other animals.

A much more scenic, though slightly longer route is the Main Range Track, which leaves from Charlotte Pass, crosses the Snowy River and heads up past Hedley Tarn and Blue Lake before getting to Kosciuszko. This can be further lengthened into the 22-kilometre Lakes Walk for a strenuous though very rewarding hike, which includes the summit of Mount Carruthers.

Other great walks range from quick strolls such as the 500-metre Snow Gums Boardwalk at Charlotte Pass, through to short walks with great views such as the 5-kilometre Porcupine Track from Perisher, and multi-day backpacking trips, such as the 650-kilometre Australian Alps Walking Track (*see* Australian Capital Territory/ Hiking and bushwalking), the 440-kilometre Hume and Hovell Walking Track from Yass to Albury or sections of the 5330-kilometre Bicentennial Trail. Even if setting out on a warm summer day, hikers should take a windcheater or other warm clothing, as conditions can change quickly.

Hume and Hovell Walking Track: www.lands.nsw.gov.au

Ice-climbing

In winter, the frozen cliffs around Blue Lake provide one of the only places in Australia to learn and perfect the art of ice-climbing. Multi-day courses involve a hike in with heavy packs, and camping out in the national park in very cold conditions, as you learn how to climb with ice-axes and crampons. Very few operators are qualified to teach these skills. Both the following operators are based in Katoomba.

High 'n wild: (02) 4782 6224; www.high-n-wild.com.au

Australian School of Mountaineering: (02) 4782 2014; www.asmguides.com

Camping on the Blue Lake and Kosciuszko Peak Overnight Walk

Platypus-watching

If you believe the hype, Bombala is the platypus capital of Australia and the locals stop just short of guaranteeing you a sighting. The best spot is the Platypus Reserve on the Bombala River (off Delegate Road) in the early morning or late afternoon, but the shy aquatic mammal can be seen at any time of the day in many of the area's creeks and rivers.

Rafting

The main whitewater rafting season is during the snowmelt from September to December, but the drought in recent years and small water releases from the Snowy Hydro Electric Scheme has made most rafting impractical. If the rivers are running, there are suitable trips for all ages, and the following operators offer a variety of day and overnight trips.

Rapid Descents, Khancoban: www.rapiddescents.com.au

Upper Murray White Water Rafting, Cooma: 1800 677 179; www.raftingsnowymountains.com.au

Jindabyne Adventure Bookings: 1300 736 581; www.jab.net.au

Sailing, Lake Jindabyne

Generally only offered November to April, this is a novel way to experience Lake Jindabyne. Tuition and the hire of catamarans and sailboards are available next to the Snowline Caravan Park.

Boat and sailboard hire: (02) 6456 1195

Snowshoeing

Snowshoes offer an easy and fun way to explore the snow and generally prevent you from sinking into it, making walking easier, faster and more comfortable. Snowshoes are light to carry and can be helpful at all times of the year if you are crossing large tracts of snow. Guided options range from a two-hour sunset walk along the ridgeline at Charlotte Pass, looking over the main range, to multi-day guided camping tours through the back country.

Most resorts (*see* contact details at the end of the Cross-country skiing entry, page 26) offer some limited snowshoeing and can recommend tracks for you to explore. The Mountain Adventure Centre (*see* Cross-country skiing, page 26) is a great place to start, and offers one of the best experiences – a day walk from Charlotte Pass, across the Snowy River and out to Blue Lake and back.

Snowy Mountains Touring Company

Based on an unusual concept, this company offers a personal tour guide who can accompany you, in your vehicle, explaining the history, heritage, flora and fauna of the area as you travel. Either you can drive, or they can take care of that too, as well as providing lunch and morning tea. There are fixed tour routes, or you can develop your own, taking in the places you want to see.

Tour details: (02) 6450 5600

A group sets off for some snowshoeing on Mount Kosciuszko

Wiradjuri Wonders Tours, Tumut

This full-day tour, which includes morning tea of johnnycakes with lemon myrtle syrup, and lunch of kangaroo sausages and emu burgers, offers insights into Indigenous history and heritage in the mountains. Taste bush tucker, learn about ceremonies and traditional practices, and hear Dreamtime stories about the land. Book through Elm Cottage, a property near Tumut with three self-contained cottages.

Wiradjuri Wonders: (02) 6947 5818 or (02) 6947 7025; www.visitnsw.com

Tour bookings: www.elmcottage.com.au

Hikers in Kosciuszko National Park

Whitewater rafting near Thredbo

Blue Mountains

The spectacular plunging cliffs and World Heritage listing make the Blue Mountains a hotspot for ecotourism. There are eco architects living in the area who have designed several of the accommodation places, and activities range from some of the best bushwalking in the country, to canyoning, mountain-biking, caving and picnicking. In some circles, the Blue Mountains region is incorrectly seen as a destination only for older people, but it is an absolute gem for ecotourists of all ages. For the purposes of this book, the region extends from north of Mittagong to just north-west of Mudgee.

Rock climbing on Mount York

Kurrajong to Lithgow

WHERE TO STAY

Dargan Springs Mountain Lodge, Clarence

At the soft end of ecotourism, this pleasant lodge and wellness retreat has advanced eco-certification. It is surrounded by a mountain ash forest dotted with waratahs, the habitat of wombats and wallabies. With a maximum of eight couples (no children under 14), no TV, and interaction between the guests, it has an emphasis on quiet relaxation, massage, tai chi, meditation and the option of more active pursuits, from bushwalking to rock climbing. The building has passive solar heating and cooling, and is made from recycled sawdust bricks and plantation cypress pine.

(02) 6355 2939; www.darganspings.com.au

Hatter's Hideout, Bell

Rent your own large cave in thick bush on a 3.2-hectare private reserve that feels miles from anywhere, with solar-powered lights, a composting toilet, barbecue, running water on tap and kitchen facilities. The large overhang sleeps up to 20, and is great for sitting around a fire with a guitar. What is more, part of the deal means that if the weather turns nasty, it is just a 10-minute walk away to a lovely big ramshackle lodge, made with a lot of recycled materials.

(02) 6355 2777; www.hattershideout.com.au

Wollemi Wilderness Cabins, Bilpin

These unusual self-contained cabins of various sizes feature passive solar design and are mainly constructed from recycled and salvaged materials. Although not high-class, they all have a spa and

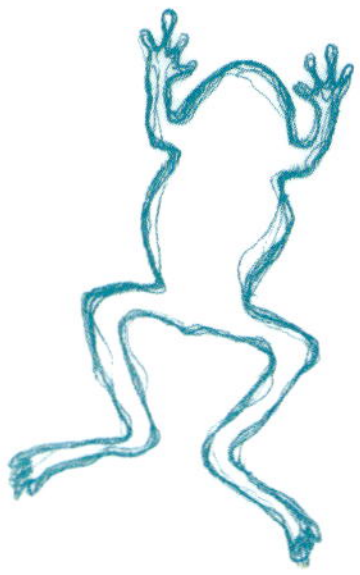

are in isolated bush settings. One has solar power, two have composting toilets, and one has won awards for environmental architecture.

0409 393 425; www.wollemiwilderness.com.au

WHERE TO EAT

Secret Creek Cafe and Restaurant, Lithgow

Hidden away at the foot of the Blue Mountains (it is a secret, after all) is this excellent cafe and restaurant that helps sustain the Australian Ecosystems Foundation, which has a focus on saving habitat and Australian wildlife. During a meal with bushfoods and Australian taste sensations (such as kangaroo eye fillets stuffed with macadamias), you can take a guided night walk of the 5-hectare, feral-proof sanctuary, seeing bounding bettongs, potoroos and the special quoll house, where eastern quolls are being bred for release back into the New South Wales bush. The property has an additional 200 hectares of bush and is involved in planting wildlife corridors in the area.

(02) 6352 1133 or 0408 695 958; www.visitnsw.com
Australian Ecosystems Foundation:
www.ausecosystems.org.au

ACTIVITIES

Canyoning

Canyoning is a combination of bushwalking, swimming, abseiling, li-loing, caving and rock climbing. It involves following a watercourse wherever it goes, particularly into dark and narrow chasms, and as a result can be a dangerous activity, particularly if water levels start rising rapidly. However, it propels participants into some of the most beautiful terrain in the Blue Mountains – deep, smooth-sided canyons that only receive direct light for an hour or so each day, freezing, swirling streams abundant in yabbies and native fish,

The dark and spectacular Claustral Canyon

fern-covered valley floors, and waterfalls spilling out into the sunlight from dark caverns.

There is a wide variety of canyoning in the region – some courses that barely wet your toes and others that are relaxing floats along rivers, while at the more extreme level, some involve difficult multi-pitch abseils down thundering waterfalls. Because of the dangerous nature of this sport, the real potential for hypothermia and the difficulty of navigating, you are strongly advised to start with a guide (*see* details below) or an experienced canyoner.

One of the most pleasant days out for inexperienced canyoners is li-loing down the Wollangambe River near Mount Wilson. It involves a little bit of rock-hopping and a steep walk out at the end of the day, but is a great introduction to the sport. More experienced canyoners head for stunning canyons with dark and difficult abseils or squeezes, including Hole in the Wall and the Claustral. If you are tackling one of the popular canyons, go on a weekday to prevent having to wait for a large group (dangerous in the freezing conditions).

High N Wild Adventures: (02) 4782 6224; www.high-n-wild.com.au

River Deep, Mountain High: (02) 4782 6109 or 0410 619 086; www.rdmh.com.au

Australian School of Mountaineering: (02) 4782 2014; www.asmguides.com

Picnicking

Take a picnic up to Mount Tomah Botanic Garden at any time of year and you will not be disappointed. At 1000 metres above sea level, it is usually cool in summer, brimming with flowers in spring, resplendent with deciduous colour in autumn, and occasionally has a dusting of snow in winter. There is rainforest, a bog garden, walks and picturesque picnic spots. Take a two-to-three-hour walking ecotour to learn about the animals, rock formations, and plants including the legendary, ancient Wollemi pine.

Further along Bells Line of Road, take the turn-off to Pierces Pass then the 1.2-kilometre walk to Walls Lookout for one of the most spectacular picnic spots anywhere – on the edge of a heart-stopping precipice that will make you dream of being a BASE jumper. There is little shade and no guardrails or fences, so it is not suitable for young, active children.

Mount Tomah Botanic Garden: (02) 4567 2154; www.bluemts.com.au

Wollemi National Park

The largest wilderness area in New South Wales, this vast landscape has rugged gorges, thick forest and – as identified recently – many hidden Aboriginal sites. Most visitors will only ever see the fringes of this 1850-square-kilometre national park, camping or walking in the known areas, such as on the T3 Walking Track near Mountain Lagoon, which offers great views of the Colo Gorge, or along the 4-kilometre section of Bob Turners Track near Colo, leading to a swim and relax on the beaches on the Colo River. The Glow Worm Tunnel is one of the premier places to see these living lights and Dunns Swamp, on the west side, is a beautiful car-camping spot with abundant birds and other animals.

Glow Worm Tunnel: www.infobluemountains.net.au

Glenbrook to Mount Victoria

WHERE TO STAY

Bunjaree Cottages, Wentworth Falls

Great for families, Bunjaree Cottages have been designed to make a small environmental footprint, with full solar power and earth-brick insulation. One is built with recycled car tyres and mud, providing even better insulation. There is a cute kids' cubby, with games and activities inside, and a romantic bathhouse, and the whole lot is set in secluded bush on the outskirts of Wentworth Falls.

(02) 4757 3096 or 0409 125 744; www.bunjareecottages.com.au

Jemby-Rinjah Eco Lodge, Blackheath

One of the first working examples of large-scale sustainable tourism to exist in Australia, Jemby-Rinjah has advanced eco-accreditation, and one of the most extensive systems of composting toilets in the country. Ten cottages, one- and two-bedroom, are surrounded by dense bush (do not get caught here in a bushfire) and just a short stroll from Evans Lookout, which offers one of the best views in the Blue Mountains. One of the cabins is solar-powered.

(02) 4787 7622; www.jembyrinjahlodge.com.au

Kanimbla View, Blackheath

Solar-powered, the two- and three-bedroom cottages here are surprisingly large inside. They are partially constructed from recycled and salvaged timbers, have composting toilets and a great view of the Kanimbla Valley from the 1.5 kilometres of bush tracks. There is a voluntary conservation agreement over about a quarter of the 5-hectare property that shelters quolls, echidnas and kangaroos. There are no TVs, but there is a tennis court and a communal spa in the glasshouse.

(02) 4787 8985; www.kanimbla.com

Old Leura Dairy

This creative collection of six buildings, which can sleep up to 30 people in various combinations, has been renovated and fitted out with all manner of recycled bits and bobs. There are old oven doors, rusted corrugated iron, timbers from an old jetty, and the communal spa is an old milk vat. The premier building is the 11-bed Strawbale House, with half-metre-thick walls made of straw, internal thermal walls, and a cooling tower. Its luxurious and contemporary eco-design makes it worth the high price. Unfortunately, it is not in a bush setting, but on the edge of suburban Leura, and the buildings are close together.

(02) 4782 0700 or 0415 900 549; www.oldleuradairy.com

Woolshed Cabins, near Blackheath

Eleven kilometres from Blackheath and surrounded by a glorious natural amphitheatre of towering sandstone walls, the Woolshed Cabins sit on 100 hectares of cleared farmland (a working cattle farm) in the Kanimbla Valley, and have absolutely sensational views. Designed in conjunction with the award-winning Eco Design Architects, the two connected, two- and three-bedroom cabins are funky, attractive and distinctly Australian, incorporating recycled timbers, corrugated iron, stringybark and a wheat silo for the bathrooms. The cabins have composting toilets and the owners have a solid environmental policy.

(02) 4787 8199 or 0404 474 304; www.woolshedcabins.com.au

ACTIVITIES

Bushwalking

Many books have been written about bushwalking in the Blue Mountains. There is certainly a wealth of choice, from gentle meanders along clifftops with jaw-dropping views and lookouts over 200-metre drops, through to multi-day challenges with gruelling descents and ascents through eucalypt forests and gorges with waterfalls and rainforest. In Blue Mountains National Park alone there are more than 140 kilometres of marked tracks. The advisory signs at the start of bushwalks suggesting how long a walk will take are generally very conservative, so if you are fit or experienced you will usually take considerably less time.

Near Blackheath, the Clifftop Walk at Evans Lookout and Grand Canyon are superb, and the challenging day walk to the delightful Blue Gum Forest from Perry's Lookdown offers a series of stunning views that can certainly be described as 'breathtaking' as you puff and pant on the way up.

Near Katoomba the Prince Henry Cliff Walk is gentle, stunning and deservedly popular. The more energetic should consider tackling the Giant Stairway and Federal Pass. The day walk to Ruined Castle – the jumble of rocks and spires near Mount Solitary – either from Narrow Neck or from Katoomba, is particularly recommended.

For those keen to carry a pack and experience a night or two in the mountains, head for Mount Solitary or take one of the many routes to camp at Acacia Flat near Blue Gum Forest. Longer, multi-day classics include the Six Foot Track (that is its width!) from Katoomba to Jenolan Caves, and the three- or four-day hike from Katoomba to Kanangra Walls in which you climb several peaks and descend 1000 metres in a single day.

Many adventure operators run guided walks to some of the best places, with revelations about the plants, animals and history along the way. Tread Lightly Eco Tours has advanced eco-certification and is well known for being one of the most environmentally dedicated operators in the mountains. Its office is solar-powered, carbon neutral and all activities focus on minimum impact and excellent interpretation of the natural environment. There are guided walks of two to eight hours tailored to ability, and night walks focusing on astronomy, glow worms, and nocturnal animals such as bats, gliders, antechinuses and wallaroos.

River Deep, Mountain High has everything from half-day guided walks to multi-day treks. Its three-day guided walk on the Six Foot Track is supported, so you only have to carry a day pack.

Tread Lightly Eco Tours: (02) 4788 1229 or 0414 976 752; www.treadlightly.com.au

River Deep, Mountain High: (02) 4782 6109; www.rdmh.com.au

Four-wheel-drive tours

Much of the Blue Mountains can be reached with a 2WD, but there are areas that can only be explored with a 4WD. Two companies have eco-accreditation: the excellent Tread Lightly Eco Tours, which has extensive environmental policies and drives a low-emission LPG vehicle; and Misty Mountains 4WD, which offers soft-adventure and harder-edge four-wheel driving, particularly for tag-along tours. Misty

Contemplating the breathtaking drop from Evans Lookout

Mountains also offers a two-hour 'breakfast with the kangaroos' tour.

Tread Lightly Eco Tours: (02) 4788 1229 or 0414 976 752; www.treadlightly.com.au

Misty Mountains 4WD: (02) 4757 2278 or 0408 263 775; www.mistymtns4wdtours.com.au

Indigenous tour

In a special day hiking in Dharug country from Faulconbridge to Springwood, Blue Mountains Walkabout will introduce you to a new way of seeing the bush. There are meditation exercises and dances, ochre painting and initiation stories, bush tucker and swimming holes. It is a sensual experience, in which you are taught to listen to, taste, smell and feel the bush and its secrets – not just see it. There are about four hours of walking on fairly rough tracks, but with a gentle and personable guide who is a former Aboriginal Discovery Ranger. This walk and other similar experiences should be almost compulsory for non-Indigenous Australians, to help us get a grasp of the Aboriginal relationship with the land.

0408 443 822; www.bluemountainswalkabout.com

*An eastern grey kangaroo (*Macropus giganteus*) at Euroka Clearing in Blue Mountains National Park*

Mountain-biking

There is a resurgence of interest in mountain-biking in the Blue Mountains, and some superb fire trails to explore. The most popular route is The Oaks Fire Trail, heading downhill from Woodford. It is a superb half- to full-day ride that can finish among the kangaroos and picnickers at Euroka Clearing, or at Glenbrook station, to catch the train back to the start. Other popular routes include Murphys and Andersons fire trails, south of Wentworth Falls, although these are technically a little harder, and the thrilling Narrow Neck Plateau near Katoomba.

Various operators offer guided mountain-biking tours, including some multi-day adventures for the really keen. Check out River Deep, Mountain High, which is a Blue Mountains Sustainable Business. High N Wild Adventures also has guided mountain-bike tours and rents mountain bikes if you want to head out on your own. Bike Minded at Wentworth Falls hires bikes, offers tips about where to go, and runs regular rides, including a mid-week off-road ride at night.

River Deep, Mountain High: (02) 4782 6109 or 0410 619 086; www.rdmh.com.au

High N Wild Adventures: (02) 4782 6224; www.high-n-wild.com.au

Bike Minded: (02) 4757 4607; www.bikeminded.com.au

Rock climbing and abseiling

In terms of eco-adventure activities, the Blue Mountains' sheer sandstone cliffs are probably most suited to dancing on the end of a rope – whether going up or down. Climbers who know what they are doing have almost infinite climbs to choose from, although some classics previously enjoyed (such as various ways up the Three Sisters) are now off-limits.

If you just want a taste of these activities, to get your heart racing and your mind clear of everything but tall cliffs and where to put your hands, start off with one of the trusted climbing operators. Most run half-day, full-day and multi-day trips for climbers of all capabilities, in areas with spectacular views.

Australian School of Mountaineering: (02) 4782 2014; www.asmguides.com

Blue Mountains Adventure Company: (02) 4782 1271; www.bmac.com.au

High N Wild Adventures: (02) 4782 6224; www.high-n-wild.com.au

River Deep, Mountain High: (02) 4782 6109 or 0410 619 086; www.rdmh.com.au

Southern Blue Mountains

WHERE TO STAY

Jenolan Cabins

These basic but cosy self-contained cabins, 6 kilometres up the steep hill past Jenolan Caves, are earth-sheltered for climate control and have composting toilets and rainwater. There are great views over the mountains, macropods that think they own the 10 hectares of private bushland, and at 1250 metres above sea level, the property occasionally gets a dusting of snow. You will need to bring almost

everything – linen, food, soap, tea, coffee – but doonas, pillows and a slow-combustion fire with firewood are supplied.
(02) 6335 6239 or 0418 619 709;
www.jenolancabins.com.au

Pine End B&B

Stay here and you can have cheese-making lessons on an organic farm committed to sustainable practices, within an hour's drive south-west of Sydney (at Belimbla Park, west of Camden). There is only one queen-bed room, and one single room, so you are guaranteed personal care by the hosts.
(02) 4657 2176 or 0412 729 403; www.pineend.com

ACTIVITIES

Jenolan Caves

The best known limestone caves in Australia, Jenolan has an extraordinary diversity of caves to explore, with tours leaving every hour or so. More than 40 kilometres of caves and 300 cave openings have been discovered here since European caving began in the early 1800s. There are guided walking tours of nine beautiful, feature-filled show caves, with well-lit, formed paths. Particularly recommended is the two-hour River Cave walk (although it has 1298 steps), and the shorter Temple of Baal. For those after a more authentic caving experience, Jenolan also offers a few introductions to caving on its 'adventure tours', with headlamps, abseiling, crawling and squeezing through tight spaces. The two-hour Plughole adventure into Elder Cave is great fun, and the six-hour tour into Mammoth Cave, with cave ladders and extensive climbing, is legendary. With every tour, you also get a free tour (with audio guide) of the Devil's Coachhouse and Nettle Cave. Among the most unusual experiences in the caves are the regular classical concerts in the Cathedral Chamber, where the sounds of string instruments resound and echo through the underworld.
(02) 6359 3311; www.jenolancaves.org.au

Kanangra–Boyd National Park

A wild wilderness of wombats, wallabies, wattlebirds and waterfalls, Kanangra is well worth the 45-minute drive past Jenolan Caves. Revel in the glorious, unfenced cliff-lines plunging to green gorges far below, and two bushwalks from the carpark: the Plateau Walk is the best, but you can complete both in a few hours. Hardened bushwalkers head out into the wilderness to places such as Mount Cloudmaker and beyond. There is a basic, wheelchair-accessible campground a few kilometres back from the cliffs.
NPWS Oberon: (02) 6336 1972;
www.environment.nsw.gov.au

Thirlmere Lakes National Park

Boasting some of the closest undisturbed lakes to Sydney, this park is great for a relaxing picnic. Lyrebirds and other feathered creatures abound.
www.environment.nsw.gov.au

Experiencing adventure caving – a Plughole Tour guide squeezes through a tight space in Elder Cave

North-east New South Wales

The north-east of New South Wales is full of opportunities for the ecotraveller. At locations such as Solitary Islands Marine Park, the warmer tropical waters and the colder temperate waters mix, resulting in a greater variety of marine life than either further north or south, with estimates of more than 700 fish species alone. There are beaches in abundance, canoeing and kayaking trips, whitewater rafting and some superb bushwalking along the Great Dividing Range in World Heritage–listed rainforests. It is a very popular region in school holidays, but even then it usually only takes a half-hour walk or paddle to get away from the crowds.

View of Pearl Beach, in Brisbane Water National Park, from Mount Ettalong Lookout

Hawkesbury River to Newcastle

WHERE TO STAY

Australia Walkabout Park, Calga

You can camp out with the 180 species of wild animal in this 32-hectare feral-proofed wildlife park that has a solid history of conservation and caring for injured and orphaned wildlife. The overnight camping experience includes provision of tents, barbecue dinner, a night and morning guided walk, and admission to the park during the day.

(02) 4375 1100; www.walkaboutpark.com.au

Bouddi National Park

This coastal national park has a couple of gems for keen campers. Tallow Beach – a 1.2-kilometre walk from the car down a steep 4WD track – will give you isolated beach camping that can feel miles from anywhere if you are lucky enough to have it on your own. Putty Beach has considerably more facilities, including barbecues and open showers, but is a lot more popular.

NPWS Gosford:
(02) 4320 4200;
www.environment.nsw.gov.au
Camp bookings: (02) 4320 4203

Callicoma Hill Eco-cabins, near Singleton

Positioned just outside Mount Royal National Park and the Barrington Wilderness, this three-bedroom wooden

cottage and rustic mudbrick bunkhouse have 80-kilometre views over the Hunter Valley. They are solar-powered (with no TV, microwave or freezer) and all wastewater is treated on site. The owners also run guided walks.
(02) 6571 1208; www.calli.com.au

Mount View Lodges, Mount View

With a careful contemporary eco-design that maximises passive solar heating and cooling, and minimises impact on the land, the one- and two-bedroom lodges here use solar hot water and rainwater. They are within a short hop of many of the Pokolbin wineries.
(02) 4998 0186; www.mountviewlodges.com.au

ACTIVITIES

Birdwatching

A reclaimed 45-hectare wetland area just 10 minutes drive from the centre of Newcastle has been Ramsar-listed and is an excellent spot to see up to 213 bird species, including more than 2000 pairs of breeding egrets. The Hunter Wetland Centre has walking and cycling tracks, canoes for hire, wildlife displays and activities for children.
(02) 4951 6466; www.wetlands.org.au

Cycling

Take a scenic two- or three-hour guided cycling tour around Newcastle, nearly all on flat bike paths, with Newcastle Bike Tours. If you want to cycle around on your own, hire from Civic Bikes, near the start of the Honeysuckle Cycling Track, and they will recommend some great rides.
Newcastle Bike Tours: 0424 168 552
Civic Bikes: (02) 4927 6277; www.civicbikes.com.au

Diving and snorkelling

There are some great little spots for both these activities if you know where to look. As always, it is best to check with local dive operators. The Scuba Shack at Toukley recommends a couple of easy shore dives and snorkelling spots, including Cabbage Tree Harbour – with its hordes of Port Jackson sharks, cuttlefish, blue groper, nudibranchs and old wives – and the swimthroughs and soft corals of Soldiers Beach.
(02) 4396 8863; www.scubashack.com.au

Kayaking

Lake Macquarie Kayaks hires kayaks by the hour from Raffertys, or will deliver kayaks to wherever you would like around the 174-kilometre circumference of the lake.
0437 772 939; www.lakemacquariekayaks.com.au

Ken Duncan Gallery

Admire the photography of Ken Duncan, one of Australia's most masterful natural landscape photographers, and other international and Australian photographers, at the largest privately owned gallery in Australia. It is on The Entrance Road in Erina Heights.
(02) 4367 6701; www.kenduncan.com.au

Last Riverboat Postman, Brooklyn

Cruise the Hawkesbury River with Australia's last official riverboat postman, delivering mail and supplies to isolated river communities. The four-hour cruise from Brooklyn explains the history and legends of the river.
(02) 9985 7566; www.hawkesburyriverferries.com.au

Sailing

Long Jetty Catamaran and Boat Hire on Tuggerah Lakes has catamarans for hire for experienced sailors or for those who just want to have a go on vessels that are reasonably easy to handle. Informal instructions and all safety equipment are provided.
(02) 4332 9362 or 0408 506 661;
www.cathire.bigpondhosting.com

Swimming

The Central Coast is best known for its beaches, and there are plenty of great ones to choose from. Terrigal and Avoca are two of the most popular, but a quieter spot for families may be Pearl Beach or Killcare. Further north, Newcastle has top beaches too – Nobbys Beach and Bar Beach are both recommended and have lifeguards year-round.

Newcastle visitor centre: (02) 4974 2999 or 1800 654 558; www.newcastletourism.com

The Great North Walk

Although it links two of Australia's most populated cities, Sydney and Newcastle, and passes through some beautiful bushland, the Great North Walk does not get the foot traffic you might expect.

A 250-kilometre, 12–16-day walk, with an offshoot to the Hunter Valley, it has beautiful sections through coastal rainforest, down gorges, through mangroves and up sandstone ridges, as well as sneaking through surprising pockets of bush on the outskirts of urban areas. There are plenty of places to get on and off the track for day walks, and quiet bush-camping areas with water.

(02) 4920 5074; www.lands.nsw.gov.au

Wine-tasting

In addition to being one of Australia's most prolific wine areas, the Hunter Valley has a handful of organic and biodynamic producers. Exercise your olfactory receptors at Tamburlaine Wines in Pokolbin, Krinklewood Vineyard in Broke and Macquariedale Estate in Rothbury. Moorebank Vineyard in Pokolbin also places an emphasis on sustainable practices. For more about these or other wineries in the area, see contact details below.

Hunter Valley Wine Country Tourism, Pokolbin: (02) 4990 0930; www.winecountry.com.au

Vines at Krinklewood Vineyard at Broke in the Hunter Valley

Newcastle to Port Macquarie

WHERE TO STAY

Banjo's Bushland Retreat, Vacy

With three self-contained lodges of various sizes and a recreation room that includes an environmental centre, this eco-accredited resort keeps nature as its focus. Even the nine-hole minigolf course weaves around the trees and kangaroos live around the tennis court. There is free mountain-bike use, and bushwalking on the 8-hectare site.

(02) 9403 3388; www.banjosretreat.com.au

Bombah Point Eco Cottages

The six beautiful cottages here, most of which are two-bedroom, have an excellent eco-design, and solar panels provide about 60 per cent of the power. The site is a wildlife refuge and is hemmed in on three sides by Myall Lakes

Cottage accommodation at Bombah Point

National Park. The cottages have rainwater tanks and sewage is treated on site with a massive worm farm and reed-bed filtration. You can hire kayaks and bikes here to explore the national park.

(02) 4997 4401; www.bombah.com.au

O'Carrollyn's Eco Village, One Mile Beach

The site here has been gradually regenerated to its former state, with hundreds of plants established, wetlands recreated and native fish reintroduced. This has seen the return of animals such as echidnas, finches and waterbirds. The nine family bungalows (disabled access) are spacious and attractive, and many of the on-site activities raise money for koala conservation.

(02) 4982 2801; www.ocarrollyns.com.au

Somewhere Unique, Wollombi

The two stand-alone, couples-only cottages here are stylish, contemporary and have passive solar design. They are eco-accredited, on an 8-hectare bushland reserve, and use only renewable energy and Greenfleet vehicles. Tariffs include free bicycles and broadband use.

(02) 4998 3257; www.somewhereunique.com.au

Tianjara, Smiths Lake

The self-contained renovated barn on this 10-hectare property sleeps five, is solar-powered and all wastewater is treated on site. What is more, if you do not feel like cooking, the owners will cook up an organic storm in their mudbrick house and bring it over.

(02) 4997 6055; www.tianjaraeco.com

Yeranda, Main Creek, near Dungog

This lush, 56-hectare property on the edge of Barrington Tops National Park has been declared a nature reserve and has a voluntary conservation agreement over the property. Two of the three isolated bush cottages – made with recycled materials and bush rock – are solar-powered, with gas appliances. There are no TVs, but sublime forest outlooks with red-necked wallabies and frogs hopping past, and sensual outdoor showers perfect for the inner naturist. There are also 4 kilometres of walking tracks on the property.

(02) 4992 1208; www.yeranda.com.au

Watching out for whales and dolphins on a Moonshadow *cruise*

*A family of tawny frogmouths (*Podargus strigoides*) at Bombah Point*

ACTIVITIES

Barrington Tops National Park

Best known for its superb bushwalking among ancient Antarctic beech forest and rainforest that receives snow several times a year, this 83403-hectare park is one of the highest spots on the Great Dividing Range and even has snow gums. There are plenty of recommended walks: the 20-kilometre aptly named Corker Trail to Careys Peak on the Dungog side; the 1-kilometre Antarctic Beech Forest Track near Gloucester; and to lookouts such as Devils Hole. You will see lyrebirds, brush-turkeys and maybe scarlet honeyeaters and noisy pitas, as well as red-necked wallabies hiding in the mist.

NPWS Gloucester: (02) 6558 1478

Birdwatching

Take a leisurely 'Breakfast with the birds' walk with Boomerang Forest Tours at Smiths Lake (book via Great Lakes Tourism). You will see some 30 bird species and possibly also whales, dingoes, kangaroos and wallabies.

(02) 6554 0757; www.greatlakes.org.au

Burning Mountain Nature Reserve

Forget global warming for a while and marvel at this coal seam, about 30 metres underground, that has been burning as hot as 1700°C for an estimated 5500 years. A 3.5-kilometre walk to the top of the mountain through open forest offers views of the surrounding area and of the vents where the smoke rises, making the mountain seem to burn. The reserve is near Wingen in the upper Hunter region.

Reserve information: (02) 6545 2300

Dolphin- and whale-watching

The waters of Port Stephens and around Nelson Bay are some of the most reliable places on the east coast to see bottlenose dolphins, and there are lots of operators who will take you out to see them. Moonshadow Cruises at Nelson Bay is eco-accredited, guarantees dolphin sightings and also runs whale-watching cruises in season. Imagine Cruises at Nelson Bay is actively involved in dolphin and whale conservation, and also eco-accredited, as is the long-running Tamboi Queen Cruises.

Moss-covered tree trunks on the rainforest floor, Barrington Tops National Park

Moonshadow Cruises: (02) 4984 9388;
www.moonshadow.com.au
Imagine Cruises: (02) 4984 9000;
www.imaginecruises.com.au
Tamboi Queen Cruises: (02) 4981 1959;
www.tamboiqueencruises.com

Dorrigo National Park

A waterfall wonderland, Dorrigo provides some of the easiest access to the World Heritage rainforests of New South Wales. The 5.5-kilometre Wonga Walk is sealed and a great introduction to this beautiful area, with chances to see catbirds, lyrebirds, paradise riflebirds, regent bowerbirds, noisy pitas, golden whistlers and plenty of brush-turkeys. The canopy skywalk is a good spot to see wompoo and rose-crowned fruit-doves.

NPWS Dorrigo: (02) 6657 2309;
www.environment.nsw.gov.au

Kayaking down rapids in Barrington Tops National Park

Kayaking

Barrington Outdoor Adventure Centre at Gloucester offers an exciting one-day tour down the Barrington River. Guides can tailor the trip for beginners or family groups, choosing a quieter part of the river where there are likely sightings of platypus, wallabies and water dragons on a leisurely paddle, or for the more intrepid, tours can be taken to a higher adrenaline level on wilder rapids. The centre also rents kayaks and canoes and does a drop-off service.

Lazy Paddles at Tea Gardens conducts two-hour kayaking tours along the Myall River, with chances to see dolphins, birds and marine life. The company also hires out kayaks and offers a drop-off service.

Blue Water Sea Kayaking in Nelson Bay also has kayaking tours, including a champagne sunset tour, a dolphin-watching kayak trip and an overnight camping excursion.

Barrington Outdoor Adventure Centre: (02) 6558 2093; www.boac.com.au

Lazy Paddles: 0412 832 220; www.lazypaddles.com.au

Blue Water Sea Kayaking: 0405 033 518; www.kayakingportstephens.com.au

Koala-spotting

In many of the bushland areas of the Port Stephens region and further north you may come across koalas, particularly in swamp mahogany trees. One of the best places to spot them is at the revegetated Tilligerry Habitat Environment Centre at Tanilba Bay, which is run by volunteers out of a strawbale building. You can go for a walk through the reserve to spy koalas on your own, or join a one-and-a-half-hour guided koala walk that can include bush tucker and boomerang throwing.

The Koala Hospital at Port Macquarie is also a must for koala lovers. Some 200 koalas are admitted to the hospital annually, suffering from chlamydia, or injuries from motor vehicles and dog attacks. The hospital is open 365 days a year and visitors are welcome at all times but a tour is conducted every day at 3pm.

Tanilba Bay centre: (02) 4984 5677

Koala Hospital: (02) 6584 1522; www.koalahospital.org.au

Mount Royal National Park

This rainforest-filled park adjoins Barrington Tops National Park, and includes part of the Barrington Tops Wilderness area. It has great walking tracks, lookouts and picnic spots in which you are likely to glimpse koalas, kangaroos and rich birdlife.

Mountain-biking

Go for a full-day's guided mountain-biking through the gorgeous Barrington Tops with Barrington Outdoor Adventure Centre at Gloucester. If you have your own mountain bike, the 30-kilometre gravel loop road in Mount Royal National Park is also recommended.

(02) 6558 2093; www.boac.com.au

Myall Lakes National Park

With the thundering ocean on one side of the dunes and quiet bird-filled lakes and waterways on the other, this is a superb park for camping and exploring. There are pleasant walks from the easy half-hour Mungo Brush Rainforest walk or the 3-kilometre-return climb up the steep Yaccaba Headland south of Hawks Nest, to the longer Old Gibber or Mungo tracks, often tackled as overnight walks.

NPWS Great Lakes: (02) 6591 0300; www.environment.nsw.gov.au

Picnicking

Slightly away from the coast there is a multitude of great picnic spots in quiet bushland, with walks through lowland rainforest and eucalypt forests. Most receive few visitors. Try Tapin Tops National Park, Boorganna Nature Reserve, Brimbin Nature Reserve and, if you are in the area, the tiny Wingham Brush Nature Reserve with its grey-headed flying-foxes, brush-turkeys and Moreton Bay figs. Free electric barbecues are down by the river.

Sea Acres Nature Reserve

This cool coastal forest, 5 kilometres south of Port Macquarie, is great for a stop and a gentle stroll, with lush rainforest extending right down to the beach. There is a 1.5-kilometre wheelchair-accessible boardwalk, which will take you into the canopy where you have a good chance of seeing some of the 100 species of birds found here, and an excellent interpretive visitor centre.

(02) 6582 3355; www.environment.nsw.gov.au

Snorkelling and diving

Nelson Bay and surrounds offer some superb snorkelling and diving. Many locations are accessible by boat only, such as beautiful Broughton Island, but there are some exceptional shore dives and snorkelling – some shore dives have even been rated among the best in the country. The easy access and plentiful marine life in the marine sanctuary at Fly Point makes it a top spot for a snorkel or easy dive, with sponge gardens, schools of bream, tarwine, mullet, big silver drummer, nudibranchs and wondrous seahorses. The pipeline, near the Fish Co-op, has moray eels, eastern rock lobsters, tropical fish during summer, cuttlefish, octopus, pipefish and more seahorses. Pro Dive at Nelson Bay can provide detailed advice and all the gear you need.

(02) 4981 4331; www.prodivenelsonbay.com

Swimming

The Port Stephens and Myall Lakes area is a superb place for swimming. Young children will love the sheltered waters around Nelson Bay, and Fingal Bay is one of the most glorious family beaches in the country. Great surf beaches are not hard to come by either – pick a spot virtually anywhere along this stretch of coast. At Port Macquarie, do not miss the delightful Flynns Beach.

*Grey-headed flying-foxes (*Pteropus poliocephalus*) in Wingham Brush Nature Reserve*

Port Macquarie to Lismore

WHERE TO STAY

Camping, Crowdy Bay National Park

With its long sweeping beaches, coastal wildflowers and pockets of rainforest, this national park is well known as a great spot to camp, particularly in summer. The main camping area is at Diamond Head, where whales can often be seen from May to October, but Kylies Beach is quieter, has a composting toilet and is a good spot to see koalas.

NPWS Port Macquarie: (02) 6586 8300; www.environment.nsw.gov.au

Lily Pily Country House, Bellingen

The owners of this stylish B&B have spent seven years revegetating and securing wildlife corridors along the riparian zone here, planting some 4000 trees and 2000 reeds, resulting in an increase in bandicoots, honeyeaters and platypus. The building with the three guest suites has passive solar design, uses solar hot water and the greywater is reused on site.

(02) 6655 0522 or 0410 576 456; www.lilypily.com.au

Trial Bay, South West Rocks

More than a caravan park, this growing resort caters to all comers and has solid environmental credentials. It has 27 cabins, including some new two-bedroom stylish ones, 138 camping sites (13 of which have private ensuites), pool, playgrounds, a cinema fitted out with old bus seats, and abundant kangaroos. It is eco-accredited, has been granted the New South Wales Gold Gumnut environmental award, has been involved in local wetland conservation, planted thousands of native trees and is good at doing a lot of

Smoky Cape Lighthouse marks the end of the coastal bushwalk from Little Bay

the little things that can make a big difference in a park this size (such as worm farms and energy- and water-saving practices). You can choose to rent canoes or bikes, swim or go for a bushwalk.

(02) 6566 6142 or 1800 670 060; www.trialbay.com.au

Yaraandoo, east of Armidale

Located 70 kilometres east of Armidale, off Waterfall Way, this well-constructed centre has quick access to three iconic national parks (New England, Cathedral Rock and Guy Fawkes River). Primarily a conference centre used for large groups, it also has a lovely self-contained apartment, double rooms, twin rooms and bunk rooms to rent (including disabled facilities). The 108-hectare property features bushwalks and a feral-proof enclosure – at times used for the conservation of native animals – and you are likely to see red-necked wallabies and kangaroos hopping around. The main building is made with rammed earth, compressed straw and recycled timbers, and reuses wastewater to flush the toilets. At 1300 metres in altitude it can be freezing cold, and the swirling mists can be a delightful surprise even when the coast is warm.

(02) 6775 9219; www.yaraandoo.com.au

ACTIVITIES

Armidale Bicentennial Arboretum

Armidale Bicentennial Arboretum, a dozen blocks from the centre of town, has thousands of native plants, walking tracks, picnic shelters and aquatic gardens with a waterfall.

Birdwatching

There are a couple of top birdwatching spots in the New England area. One of the most spectacular is an all-weather bird hide among masses of waterbirds at Quipolly Dam, about 18 kilometres north-east of Quirindi. Mother of Ducks Lagoon at Guyra is a freshwater wetland inside a volcanic crater and a good spot to see Japanese snipe. Dangars Lagoon is also well regarded and has a large bird hide and some big snakes lurking in the long grass.

Back down on the coast, do not miss Muttonbird Island Nature Reserve near Coffs Harbour Marina. As well as being home to thousands of migratory wedge-tailed shearwaters, and a great vantage point for whale-watching, it has storm petrels, lesser frigatebirds and a range of other seabirds.

Bush-tucker tasting

Sample some Australian bushfoods at Valley of the Mist near Macksville, a farm dedicated to sustainable methods. You will taste bush fruits, nuts, herbs and condiments and have a tour of the farm. You can also take a canoe tour of the wetlands to see a host of wildlife, including jabirus, swamp wallabies and black swans.

(02) 6568 3268 or 0428 683 268; www.valleyofthemist.com.au

Bushwalking

For a classic coastal walk with beautiful beaches, rainforest and stunning wildflowers in spring, walk the coastline south from Little Bay to Smoky Cape Lighthouse through Hat Head National Park. It will take all day to trek the 20 kilometres there and back, and possibly longer if you stop for too many swims. If you are in South West Rocks in spring and want something a little shorter, make sure you walk up Monument Hill for the stunning wildflowers and coastal views.

Canoeing and kayaking

Rent a canoe, kayak or even a tyre tube and go floating down Goolang Creek for about 6 kilometres. You can leave your car down there with a trailer, or Nymboida Canoe

Stylish cabins at Trial Bay resort

Swimming at Diamond Head in Crowdy Bay National Park

Centre at Coffs Harbour will pick you up in their 20-seater bus. They will also fit you out for more advanced canoeing and kayaking trips, including overnight excursions on the legendary Nymboida River. You can camp on the 40 hectares of grounds near the centre. For a pleasant, quiet kayaking tour on a pristine estuary with stingrays, birds and the odd bull shark, join the afternoon paddle in Bongil Bongil National Park south of Coffs Harbour. Liquid Assets will even pick you up from your accommodation. They also do a morning sea-kayaking trip in Solitary Islands National Park in which you are likely to see dolphins and sea-eagles, and occasionally turtles sticking their heads out of the water.

Evans Head Kayak Adventures runs a pleasant paddle with a strong environmental focus and a visit to the headquarters of the admirable Australian Seabird Rescue. Bellingen Canoe Adventures offers canoe hire or a range of guided tours on flatwater or easy rapids, including a Full Moon Tour in which you might see nocturnal animals such as possums, koalas, bats and birds.

Nymboida Canoe Centre: (02) 6649 4155; www.nymboidacanoecentre.com
Liquid Assets: (02) 6658 0850; www.surfrafting.com
Evans Head Kayak Adventures: (02) 6682 6229 or 0410 016 926; www.evansriverkayaks.com
Bellingen Canoe Adventures: (02) 6655 9955; www.canoeadventures.com.au

Cathedral Rock National Park

The main feature of this 10 920-hectare park is the exhilarating walk to the top of Cathedral Rock, with a magnificent 360-degree view that is well worth the climb. Round Mountain, at 1584 metres, is the highest point north of the Snowy Mountains in New South Wales. You can camp nearby in a basic campground unsuitable for caravans.

NPWS Dorrigo: (02) 6657 2309; www.environment.nsw.gov.au

Cycling

A 5-kilometre bicycle track leads from Harris Park in Armidale to the University of New England. Bikes can be hired from Armidale Bicycle Centre or the University's Sports Union. The 26-kilometre-return ride from Coffs Harbour Jetty to Sawtell is recommended for intermediate cyclists, and passes by a velodrome and mountain-bike circuit. Coffs Harbour has several places to hire bikes, including Bob Wallis Cycles. The company provides maps and will give more recommendations.

Armidale Bicycle Centre: (02) 6772 3718
Sports Union: (02) 6773 2316
Bob Wallis Cycles: (02) 6652 5102

Diving and snorkelling

Experienced divers know and love Fish Rock Cave at South West Rocks, one of the best dive

Kayaking in Bongil Bongil National Park

Ebor Falls in Guy Fawkes National Park

Escarpment in Guy Fawkes National Park

sites in Australia. At 120 metres long, it is one of the largest ocean caverns in the Southern Hemisphere, and contains endangered grey nurse sharks, corals, crayfish, clownfish and bullseyes. The Fish Rock Dive Centre will get you there and assist with other great dives in the area, including the shallow shore dive at Ladies Reef. There is also excellent snorkelling around the boulders off the main beach and in Horseshoe Bay.

The Solitary Islands Marine Park was the first marine park established in New South Wales and is one of the state's largest, stretching 75 kilometres along the coast and covering more than 70 000 hectares. As it is one of the meeting points of the tropical waters and the cooler temperate waters, it has an extraordinary number of fish species – probably 700 or more. It also has some special grey nurse shark covens, sea turtles and dolphins. To explore this extraordinary area on or below the water, you will need to have access to a boat. Jetty Dive at Coffs Harbour can get you to some of the key spots.

Fish Rock Dive Centre: (02) 6566 6614; www.fishrock.com.au

Jetty Dive: (02) 6651 1611; www.jettydive.com.au

Guy Fawkes National Park

Do not miss the spectacular double-drop Ebor Falls in this park that abuts Cathedral Rock National Park. There are some short strolls well worth doing, and longer hikes for those wanting more of a boot fest.

NPWS Dorrigo: (02) 6657 2309; www.environment.nsw.gov.au

Houseboating

Although large chugging houseboats can be an environmental no-no, Macleay River Houseboats at Kempsey are small – designed for just two people – use relatively clean

NATURE WATCH Floyd's grass (*Alexfloydia repens*) is an attractive purple-flowering grass found only in the Coffs Harbour area, and as its distribution is restricted almost entirely to about a metre above sea level, it is at risk from global warming. It is the sole food of the endangered black grass-dart butterfly (*Ocybadistes knightorum*).

four-stroke petrol motors, have solar-powered electricity and the effluent is kept on board to be pumped off later. The houseboats are fully self-contained, have a barbecue and DVD player and are probably cheaper than you would expect. Fresh produce is never far away, with towns, villages and riverside hotels on the banks of the Macleay River.

0407 674 998; www.macleayriverhouseboats.com.au

New England National Park

If the swirling fog at 1500 metres in altitude does not stop you, you can score superb views in this park from Point Lookout (wheelchair accessible), Banksia Point or Wrights Lookout. There are some easy wanders through the bush around the lookouts, or take one of the longer tracks in more than 20 kilometres of graded trails through Antarctic beech and eucalypt forest. The 72 241-hectare park also has basic camping at the Thungutti camping ground.

NPWS Dorrigo: (02) 6657 2309; www.environment.nsw.gov.au

Oxley Wild Rivers National Park

This wild, rugged and spectacular park of 90 000 hectares is home to the 260-metre Wollomombi Falls, the highest in New South Wales (although falling into a fairly unattractive bowl), and the beautiful Dangars Falls. Both have excellent picnic facilities nearby and gas barbecues. There is a plethora of short, medium and longer walks, most of which take in a waterfall and a lookout or two, and the gorges and cliffs are home to the largest known population of brush-tailed rock-wallabies – an estimated 10 000 or so.

For long guided walks in this awesome area, try Wild River Walks, which has a long day walk and an overnight walk, with camping in the bottom of a gorge.

Wild River Walks: (02) 6778 0337

Picnicking

This is such an attractive area that you will find no shortage of places to throw the rug down – whether on a beach, a headland, or a patch of quiet forest floor. One spot worth checking out is the beautiful North Coast Regional Botanic Garden at Coffs Harbour. It has 20 hectares packed with plants from Australia and around the world, 5 kilometres of walking tracks, including through a rainforest, some lovely picnic areas, and is free.

Look at Me Now Headland in Emerald Beach has plenty of kangaroos and views of the Solitary Islands. Smoky Cape Lighthouse has superb views and free electric barbecues and, if you get it on a calm day, it is quite splendid.

Botanic garden: (02) 6648 4188; www.botanicgarden.coffsharbour.nsw.gov.au

Rafting

Although it used to have many rafting companies, Coffs Harbour is now home to only one: Liquid Assets. This operator offers a family-friendly half-day outing, a peaceful platypus-watching raft and a more radical full-day outing for those aged over 14, as well as an overnight experience.

(02) 6658 0850; www.surfrafting.com

Washpool National Park

Considered to be at biological crossroads, this stunning area gets many species towards the edges of their ranges. Take one of the walks – either the 8.5-kilometre Washpool Walk to Summit Falls and Washpool Lookout through warm temperate rainforests or the 1.5-kilometre Coombadjha Nature Stroll to a swimming hole – and you are likely to see a huge range of birds (the rare rufous-scrub bird is one of the bird species found here) land mullets, snakes and maybe even platypus and pademelons. There are a couple of basic campgrounds.

NPWS Glen Innes: (02) 6739 0700; www.environment.nsw.gov.au

Wine-tasting

Wright Robertson of Glencoe is a certified organic vineyard and uses no irrigation. At the cellar door you can try their range of mainly red and fortified wines.

(02) 6733 3255; www.wrightwine.com

Lismore to Queensland border

WHERE TO STAY

Crystal Creek Rainforest Retreat

Located near Murwillumbah and surrounded on three sides by World Heritage–listed national parks, this secluded couples-only resort on the Queensland border has minimal-impact, self-contained bungalows and cabins. Sixty per cent of the 102-hectare property has been set aside in a voluntary conservation agreement, protecting 25 species of rare and threatened plants and the habitat of 15 species of vulnerable birds, mammals, reptiles and amphibians. The owners have planted more than 16 000 trees on the former banana plantation and there are 8 kilometres of bushwalks to old-growth forests.

(02) 6679 1591; www.ccrr.com.au

Emerald Valley Villa

Nestled in the hinterland some 25 minutes drive from Byron Bay, this is way up the high end of ecotourism in this country. You can rent your own five-star palace (they call it a villa), complete with pool, courtyard, four large bedrooms with their own lavish bathrooms, large entertaining area, and 35 hectares of mini-botanic gardens and rainforest to wander

Stand of coachwood (Ceratopetalum apelatum) in the warm temperate rainforest of Washpool National Park

White-throated treecreeper (Cormobates leucophaeus) in Guy Fawkes National Park

through. They will even bring in masseurs and chefs if you wish. The place was created by Michael Robison, founder of environmental organisation The Emerald Planet Trust, and also founder of the carbon-offset company Climate Friendly. The site uses only green power, is 100 per cent carbon neutral, has solar hot water, is water self-sufficient, has an organic vegetable garden, preserves rainforest, and the bulk of the furniture is made from recycled timber. It is not a place for the light of wallet.

(02) 6684 9398; www.emeraldvalleyvilla.com

ACTIVITIES

Bushwalking

There is a range of gentle and more challenging walks in this area through rainforests, gorges and coastal environments. Take the boardwalk through Victoria Park Nature Reserve at Alstonville to see some of the last remaining remnants of the subtropical rainforest that once covered most of northern New South Wales. Explore stunning coastal scenery in Broadwater, Bundjalung and Yuraygir national parks. Or head up into the hinterland for some more serious walking in Border Ranges or Nightcap national parks. Of course, Mount Warning is one of the most spectacular destinations in the area, but the Bundjalung people ask that you do not climb it.

Diving and snorkelling

Although there is not much in the way of shore dives or snorkelling around Byron Bay, the nearby Julian Rocks Marine Reserve is a top spot if you can get on a boat, with sea turtles, eagle rays, corals, grey nurse and leopard sharks, cuttlefish and more than 500 species of fish. Byron Bay Dive Centre will take you there.

Shaws Bay near Ballina is sheltered for reasonable snorkelling and, for the more experienced, 'The Moat' extends for around 1.5 kilometres along Seven Mile Beach.

Byron Bay Dive Centre: (02) 6685 8333 or 1800 243 483; www.byronbaydivecentre.com.au

Kayaking

Byron Bay Kayaks guarantees you will see dolphins, whales and/or turtles on their two-hour kayak tours around Byron Bay Marine Park. Ballina Kayak Tours also runs a daily three-hour trip in which you are likely to see bottlenose dolphins, sea-eagles and other wildlife.

Byron Bay: (02) 6680 9555;
www.capebyronkayaks.com
Ballina Kayak Tours: (02) 6685 3722

Mountain-biking

From Byron Bay, Mountain Bike Tours will take you on guided all-day tours through beautiful forest tracks in Nightcap National Park and other local national parks. The guides offer interpretation of the environment and history as you go, and part of your fee goes to Rainforest Rescue. Multi-day mountain-biking tours are also offered, and you can hire bikes if you want to get muddy on your own.

1800 122 504 or 0429 122 504;
www.mountainbiketours.com.au

Wildlife tours

For one of the most innovative wildlife tours in this country, join Vision Walks on their nocturnal walk in Nightcap National Park, with $1000-night-vision glasses as used by the military. You have an incredible advantage over the animals, in that you can see them clearly (in monochrome) but you are not using a spotlight. Animals include possums, pademelons, tawny frogmouths, koalas, tree mice and frogs. Vision Walks will pick you up from your accommodation in the Byron Bay area, and provide detailed natural history

Emerald Valley Villa in the hinterland behind Byron Bay

information along the way. They also do day walks and half-day tours.

On a six-hour wildlife tour with Byron Bay Wildlife Tours you are guaranteed of seeing at least seven species of mammal in the wild, including kangaroos, koalas, wallabies, pademelons, flying-foxes and often dolphins and humpback whales. The tour, in a small LPG-powered bus, also takes in reptiles, birds and other wildlife around the Byron Bay area.

Vision Walks: (02) 6687 4237 or 0405 275 743; www.visionwalks.com

Byron Bay Wildlife Tours: 0429 770 686; www.byronbaywildlifetours.com

Wildlife-watching

No need to get out on a boat here to spy migrating whales – there are plenty of great vantage points on headlands, including around Cape Byron Lighthouse and at Pat Moreton Lookout at Lennox Head, during May–June and October–November.

If you want to try whale-watching under the quietness of sail rather than motor, try Baysail at Ballina between June and November. The company also runs a powerboat whale-watching tour in which the data collected is provided to Southern Cross University for conservation and protection of whales. Out of whale-watching season, you can also join the ecotourism award-winning enterprise for a half-day or longer sail in the area, where you may encounter animals such as dolphins, turtles and rays. If the day is peaceful and calm, you will experience the serenity of being on the water, or if the winds are up it can be quite exhilarating.

Renowned birdwatching spots in this area include Clarrie Hall Dam west of Murwillumbah, and Terranora Inlet and Fingal Headland, both near Tweed Heads.

Byron Bay visitor centre: (02) 6680 8558; www.visitbyronbay.com

Baysail: (02) 6626 6889 or 1300 857443; www.baysail.net.au

Western New South Wales

Over the Great Dividing Range, New South Wales is full of natural treasures, although the distances between them can be daunting. Like much ecotourism, you are often best to base yourself in one area and explore it well, rather than skipping over the surface of the whole state. In the far west, near Broken Hill, the ancient mysteries of the World Heritage–listed Mungo National Park call for careful exploration and thought, and speedy travellers are often blinded to the beauty and life hidden in the red sand dunes of places such as Sturt National Park.

In this region there are a surprising number of hidden wetlands and bird haunts, cycling tours and organic farms. The ancient sound of the clapstick and corroboree echoes through the area's abundant Aboriginal campsites and art sites. Most travellers are advised to avoid summer in the far west as temperatures can reach 50°C. In winter, however, nights can get below freezing. With clear open skies and the home of some of Australia's biggest telescopes primed for stargazing, it is a region to open your eyes to horizons and eco-possibilities – the sky is the limit.

Walls of China in Mungo National Park

NATURE WATCH Lake Keepit State Recreation Area near Gunnedah is the only known habitat of the last 150 or so Lake Keepit hakea (*Hakea pulvinifera*), a spiky shrub that has small yellow–white flowers in September–October. The oldest specimens are believed to be hundreds of years old; www.threatenedspecies.environment.nsw.gov.au

Near Coonabarabran

ACTIVITIES

Exploring Warrumbungle National Park

There are walking tracks to suit all walkers in this dramatic volcanic park, from 1-kilometre strolls along paths suitable for strollers and wheelchairs, through to multi-day adventure hikes traversing steep and rough terrain. The 12.5-kilometre Breadknife Grand High Tops walk is the park's classic, with stunning views over the iconic 100-metre-high volcanic spire. Rock climbers used to love climbing this feature, but now are banned. However, they can still often be seen on the impressive cliffs elsewhere in the park. As in many New South Wales national parks, mountain-biking is permitted on fire trails, but not on walking tracks.

There is a range of campsites in the park, including The Woolshed, suitable for small-to-medium-sized groups. It can hold 55 at a pinch, and has power, lighting, a composting toilet, drinking water (untreated) and privacy from other campers. Other main sites also have toilets and Blackman has hot showers.

Indigenous Discovery Rangers run guided walks, where they describe bush tucker of the area and traditional lifestyles. A three-hour, easy walk to Tara Cave, a shelter used by the Gamilaroi people for thousands of years, is particularly recommended.

Warrumbungle Visitor Centre: (02) 6825 4364; www.environment.nsw.gov.au

Koala-spotting

Coonabarabran is home to one of the healthiest koala colonies in the state, and the solitary mammals are often seen in and around the town. Try the Porcupine Reserve and while there check out the view over the Liverpool Plains from the lookout.

Mount Kaputar National Park

This dramatic volcanic area has the 1510-metre Mount Kaputar at its peak, with superb views over about one-tenth of New South Wales. There are plenty of picnic areas, various lookouts and a range of bushwalks, from less than a kilometre to all-day treks. Two campgrounds have hot showers.

NPWS Narrabri: (02) 6792 7300; www.environment.nsw.gov.au

The awesome magma edge of The Breadknife towers 100 metres above Warrumbungle National Park

Didgeridoo player in sandstone caves at Pilliga Nature Reserve

Pilliga Nature Reserve

The Pilliga is the largest area of continuous temperate woodland on the Australian continent. Nearly half of this birdwatching mecca – almost 2500 square kilometres – is managed by the National Parks and Wildlife Service and the rest by State Forests. Its cypress pines, ironbark and Pilliga box trees surround many Aboriginal campsites and some rock shelters, with engravings, rock art and stone implements. As always, do not disturb any items you find. Pick up a copy of 'Bird Routes of Baradine' and the Pilliga brochure from the visitor centre then go for a picnic with your binoculars at the ready. Keep an eye out for turquoise parrots, glossy black-cockatoos and koalas. You may also spot mallee fowl, red-backed kingfishers, diamond firetails, and even a rare regent honeyeater. Make sure you include the waterbird haven of Yarrie Lake on your tour.

During the school holidays, and at other times on request, you can join a five-hour tag-along Aboriginal Discovery Tour. Bush campers are welcome in the reserve, but there are no camping facilities.

Visitor centre: (02) 6843 4000;
www.environment.nsw.gov.au
Warrumbungle Visitor Centre: (02) 6825 4364

Stargazing

Because of its combination of clear skies, altitude and distance from city lights, Coonabarabran is the astronomy capital of Australia. There are various ways to explore space here, from simply gazing skyward with a pair of binoculars while you camp, to touring the advanced facilities and technology at Siding Spring Observatory, the largest optical telescope in Australia. June and July are the best months for stargazing, but nights will be cold. Siding Spring Observatory does not offer any night activities, but there is an exhibition with information and activities about the pioneering work undertaken here and you can see the massive 3.9-metre telescope of the Anglo Australian Observatory.

The Warrumbungles Observatory offers day-viewing of sunspots, planets and some stars (yes, if the telescope is powerful enough you can still see stars during the day), as well as night shows where you will explore galaxies, nebulae and other worlds.

Siding Spring: (02) 6842 6211; www.mso.anu.edu.au
Warrumbungles Observatory: 0488 425 112;
www.tenbyobservatory.com

Near Dubbo

ACTIVITIES

Picnicking

Throw a rug down in the 167-hectare Burrendong Botanic Gardens and Arboretum near Wellington, and take in the fragrance of an estimated 2500 native plant species.

Botanic gardens: www.burrendongarboretum.org
Dubbo Visitor Centre: (02) 6884 1422 or 1800 674 443; www.dubbotourism.com.au

Taronga Western Plains Zoo

Australia's premier open-range zoo has some 1500 animals, many of them endangered, on 300 hectares of large, open areas and bushland. The zoo is involved in breeding and research programs for rare Australian and other animals.

You can cycle the 6-kilometre loop road, passing a vast number of creatures such as gibbons, giraffes and rhinoceros. For an extra-special encounter, stay on-site at the zoo in four-person safari lodges, where you can listen to the wildlife all night and go on exclusive behind-the-scenes tours, including a chance to hand-feed the giraffes. All the profits from Zoofari Lodge go back into education, conservation and protection of wildlife around the world.

(02) 6881 1488; www.zoofari.com.au

Wellington Caves

There are only two main caves to view here but they contain the Southern Hemisphere's largest known stalagmite – 15 metres in height and 32 metres in circumference. These caves also contain the largest deposit of Plio-Pleistocene mammal fossils in Australia, as well as fossils of corals and marine snails.

Wellington Visitor Centre: (02) 6845 1733 or 1800 621 614; www.visitwellington.com.au

Near Tibooburra

ACTIVITIES

Sturt National Park

Those desiring peace and solitude on their eco-holiday can camp among the rolling red sand dunes of the Strzelecki Desert. There are flat-topped mesas and spectacular jump-ups, granite tors and wide open spaces with red kangaroos and abundant wildflowers after rain. Four-wheel-drives are not needed in dry weather as there are loops for 2WD vehicles and 2WD campsites with free gas barbecues, but you need to bring your own water. You can also stay in bunk-style shearer's quarters or the homestead at Mount Wood station, in the far south-east corner of the park.

Tibooburra Visitor Centre: (08) 8091 3308

A giraffe at Taronga Western Plains Zoo

Camping in Sturt National Park

Walking across the Mungo dunes with Harry Nanya Tours

Near Broken Hill

WHERE TO STAY

Camping

Camping under the stars is one of your best options around this area, but several of the national parks also have shearer's quarters if you want to be under cover and have access to a kitchen (*see* national parks in Activities below).

Mungo Lodge

If you want a more up-market alternative, try Mungo Lodge, near Mungo National Park. Owned by Indigenous Business Australia, this has 16 recently refurbished units with ensuites, a windmill and solar panels that supply electricity, and all water is recycled to a high level of purity. There is a restaurant and bar.

(03) 5029 7297; www.mungolodge.com.au

ACTIVITIES

Kinchega National Park

This national park along the Darling River has massive red gums and a series of lakes and billabongs beside red dunes that can attract a variety of birdlife. There is some good camping, and occasionally the opportunity to have billy tea and johnnycakes with the Barkindtji elders.

NPWS Broken Hill: (08) 8080 3200

Mungo National Park

At the centre of the Willandra Lakes World Heritage Area, Mungo was listed in 1981 because of its special archaeological and geomorphologic features, including some of the world's oldest evidence of human life, in the skeletons, tools, shell middens and animal bones that have been found. Many of these have been preserved in then eroded out of the feature known as the Walls of China.

A two-hour tag-along interpretive driving tour with a Paakantji, Ngyiampaa or Mutthi Mutthi Discovery Ranger to the Walls of China is one of the best ways to appreciate and understand this incredible environment, including the 60 000 or more years of Aboriginal history and the compelling story of survival associated with the rise and fall of the lake.

For a full-day driving tour of Mungo's features with an Aboriginal guide, try the Aboriginal-owned Harry Nanya Tours, which also offers sunset tours.

Campsites are fairly basic at Mungo, but there are flush toilets and hot showers at the Visitor Centre. Up to 26 people can also stay in bunk rooms in the Shearer's Quarters, which has a communal kitchen.

Discovery ranger tour: (03) 5021 8900
Harry Nanya Tours: (03) 5027 2076; www.harrynanyatours.com.au
NPWS Buronga: (03) 5021 8900

Mutawintji National Park

Mutawintji National Park and the nearby Mutawintji Historic Site are brimming with Aboriginal rock art and engraving sites. The local Aboriginal Land Council conducts three-hour guided tours from April to October, usually Wednesdays and Saturdays. The national park also contains colourful gorges, perfect for isolated bush camping.

NPWS Broken Hill: (08) 8080 3200 or (08) 8080 3560

Remote four-wheel-drive tour

Some of Tri-State Safaris' tours have advanced eco-certification and provide a way to get out to some of the remotest parts of the state. They range from a two-hour sunset tour from Broken Hill, to multi-day tours of Kinchega, Mutawintji, Sturt and Mungo national parks.

(08) 8088 2389; www.tristate.com.au

Near Mudgee

WHERE TO STAY

Turon Gates, Capertee

Turon Gates has solar and gas-powered cabins and cottages on 2400 hectares of bushland. You can mountain-bike, swim in the Turon River, bushwalk or just laze around.

(02) 9969 3818 or (02) 6359 0142; www.turongates.com

ACTIVITIES

Cycling tours

Green Pedal Tours offers a great range of self-ride or guided and fully supported cycling tours, including tours to vineyards that will forward your purchases for free. The tours range from half-day family-friendly rides to multi-day 'wilderness rides' such as the 173-kilometre, four-day tour into Wollemi National Park and to Dunns Swamp (*see* Blue Mountains/Wollemi National Park). And after a day in the saddle, there is no camping – accommodation is in B&Bs and cottages.

(02) 6372 0999 or 0404 594 893; www.greenpedaltours.com.au

Cycling around the Mudgee vineyards with Green Pedal Tours

Wine-tasting

Mudgee is probably best known for its vineyards and wine, and there are a growing number of organic wineries, including Botobolar, Lowe Family Wines, Martins Hill and Thistle Hill. Broombee also has organic fruit and olives.

Mudgee Visitor Centre: (02) 6372 1020; www.mudgeewine.com.au

Near Bathurst

WHERE TO STAY

Clonturkle Sanctuary

Join the experiment in sustainable living and tourism at Clonturkle Earth Hamlet and Forest Sanctuary. Located at Yetholme, there are four cabins set on 240 hectares of mostly eucalypt forest, with 15 kilometres of walking tracks on the property.

(02) 6337 5226 or 0418 976 313; www.clonturklesanctuary.com.au

Near Wagga Wagga

ACTIVITIES

Birdwatching

Fivebough and Tuckerbil Wetlands are Ramsar-listed, and among nearly 200 birds spotted here are brolgas, black-winged stilts and painted snipes. Fivebough has 5 kilometres of walking tracks, with bird hides along the way.

(02) 6953 2541; http://fivebough.org.au

Koala-spotting

Koalas have thrived at Narrandera since they were released in 1972. At Narrandera Nature Reserve you should be able to spot a few.

Narrandera Visitor Centre: (02) 6959 1766

The Rock Nature Reserve

A 3-kilometre nature trail leads to a lookout at the top of the reserve's namesake, which towers 250 metres above the surrounding countryside, and from it you can see the Australian Alps.

The Rock Visitor Centre: (02) 6966 8100

Northern Territory

It is easy to see the Northern Territory as a tale of two landscapes: the humid wetlands of the Top End, where waterbirds and wildlife abound, and the stark, dusty red centre, with its striking rocks and gorges. But of course it is not as simple as that, with savannah and beaches, islands and ranges, dunes and stony deserts, fire and rain.

Ecotourism in this state has a strong focus on links with Indigenous heritage, more intact here than in many other areas. New and innovative tourism approaches are combining with these ancient ways to provide some very special experiences for the ecotraveller.

THE TOP END, home of vast cattle and buffalo stations, has abundant wildlife and authentic Aboriginal experiences in places such as Arnhem Land and Kakadu.

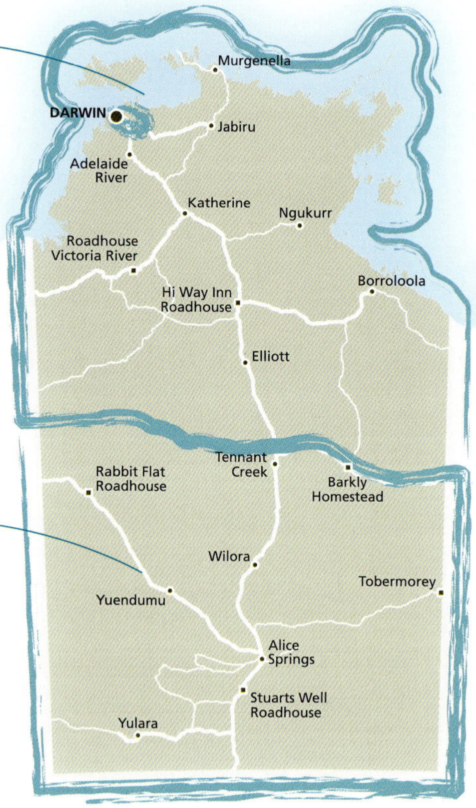

HEART OF THE COUNTRY is perhaps the most iconic of all Australia's landscapes. With the few tourism operators spread widely, ecotourism is still small but growing.

Tourism Top End: Cnr Mitchell and Knuckey sts, Darwin; (08) 8936 2499 or 1300 138 886; www.tourismtopend.com.au

Central Australian Tourism Industry Association: 60 Gregory Tce, Alice Springs; (08) 8952 5800 or 1800 645 199; www.centralaustraliantourism.com

Parks and Wildlife Commission Northern Territory (PWCNT): (08) 8999 5511; www.nt.gov.au/nreta/parks/

Parks Australia/Kakadu: (08) 8938 1120; www.environment.gov.au/parks/kakadu

Parks Australia/Uluṟu–Kata Tjuṯa: Cultural Centre (08) 8956 1128; Park Administration (08) 8956 1100; www.environment.gov.au/parks/uluru

TOP TEN

1 Spend five days soaking up Aboriginal culture on Pitjantjatjara lands in the Angatja Bush College, departing from Ayers Rock Resort

2 Soak under the stars at the meeting point of the cool and hot waters of the Tjuwaliyn (Douglas) Hot Springs

3 Help clear remote Arnhem Land coastline of marine debris alongside Yolngu rangers

4 Trek the legendary Larapinta Trail

5 Share a meal with an Indigenous family in a solar-powered resort in Kakadu

6 Cool off at Butterfly Gorge, Leliyn (Edith Falls) or one of the other top swimming spots

7 Canoe up Katherine Gorge and beyond

8 Spoil yourself at the new Indigenous-owned resort on Groote Eylandt

9 Gaze down from dizzying heights while on the Kings Canyon Walk

10 Sail out of Darwin to a nesting flatback turtle site

*Flatback turtle (*Natator depressus*) hatchling heading for the water on Bare Sand Island*

*The frilled lizard (*Chlamydosaurus kingii*) inhabits the woodlands of the Top End*

Darwin

In the heat and humidity of Darwin, where the whirr of air-conditioners continues in many establishments 24/7, there are some new and innovative ecotourism ventures cropping up, but certainly room for much more. The area around Darwin is rich in wildlife, beauty and Aboriginal heritage, so there is much here to protect. When visiting the capital you need to get out and about, for instance, taking in the birdlife at Fogg Dam, 70 kilometres away – an easy day trip.

WHERE TO STAY

Darwin Central

One of the first things you may notice about Darwin Central in comparison to other nearby hotels is its surprisingly small windows – part of its energy-efficient design. It was recently declared one of Darwin's greenest hotels for some of its initiatives.

21 Knuckey St; (08) 8944 9900 or 1300 364 263; www.darwincentral.com.au

Feathers Sanctuary

The owners of this quiet B&B, 10 minutes drive from the centre of town, are wildlife carers and often have injured birds such as jabirus on site. Their dug-out lagoon is also home to a wide range of birds, including whistling-ducks, cranes and egrets. The stylish huts are supplied by solar hot water, and all wastewater is fully recycled on site.

49A Freshwater Rd, Jingili; (08) 8985 2144 or 0408 895 512; www.featherssanctuary.com

WHERE TO EAT

Saffrron

This Indian restaurant in Parap uses biodegradable plates and bowls made from sugarcane fibres, and buys nearly all ingredients locally.

Shop 14, 34 Parap Rd, Parap; (08) 8981 2383; www.saffrron.com

← *Darwin Central Hotel*

Biodegradable plates are a feature of eco-friendly Saffrron restaurant →

ACTIVITIES

Cycling

Although the humidity might prevent you from wanting to do any exercise at all, the advantage of cycling is that you get a cool breeze as you go, and Darwin is relatively flat. Join a relaxing, guided three-hour cycle with Darwin Walking and Bicycle Tours to places such as the Botanic Gardens and Fannie Bay Beach, with lots of rest stops and information on everything from birdlife to history. If you want to head out on your own, the company will hire and drop off bikes to your accommodation. As the name suggests, there are also guided walking tours.

(08) 8942 1022; www.darwinwalkingtours.com

Fogg Dam Conservation Reserve

This incredible site 70 kilometres east of Darwin is believed to have the highest known biomass of predators and prey of any ecosystem on earth, and is teeming with water pythons and their primary food of choice, dusky rats. Vast numbers of birds also congregate here so it is a favourite haunt for birdwatchers. There are several walks, including the 2-kilometre Woodlands to Waterlily Walk and the 3.6-kilometre Monsoon Forest Walk, and regular guided night walks, in which you will probably encounter snakes, rats, turtles and owls.

Arnhem Hwy; (08) 8988 8009; www.nt.gov.au

George Brown Darwin Botanic Gardens

This 42-hectare tropical paradise, just north of Mindil Beach, includes sections of monsoon forest, dunes, mangroves and open woodlands. It is a great place for a stroll and introduction to the flora of northern Australia.

Geranium St; (08) 8981 1958; www.nt.gov.au

Swimming

Swim among the barramundi, turtles, agile wallabies and ibis at the 283-hectare Howard Springs Nature Park, 35 kilometres out of Darwin. There is a short, informative walk and plenty of shady picnic and barbecue spots, as well as a toddlers' pool.

A little further out of town is the Berry Springs Nature Park, which has two beautiful spring-fed pools to swim in, and a small waterfall fringed by pandanus and monsoon rainforest, as well as barbecues, picnic areas and walking tracks. Take a tip from the locals and swim with goggles to see some of the fish and other aquatic animals.

Howard Springs NP: (08) 8983 1001; www.nt.gov.au
Berry Springs NP: (08) 8933 6310; www.nt.gov.au

Mangrove Route's wildlife cruise boat Snubfin *is named after Australia's only endemic dolphin species, the Australian snubfin (*Orcaella heinsohni*), a family of which lives in Darwin Harbour*

Wildlife tours

Powered by wind alone, City of Darwin Cruises' eco-accredited catamarans can take you to dugongs, dolphins and, from May to September, nesting flatback turtles. Cruises range from three hours to multi-day experiences.

With Mangrove Route you can visit nesting sites of flatback and olive ridley turtles or search for dolphins on a vessel that takes a maximum of 21 passengers.

City of Darwin Cruises: Stokes Hill Wharf; 0417 855 829 or 0418 480 095 or 0401 118 777; www.cityofdarwincruises.com.au
Mangrove Route: (08) 8942 3995; www.mangroveroute.com

The Top End

Until recently, ecotourism in the Top End has been something of a sleeping giant. However, in the past couple of decades, Territorians have increasingly realised how special their wildlife, authentic Indigenous culture and landscapes are – and not only how important these features are to preserve, but how attractive they are to tourists. Although World Heritage treasures such as Kakadu National Park will continue to be major drawcards, the Territory is starting to offer more diverse experiences, particularly in the luxury market. Take a look at the options on isolated stations, in bush camps and at places such as Groote Eylandt.

Stokes Range soars above the Victoria River in Gregory National Park

Top End tours

Because of the distances, logistics and permits required to obtain access to areas such as Arnhem Land, ecotravellers in the Northern Territory should consider some of the great organised tours on offer. Travelling with a small group will probably reduce your individual carbon footprint, and can take much of the stress out of a holiday. There are plenty of operators, but some are particularly recommended. Odyssey Tours and Safaris is eco-certified and runs a special seven-day Top End safari through Kakadu and Arnhem Land, staying in semi-permanent and permanent safari camps. Wilderness Adventures is also eco-certified and runs small, nature-based tours. Other companies that offer small, private tours with a focus on nature and Indigenous culture include Guided by Nature and Venture North.

Odyssey Tours and Safaris: (08) 8984 3450 or 1800 891 190; www.odysaf.com.au
Wilderness Adventures: (08) 8941 2161; www.wildernessadventures.com.au
Guided by Nature: (08) 8983 2797; www.guidedbynature.com.au
Venture North: (08) 8927 5500; www.northernaustralia.com

Darwin to Katherine

WHERE TO STAY

Bamurru Plains

If you want to use air-conditioning in the beautiful high-class safari suites here, you have to pay extra. That is just one of the unusual environmental policies at this resort on a working buffalo station on the edge of Kakadu National Park. Hot water and more than 60 per cent of the power needed in camp is solar generated. Local products are used wherever possible, and the operation donates to the Australian Wildlife Conservancy.

(02) 9571 6399 or 1300 790 561;
www.bamurruplains.com

Kakadu Culture Camp

This Aboriginal-owned-and-operated camp in the heart of Kakadu is 100 per cent solar-powered, including the bore pump. It has solar hot water and 40 solar panels providing electricity. From May to November you can stay in one of the spartan safari tents or camp, sharing three-course meals of crocodile, kangaroo or buffalo meat, or anything else with the Bininj people who live and work here. There is a range of cultural and natural heritage tours, including the only night-time tour in Kakadu.

0428 792 048; http://kakaduculturecamp.com

ACTIVITIES

Indigenous tours

About 100 kilometres east of Katherine, the Aboriginal community of Manyallaluk is open for day tours in which you will learn about bush tucker, bark painting, fire lighting, spear throwing and traditional basket weaving. The road is suitable for 2WD vehicles for most of the year, or you can get picked up in Katherine.

Gecko Canoeing: (08) 8972 2224 or 1800 634 319;
www.geckocanoeing.com.au

Litchfield National Park

Less than a couple of hours drive from Darwin, this special park near Batchelor has a stunning mix of Top End terrain, including waterholes where you can swim, and some magnificent waterfalls. You need a 4WD to get to the south part of the park and places such as the haunting Lost City sandstone formations, but the rest can be reached by a sealed road. The park offers plenty of great camping, picnicking and walking, including the 39-kilometre Tabletop Track, which can be done in two to five days, or sections done as day walks.

PWCNT Batchelor: (08) 8976 0282; www.nt.gov.au

Kakadu National Park

This World Heritage–listed national park covers 19000 square kilometres and is overflowing with Aboriginal culture, wildlife, wetlands and around 1000 species of plant. Its terrain

A herd of buffalo at Bamurru Plains

Relaxing by the pool at Bamurru Plains resort

includes eucalypt woodlands and forests, flood plains, monsoonal rainforests, sandstone gorges and gullies, rivers and streams, billabongs and mangroves, and its animals range from dingoes to dugong, and jacanas to jabirus. There are bird hides at the Mamukala Floodplain in the South Alligator area. There are plenty of camping areas, some only accessible in the Dry.

Yellow Water Cruises With a reputation as one of the best tours in Kakadu, this operator is eco-accredited and works with Parks Australia in monitoring weeds and wildlife.

Parks Australia: (08) 8938 1120; www.environment.gov.au

Yellow Water Cruises: (08) 8979 0145; www.yellowwatercruises.com

Hiking

Willis's Walkabouts run a huge range of guided bushwalking tours in Kakadu, the Top End and elsewhere. The trips are graded in different levels, but are generally aimed at fit people who can carry a moderately heavy pack for distances and do not mind roughing it a bit to see some spectacular, little-travelled parts of the bush.

(08) 8985 2134; www.bushwalkingholidays.com.au

Nitmiluk (Katherine Gorge) National Park

Visitors to this 2928-square-kilometre national park are drawn to the stupendous Katherine Gorge, with its walls of sandstone up to 200 metres high, and freshwater crocodiles and three turtle species that poke their heads out of the water. But the park has other treasures. Leliyn (Edith Falls) has picturesque waterfalls and pools that are great for swimming and the Jatbula Trail offers superb overnight hiking (*see* below).

Canoeing Have a casual paddle in the main gorge in Nitmiluk for four hours, or aim to get to the end of the fourth gorge in a 16-kilometre, eight-hour round trip. Canoes can be hired at the Gorge with Nitmiluk Tours, but booking is recommended during the busy June–September season. Keen canoeists can also take out canoes overnight, camping in one of the designated camping areas for canoeists.

Rockpools at Gunlom in Kakadu National Park

Out of the park but still on the stunning Katherine River, Gecko Canoeing runs three-to-seven-day guided canoeing adventures, supplying everything you need, including a cook! The popular three-day trip involves 40–55 kilometres of paddling, and the longest trips are up to 120 kilometres.

Hiking Experience the spectacular range of terrain that Nitmiluk has to offer on the 58-kilometre, four-to-five-day Jatbula Trail. The track is well marked and popular, only open in the dry season, and campsites are restricted to ten campers, so you will need to book. It takes in stunning waterfalls, rock-art sites and butterfly-filled gorges. Nitmiluk Tours provides transport for hikers from Katherine, and will provide a ferry service across the Katherine River to the start of the walk. The company also provides a range of cultural and wildlife tours. Gecko Canoeing has a guided five-day walk on the Jatbula Trail (you need to carry a pack).

PWCNT Nitmiluk: (08) 8972 1886; www.nt.gov.au

Nitmiluk Tours: (08) 8972 1253; www.nitmiluktours.com.au

Gecko Canoeing: (08) 8972 2224 or 1800 634 319; www.geckocanoeing.com.au

Arnhem Land

WHERE TO STAY

There are limited opportunities to get into Arnhem Land and permits are needed. Two of the few operators that run remote bush camps and lodges with Aboriginal cultural and nature tours are Davidson's Arnhemland Safaris, in the west of Arnhem Land, and Arnhemland Barramundi Nature Lodge near Maningrida.

Davidson's Arnhemland Safaris: (08) 8927 5240; www.arnhemland-safaris.com

Arnhemland Barramundi Nature Lodge: (08) 8983 1544; www.barralodge.com.au

Dugong Beach Resort

This new, exclusive resort is owned by the Groote Eylandt traditional landowners and features cultural tours and interaction with local people. On a 'traditional boating tour' mud crabs and other shellfish are speared and cooked in a traditional way for you to eat.

(08) 8987 7077 or 1800 877 077; www.dugongbeachresort.com.au

ACTIVITIES

Arnhem Land Coast Sailing Expedition

In a trip mainly under sail on a catamaran, you will travel the Arnhem Land coastline to the Cobourg Peninsula then across the Timor Sea to the Tiwi Islands. The seven-day trip runs May to October, and you can become involved in the sailing, or sit back and relax.

(02) 8270 8400 or 1300 720 000; www.worldexpeditions.com/au/

Arnhem Land marine rescue project

On this amazing expedition, you will join Yolngu rangers in removing marine rubbish, such as discarded fishing nets and thousands of thongs, bottles and plastic bags, from remote stretches of the Arnhem Land coastline, freeing animals such as turtles. The six-day trip combines this important work with immersion in the Yolngu culture, including a day when men and women separate to learn about the traditional roles of each group.

(02) 8270 8400 or 1300 720 000; www.worldexpeditions.com/au/

A remote beach on the Gove Peninsula in Arnhem Land

Bawaka Cultural Experiences

This Indigenous-owned-and-run tourism operation is gradually opening up a variety of extraordinary experiences with Arnhem Land's Aboriginal people on the Gove Peninsula. One of the programs is an overnight experience for women only, called the dillybag program. In it, participants learn about history, art, beliefs, customs, spirituality, medicine, food collection, cooking and the Yolngu women's connection and affiliation with the land. Visitors stay in solar-powered houses, or can sleep outdoors. There is also a men's 'hunting and men's business' program, for one or two days.

(08) 8987 0429; www.yolngutourism.com

Aboriginal rock paintings at the Nganalam Art Site in Keep River National Park, west of Timber Creek

Beyond Katherine

ACTIVITIES

Butterfly Gorge Nature Park

One of the best swimming waterholes in the Top End, the main pool here is deep and big enough to swim laps. It is a bit of a walk from the car, but the rewards are towering paperbarks, rock walls with ancient art and crow butterflies flitting overhead. It is a top spot for a picnic.

PWCNT Batchelor: (08) 8976 0282; www.nt.gov.au

Gregory National Park

The Northern Territory's second-largest national park is believed by many to be more beautiful than Kakadu, with spectacular ranges and gorges. There are some roads accessible to two-wheel-drive vehicles, but the majority of tracks are 4WD only. There are plenty of camping sites, but few facilities.

PWCNT Timber Creek: (08) 8975 0888; www.nt.gov.au

Katherine Visitor Centre: (08) 8972 2650

Keep River National Park

A small but precious national park near the Western Australian border, Keep River treasures some great little secrets. Near the campgrounds it has sandstone formations like the famous Bungle Bungles across the border, and it has exceptionally fine views along the 2-kilometre Gurrandalng walk and from Jarnem Lookout. In the dry season you should be able to get to the camping areas with a 2WD.

Park ranger: (08) 9167 8827; www.nt.gov.au

Tjuwaliyn (Douglas) Hot Springs

An ancient place of Wagiman women's ceremonies, these hot springs are too hot to touch where they come out of the ground, but provide a relaxing soak further downstream at the junction of a cool creek. There is a large camping area with toilets, barbecues, firewood, picnic tables and water.

PWCNT Batchelor: (08) 8976 0282; www.nt.gov.au

Heart of the country

A quiet moment by a pool, within sight of the hulking form of Uluru. The reverence of the natural cathedral of Palm Valley. The pulse-quickening rush when peering over the edge of the red cliffs of Kings Canyon. Natural treasures like these are the keys to ecotourism in Central Australia. Awareness of environmental impact is slowly causing change in this region, with more operators becoming partly solar-powered and taking other positive steps. As in the Top End, Indigenous experiences here are a vital and growing part of the ecotourism industry.

Surveying the view from the rim of Kings Canyon

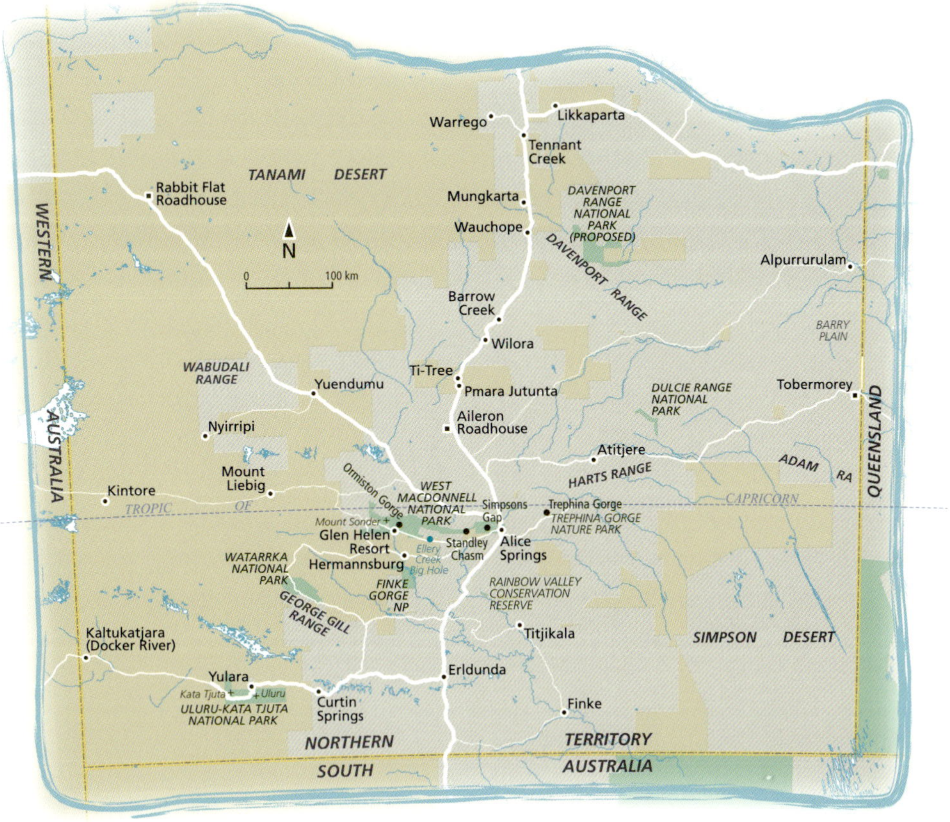

Heart of the country tours

Driving times to Uluru and Kings Canyon surprise many travellers who expect to stay in Alice and pop out for a 'visit' to the Rock. If long-driving distances daunt you, or you are not an experienced four-wheel driver and want to go to places such as Palm Valley, join a tour with an eco-accredited operator such as Alice Springs Holidays.

Experienced 4WD tour operators can also get you safely into more remote areas of the desert country. Try the eco-accredited company Way Out Back, in particular its birdwatching and Aboriginal cultural tours.

Ossies Outback 4WD Tours is also eco-accredited and runs remote tours through desert country, especially the Simpson Desert. They dig a proper bush toilet every night, solving problems of toilet paper blowing around the bush and being dug up by dingoes.

GREEN TRAVEL TIP Dingoes and some other animals often dig up human waste and toilet paper if it is buried shallowly. This can lead to used toilet paper blowing around bush campsites and along bush tracks. To prevent this, if it is safe to do so, burn your used toilet paper in the deep hole you have dug before filling it in. Just be careful of spinifex, as it is very flammable.

Alice Springs Holidays: (08) 8953 1411 or 1800 801 401;
www.alicespringsholidays.com.au
Way Out Back: (08) 8952 4324 or 1300 551 510;
www.wayoutback.com
Ossies Outback 4WD Tours: (08) 8952 2308;
www.ossies.com.au

Alice Springs and surrounds

ACTIVITIES

Alice Springs Desert Park

More than a zoo, this superb facility will introduce you to the plants, animals and people of the central Australian deserts and is well worth the entry price. The changing daily schedule includes wildlife talks, bush-tucker tastings, traditional storytelling, nocturnal tours and dawn birdwatching tours.

Larapinta Dr, Alice Springs; (08) 8951 8788;
www.alicespringsdesertpark.com.au

Alice Springs Telegraph Station

As well as visiting the heritage sites in the historical reserve, go for a walk along one of the tracks, where rock-wallabies and other wildlife can often be seen. It is also a nice spot for a picnic and free electric barbecues are provided. The reserve is located just 3 kilometres north of town.

Telegraph Station Rd (off Stuart Hwy); www.nt.gov.au

Alice Springs walking tour

Take Foot Falcon's two-hour walking tour around Alice Springs, learning about the history and culture of the region with long-term Alice Springs resident, teacher, writer and historian, Linda Wells. A highlight of the tour is sitting in the legendary Todd River bed, listening to some of Linda's poetry.

(08) 8953 4015 or 0427 569 531; f.falcon@bigpond.net.au

Birdwatching

Surprisingly, the Alice Springs Sewage Ponds, with a year-round supply of water, is one of the best places to watch birds in this region. There is even a decent bird hide, and although you certainly should not swim or wade, the ponds look like a harmless series of dams. If you like birds, do not miss this experience, bizarre as it sounds, late in the afternoon. You will need to leave a deposit for a key at PowerWater.

PowerWater: Greatorex Bldg, cnr Bath and Parsons sts, Alice Springs; (08) 8951 7340;
www.powerwater.com.au

Cycling

Hop on the 40-kilometre-return bike track that heads out from Flynn's Grave on the outskirts of town to Simpsons Gap. It is generally flat and provides an unexpected way to see the hills and ranges encircling Alice Springs as you cycle through woodlands of river red gums, mulga and witchetty bush. There are 18 interpretive signs along the way, rest points and two places to get drinking water. Bikes can be hired from Toddys Backpacker Resort. Jungala Enterprises conducts four-hour, guided cultural tours along the route, on painted mountain bikes.

*An emu (*Dromaius novaehollandiae*) in the landscape, with Mount Connor in the background*

Aboriginal cultural tour in Alice Springs Desert Park

Solar city

As one of five Australian cities in the Solar Cities program, Alice Springs is undergoing a power revolution. With $36 million being handed out to residents and business to change their power consumption to more sustainable technologies, solar hot water heaters and panels are popping up everywhere. Tourists will also notice some large, shiny parabolic 'solar concentrators' at the airport and just out of town, which focus the sun's rays to generate power. If you want to learn more, visit the Smart Living Centre in Todd Street, with changing displays, and the Desert Knowledge Precinct with new solar technology displays (see Activities).

(08) 8950 4350; www.alicesolarcity.com.au

For a tougher desert cycling experience, try 14 days with the Adventure Collective, nearly all on dirt roads, from Alice Springs to Cooper Pedy, through the Simpson Desert. It is supported all the way by vehicle and you are likely to be the only ones out there. Other multi-day, supported, desert-cycling options include the MacDonnell Ranges and Uluṟu area.

Toddys: (08) 8952 1322 or 1800 027 027; www.toddys.com.au

Jungala: 0415 815 033; www.jungala.com.au

Adventure Collective: (08) 8357 3935 or 1300 948 911; www.adventurecollective.com.au

Desert Knowledge Precinct

Examine up close a range of different solar-power technologies at the Desert Knowledge Precinct on the outskirts of town. This $3 million facility will demonstrate tracking devices, solar concentrator dishes and a variety of other technology in an interactive display.

South Stuart Hwy; (08) 8959 6000; www.desertknowledge.com.au

Finke Gorge National Park

This 460-square-kilometre park, with its hidden oasis Palm Valley, is home to many unique plant species, including the red cabbage palm (*Livistona mariae*), of which there are only about 3000 adult plants. The rough track in is only suitable to 4WD, but it is worth joining a tour (*see* tours, page 75) or renting a 4WD to spend some time in this very special place. The main campsite has toilets, hot showers and barbecues.

PWCNT Alice Springs: (08) 8951 8211; www.nt.gov.au

PWCNT Finke Gorge: (08) 8956 7401

Hiking

Now known as one of the best arid-zone treks in the world, the 220-kilometre Larapinta Trail goes from Alice Springs to Mount Sonder, and can be done in 12–15 days by experienced hikers. Walkers are advised to use the Walker Registration Scheme prior to departure. They need to be prepared for freezing nights and

*Red cabbage palms (*Livistona mariae*) line the course of the Finke River at Palm Valley*

Ghost gums in West MacDonnell National Park

hot days with little shade, and the rocky track is best handled with firm-soled boots. Do not despair if you cannot handle carrying a heavy pack for that distance. There are several Larapinta walking tour operators who provide a 'best of' package. They transport you to and from the best sections, carry the bulk of your gear between campsites and provide a knowledgeable guide during the day. You still get to camp out under the stars. Trek Larapinta offers a range of Larapinta tours from three to 20 days. It is an eco-accredited, carbon-neutral business that uses solar panels in campsites and works with Indigenous communities through the Central Land Council. Jungala Enterprises is the only Aboriginal-guided tour on the Larapinta, and you can do single days, overnight excursions or week-long adventures.

Overnight Walker Registration Scheme: 1300 650 730; www.nt.gov.au

Trek Larapinta: 1300 724 795; www.treklarapinta.com.au

Jungala: 0415 815 033; www.jungala.com.au

Indigenous tours

The Aboriginal-owned-and-operated RT Tours runs a range of tours up to a nine-day experience. Operator Bob (Penunka) Taylor is an ex-chef, and also offers a bush restaurant experience in the MacDonnell Ranges, in which you are picked up from Alice, and taken out for a three-course meal with bush influences, cooked over a mulga fire. After dinner you will go looking for wildlife.

(08) 8952 0327 or 0438 532 118; www.rttoursaustralia.com.au

Newhaven Sanctuary

Jointly run by the Australian Wildlife Conservancy and Birds Australia, the 2620-square-kilometre Newhaven Sanctuary was previously a cattle station, and now is run solely to preserve the 160 bird species, four threatened mammal species and other wildlife here. It is very remote, 360 kilometres west of Alice Springs, near the tiny community of Nyirripi, and the campground, with toilets and showers, is only open between April and November, but it holds a magnificent desert ecosystem of claypans, dunes, spinifex, jump-ups and salt lakes. You need a 4WD.

(08) 8964 6000; www.awc.org.au

Olive Pink Botanic Gardens

A top little spot for a picnic and a gentle meander, this interesting site has more than 250 species of central Australian plants identified, and is often alive with myriad birds.

Tuncks Rd, Alice Springs; (08) 8952 2154; www.opbg.com.au

Stargazing

In a night that combines scientific knowledge about the stars with traditional storytelling, telescope viewing and coffee under the stars, head to the Milky Way Cafe 12 kilometres out of Alice, and the Spirit of the Night Sky tour.

Tour bookings: (08) 8950 3030; www.ananguwaai.com.au

Trephina Gorge National Park

Trephina Gorge has ghost gums growing on sheer quartzite cliffs, sandy watercourses lined by magnificent river red gums, swimming holes, top camping with drinking water and gas barbecues, and some fantastic walks – the two-hour Chain of Ponds walk is an absolute gem.

PWCNT Alice Springs: (08) 8951 8211; www.nt.gov.au

West MacDonnell National Park

Most Alice Springs tourists will pop out to West MacDonnell National Park, dipping into key sites that are generally just off the road: Simpsons Gap, Standley Chasm, Ellery Creek Big Hole, Ormiston Gorge and Glen Helen Resort. Each of these has excellent short walks in which you have a fair chance of seeing rock-wallabies and abundant birdlife. But rather than hurtling around seeing everything in a day before racing back, take a swag or tent, or hire a campervan, and camp at one of the top spots. You will have far more chance of seeing a wider range of wildlife, hearing dingoes howl, and watching the bush come alive in the crisp early morning. You will also have more of a chance to go for a longer hike on a section of the extraordinary Larapinta Trail (*see* Hiking above). In summer you can take a dip in some of the waterholes, which can be extremely cold.

PWCNT Alice Springs: (08) 8951 8211; www.nt.gov.au

South of Alice

WHERE TO STAY

Gunya Titjikala

The five deluxe safari tents here, on the outskirts of the remote Titjikala community, are raised on platforms with private decks that overlook the red sands of the Simpson Desert. The whole facility is solar-powered and the ensuites have bioseptic flush toilets that purify everything to clear water. All staff are

The sheer-sided walls of Standley Chasm

local Indigenous people, and 50 per cent of all profits go directly to the Titjikala Foundation, which focuses on health, education, and school retention initiatives. You can go on walks or bush-tucker gathering with the locals, take part in dot-painting workshops and share stories around a campfire. The resort is only accessible by 4WD, but transfers from Alice Springs can be arranged.

(02) 9211 2322 or 1300 135 657; www.gunya.com.au

Kings Canyon

Kings Canyon Wilderness Lodge, run by APT on Kings Creek Station adjacent Watarrka National Park, has luxury tented cabins that are partly run on solar power. Kings Creek Station itself has a range of camping sites and permanent tents with great views of the George Gill Ranges. About 80 per cent of the power needs at Kings Canyon Resort, inside the park, is supplied by solar power.

(03) 9277 8555; www.aptouring.com.au

(08) 8956 7474; www.kingscreekstation.com.au

(08) 8956 7442 or 1300 134 044; www.kingscanyonresort.com.au

An Aboriginal guide explains the uses of native plants at Uluru

Uluru and Kata Tjuta

In terms of accommodation providers, options are very limited at Uluru and camping is not permitted in the park, but thankfully Ayers Rock Resort has been developed with a wide variety of options, from five-star luxury to simple cabins and camping. The resort features large sails to assist with passive cooling, has established the Mutitjulu Foundation to help the local Anangu people, and treats its wastewater back to an irrigation standard.

(02) 8296 8010; www.ayersrockresort.com.au

ACTIVITIES

Indigenous tours

Join dot-painting workshops, sunrise viewing of Uluru and breakfast with Anangu people, or one of the other Anangu Tours and you will learn about the lifestyle and Tjukurpa lore of Uluru's people, including bush tucker, traditional ways of living and bush skills.

Desert Tracks conducts a one-day tour from Ayers Rock Resort to Cave Hill, perhaps the largest and most significant art site in Central Australia, and site of the Seven Sisters Tjukurpa. But their most exciting tour is the five-day Angatja Bush College, in which you travel into Pitjantjatjara country, camp out, learn how to make traditional weapons and tools, discover some of the creation stories, songlines and dances, and forage for honey ants and other bush tucker.

In the Kings Canyon area, learn about the local rock art, bush tucker and people of the Kings Canyon area at the Wallace Rockhole Tourist Park, an Aranda community. There are also dot-painting workshops, and you can stay in one of the two simple cabins or in the camping area.

(08) 8956 2123; www.ananguwaai.com.au
(08) 8656 2563; www.deserttracks.com.au
(08) 8956 7993; www.wallacerockholetours.com.au

Rainbow Valley Conservation Reserve

If Uluru has not sated your appetite for rocks that change colour at sunset, camp out at this reserve 100 kilometres south of Alice. Part of the

'Sounds of Silence' dinner preparations at Ayers Rock Resort, with Uluru in the background

Sunset lights up the brilliantly coloured domes of Kata Tjuta

James Range, the pretty sandstone cliffs here have different coloured bands. Access is only recommended for 4WDs as there are a few sandy stretches on the 22 kilometres of unsealed road.

PWCNT Alice Springs: (08) 8951 8211; www.nt.gov.au

Uluṟu–Kata Tjuṯa National Park

To respect the Anangu people's wishes, and not climb Uluṟu, does not mean you will miss out, because this iconic national park is full of great experiences and things to keep you occupied for days. The 10-kilometre walk around the base of Uluṟu is flat, marked by informative signs and gives you a constantly changing, peaceful perspective of the monolith away from the crowds at the carpark. At Kata Tjuṯa, the 7-kilometre Valley of the Winds and shorter Walpa Gorge walk are both worth doing. The excellent cultural centre is made of locally produced mud bricks and offers cultural and bush-tucker sessions and plant walks. There are free ranger tours and dawn and sunset viewing of the Rock or Kata Tjuṯa as they are undergo various colour changes.

Parks Australia: (08) 8956 1100;
www.environment.gov.au
Cultural Centre: (08) 8956 1128

Watarrka National Park

On the steep climb in the heat, you may think you are going to have a heart attack, but the view from the top of the 6-kilometre Kings Canyon Walk, or rim walk, is definitely worth it, with plunging red cliffs and lush green vegetation below. Halfway along the rim, with its rocky domes and incredible views 100 metres straight down into Kings Canyon, is the Garden of Eden waterhole, where you can cool off. If this taste leaves you wanting more, strap on a pack and tackle the 22-kilometre Giles Track.

PWCNT Watarrka: (08) 8956 7460
PWCNT Alice Springs: (08) 8951 8211; www.nt.gov.au

The road to Mount Connor, some 100 kilometres east of Uluṟu

Near Tennant Creek

ACTIVITIES

Davenport Range National Park

Although little known, some describe this as the most beautiful national park in the state. It only has basic camping facilities, but features beautiful permanent waterholes that attract abundant wildlife and are great for swimming. You will need a 4WD with high clearance to get to most areas.

PWCNT Alice Springs: (08) 8951 8211; www.nt.gov.au

Nyinkka Nyunyu Art and Culture Centre

This centre, situated in Paterson Street, incorporates an Aboriginal art gallery and museum. As well as great art and information about the Indigenous people of the Tennant Creek area, there are bush-tucker tours and occasional performances, and a landscaped garden with bushfoods.

Culture centre: (08) 8962 2699;
www.nyinkkanyunyu.com.au
Performance manager: (02) 8962 2221

Queensland

Ecotourism is probably at its strongest in Queensland. With a real focus on protecting the World Heritage–listed rainforests and the Great Barrier Reef, Tourism Queensland and individual operators have diligently worked to improve the sustainability of tourism, and promote the state's outstanding natural values. In addition, Ecotourism Australia has its home in Queensland, leading to greater awareness and more eco-accredited operators here than elsewhere.

The state is also home to some of the largest and longest-running ecotourism ventures in the country. Whether kayaking, bushwalking, snorkelling, camping on remote islands or joining a dinosaur dig, there is bound to be something in this vast state for every ecotourist.

FAR NORTH QUEENSLAND is quite wild and remote, but still offers a range of accommodation and activities for the ecotourist, as well as multi-day 4WD tours.

REEF AND ISLANDS and the lush hinterland is a focus for ecotourists in Australia and around the world, who mainly come to see the most impressive coral reef on the planet.

SOUTH-EAST QUEENSLAND is something of a hotspot for ecotourism, with ventures located around the ranges covered in World Heritage rainforests, and in the green belt of the greater Brisbane area and sand islands of Moreton Bay.

SAVANNAH AND OUTBACK covers an enormous area, and opportunities for ecotourists are fairly widespread.

Brisbane Visitor Information Centre: Cnr Albert and Queen sts, Queen Street Mall, Brisbane; (07) 3006 6200 or (07) 3006 6290; www.ourbrisbane.com

Queensland Parks and Wildlife Service (QPWS): (07) 3227 7111

Environmental Protection Agency (EPA): 160 Ann St, Brisbane; 1300 130 372; www.epa.qld.gov.au

TOP TEN

1. Rescue and monitor endangered marine turtles on remote coastline near Mapoon
2. Paddle a canoe through luscious Boodjamulla (Lawn Hill) National Park
3. Go on a remarkable dinosaur dig for a week with palaeontologists, leaving from Winton
4. Experience one of the great outback train journeys, with the *Gulflander*, the *Savannahlander* or the *Westlander*
5. Stay on a large, organically run cattle station near Kilcowera in the far south-west
6. Play and picnic in one of Brisbane's parks, in particular Brisbane Forest Park or Mount Coot-tha Forest
7. Swim with dwarf minke whales on a multi-day diving expedition on the Great Barrier Reef
8. Spend several days soaking up the culture and rich wildlife of the Aurukun Wetlands on the west coast of Cape York Peninsula
9. Whale-watch at Hervey Bay
10. Explore the magnificent Whitsunday Islands by kayak or yacht

GREEN TRAVEL TIP If you have a great travel experience with an operator who is being environmentally responsible, spread the news! By pointing people towards the best operators, you will encourage others to lower their environmental impact when they embark on their holidays.

Brisbane

City of dragons and brush-turkeys, koalas and bull sharks, Brisbane has a delightful array of sizeable parks and bush areas housing all sorts of wildlife and opportunities for ecotravellers. Join up to 24 species of migratory wader that visit the Greater Brisbane area each year. It is well worth exploring the river and surrounds, either by ferry, kayak or cycling on the bike paths, and visiting at least one of the large regional parks. Picnickers and families with active children will love the variety of outdoor fun on offer, and Brisbane is a great spot to launch an eco holiday in south-east Queensland, Fraser Island or the southern parts of the Great Barrier Reef.

WHERE TO STAY

Brisbane Marriott Hotel

By no means the greenest accommodation in this book, the Marriott still deserves inclusion as one of the better options in large hotels. It gained the Green Globe Benchmarked Bronze status and is AAA-rated for its water- and electricity-saving schemes. All general waste goes to the Ti Tree Bio energy facility to turn waste into green energy.

515 Queen St, Brisbane; (07) 3303 8000 or 1800 899 899; www.marriott.com

WHERE TO EAT

Mondo Organics, West End

Australia's first organic restaurant when it opened in 2000, Mondo Organics has a range of organic meats, including beef, chicken, duck and lamb, and the fish is chosen for the sustainability of the catch. The grains and some of the fruit and vegetables are also organic.

166 Hardgrave Rd, West End; (07) 3844 1132; www.mondo-organics.com.au

Main Beach on North Stradbroke Island

Cycling along the boardwalk at Kangaroo Point

ACTIVITIES

Birdwatching

Although Brisbane is not the hottest birdwatching destination in the country, there are several pleasant surprises for some avian magic. Try the 380-hectare Tinchi Tamba Wetlands on Moreton Bay, which has walking and canoe trails, and a bird hide from which you may see collared kingfishers, mangrove honeyeaters, striated herons, avocets, royal spoonbills and Pacific herons. The Boondall Wetlands also has a series of boardwalks and tracks, and a good population of eastern curlews that feed there between September and April before flying to Siberia. There are free, guided walks every weekend, and occasional guided canoeing trips.

Mirrabool on Moreton Island (*see* Moreton Island below) is also known as an excellent place to see some of the many stints, curlews and other waders that arrive here from Siberia during spring, staying until April.

Tinchi Tamba Wetlands: Brisbane City Council (07) 3403 8888; www.brisbane.qld.gov.au

Boondall Wetlands: via Gateway Arterial Rd (take Boondall Entertainment Centre exit); (07) 3403 1490; www.ourbrisbane.com

Brisbane Forest Park

More than 800 plant species grow in this 28 500-hectare park, which includes subtropical rainforest, open woodlands and scribbly gum forests. There are numerous short to medium-length walks to lookouts, waterfalls and rainforest pockets, and ten walk-in bush camping sites.

Park HQ: 60 Mount Nebo Rd, The Gap; (07) 3300 4855 or 1300 723 684; www.epa.qld.gov.au

Cycling and mountain-biking

Brisbane has a growing network of great cycling trails and some excellent rides for tourists – a five-to-20-kilometre ride along the shores of the Brisbane River comes highly recommended. There is also a great ride from the Brisbane Entertainment Centre to Nudgee Beach via the Boondall Wetlands and a lookout. You can hire from several places, including Riverlife at Kangaroo Point and Valet Cycle Hire in the Botanic Gardens. Both these operators will provide you with some great ideas for a ride suitable to you, and Valet Cycle Hire will also deliver the bike to your accommodation.

One of the most exciting places for mountain bikers is Daisy Hill State Forest, with a range of tight, twisty tracks through the forest. If you have any time to look up you may also spot the odd koala.

A little outside the city, a 148-kilometre rail trail between Ipswich and Blackbutt is being progressively developed and opened to explore the scenic Brisbane Valley and the Blackbutt Range. At the time of publication about a quarter of the lovely route was open – you will need to obtain a key to unlock the gate (to prevent trail-bike riders and four-wheel drivers from entering).

Riverlife: (07) 3891 5766; www.riverlife.com.au

Valet Cycle Hire: 0408 003 198; www.cyclebrisbane.com

Mountain-bike riding: www.mtbdirt.com.au

Rail trail: (07) 4163 0633; www.railtrails.org.au

Indigenous concert

Riverlife Mirrabooka perform ancient stories and dance twice a week during a day concert and a night concert at Kangaroo Point. Witness traditional fire-starting techniques and try traditional Indigenous instruments such as the didgeridoo and clapsticks.

(07) 3891 5766; www.riverlife.com.au

Feeding the dolphins at Tangalooma Island Resort

Kayaking and canoeing

Take a kayak for a paddle along the Brisbane River and the brownish water will prevent you from seeing the many bull sharks or other marine life swimming below the surface, but it is a great way to see the city. Riverlife at Kangaroo Point hires kayaks, and also runs a popular sunset/night kayaking trip where the city lights come on as flying foxes come out to play.

Ipswich Canoe Hire has kayaks and canoes for hire and runs a drop-off and pick-up service if required. They recommend a half-day paddle from Fernvale to Twin Bridges.

Riverlife: (07) 3891 5766; www.riverlife.com.au

Ipswich Canoe Hire: (07) 3201 7075

Moreton Island's Tangalooma wrecks, a popular diving site

Moreton Island

Almost completely protected by national park, this sand island is reached by ferry from Scarborough or the Brisbane River, and if you keep an eye out you may spot dugong, turtles and bottlenose dolphins on the way. Once there you can climb to the 285-metre summit of the world's tallest, stabilised sand dune on the 2.5-kilometre Mount Tempest Track or take one of the other walks to perched lakes. Other pursuits include snorkelling, swimming and a guided cruise or tour with Tangalooma Island Resort – including the extended cruise in which you can hand-feed wild dolphins at the end of the day. Tangalooma Island Resort also hires out snorkelling and diving gear, runs snorkelling tours, a fantastic eco kids club, and the Tangalooma Marine Education and Conservation Centre. Dolphin Wild also runs cruises and snorkelling tours to see the marine life. There are five campgrounds and four beach-camping zones on the island.

Tangalooma Island Resort: (07) 3637 2000 or 1300 652 250; www.tangalooma.com

Dolphin Wild: (07) 3880 4444; www.dolphinwild.com.au

Mount Coot-tha Forest

The largest natural area in Brisbane, this 1500 hectares of open eucalypt forest holds more than 18 kilometres of walking tracks, 12 kilometres of mountain-biking tracks and a further 31 kilometres of multi-use tracks. Although the bushland itself is not stunning, it boasts some beautiful waterfalls after rain, golden wattles and other wildflowers in spring, and superb views over Moreton Bay, Stradbroke Island and the city. There are plenty of picnic areas too, including at Simpson and J C Slaughter falls.

Brisbane City Council: (07) 3403 8888; www.brisbane.qld.gov.au

North Stradbroke Island

North Stradbroke is known among Brisbane wildlife- and beach-lovers as a great place to get away for a weekend or even just a day. You can get there by vehicular ferry from Cleveland, and enjoy beaches such as the 32-kilometre Main Beach and the family-friendly Cylinder Beach. Spy whales from June to November on the 30-minute North Gorge Headland Walk, walk the

The view from Point Lookout on the North Gorge Headland Walk, North Stradbroke Island

2 kilometres through Blue Lake National Park to Blue Lake or visit any of the spring-fed lake areas on the island. Stradbroke Island Holidays can organise everything from bike hire to the ferry trip and lunch.

Alternatively, you can go for a three-hour combined kayaking and snorkelling tour with Straddie Adventures. They also hire out kayaks, surfboards and snorkelling gear and run 4WD tours to places such as the Aboriginal middens at Myora Springs, the lakes and the Keyholes.

You can be picked up from your accommodation in Brisbane for a six-hour 4WD tour of the island with Straddie Kingfisher Tours. Run on biodiesel, the tour includes a barbecue on the beach ('the best restaurant in the world') and opportunities to see dolphins, turtles, manta rays, koalas and kangaroos. Straddie Guides also runs half- and full-day 4WD tours, including the option for longer bushwalks.

If you want to know the best snorkelling or diving spots, check in at the Manta Lodge and Scuba Centre. They can direct you towards manta rays and leopard sharks during summer, endangered grey nurse sharks during winter, plus rays, guitar sharks, turtles, dolphins, octopus, corals, nudibranchs and hundreds of tropical fish.

Stradbroke Island Holidays: (07) 3821 0266 or 1300 303 766; www.stradbrokeholidays.com.au
Straddie Adventures: (07) 3409 8414 or 0417 741 963; www.straddieadventures.com.au
Straddie Kingfisher Tours: (07) 3409 9502; www.straddiekingfishertours.com.au
Straddie Guides: (07) 3415 3106; www.straddieguides.com
Manta Lodge and Scuba Centre: (07) 3409 8888; www.mantalodge.com.au
Visitor centre: Junner St, Dunwich, North Stradbroke; (07) 3409 9555

Playing and picnicking

Brisbane abounds in great picnic and play areas. The wet and adventure playground at Manly is one of the best in Australia for infants and the young at heart, and there is plenty of room for a picnic. Other top spots include South Bank Parklands and, in Ipswich, Queens Park, which includes a free zoo featuring Australian wildlife.

Rock climbing

Brisbane's Kangaroo Point is perhaps the friendliest city rock-climbing spot in the country, with views over the Brisbane River, a range of climbs for absolute beginners and upwards, and established anchor points (bollards) at the top of the 20-metre cliff. It is even lit up at night and on some summer nights there are climbers there past midnight. Riverlife, at the base of the cliffs, will give you instruction, as will Pinnacle Sports, or if you know what you are doing and have your own gear, go for it!

Riverlife: (07) 3891 5766; www.riverlife.com.au
Pinnacle Sports: (07) 3368 3335;
www.pinnaclesports.com.au

Wildlife tours

Araucaria Ecotours, based in Rathdowney, runs birdwatching and other wildlife tours of one to three days in and around the Brisbane area. The highly educational eco-accredited tours are designed, and usually run, by a research zoologist.

Bushwacker Ecotours is also eco-accredited and focuses on one- and two-day trips from Brisbane into surrounding islands or areas of rainforest, such as Lamington National Park, Springbrook, Fraser Island and Moreton Island. Most of the guides have a background in environmental science or research.

Ferryman Cruises runs wildlife cruises around Bribie Island and Pumicestone Passage Marine Park. A carbon-negative business, it has a strong environmental policy and contributes time and resources to Clean Up Australia Day.

During a night-spotlighting tour at Redlands Indigiscapes at Capalaba you have a reasonable chance of seeing koalas, possums and other wildlife. The tours run in school holidays – there are bushfood tours then as well – but at all times you are free to explore the 14.5-hectare site brimming with native plants and a kilometre of walking tracks, and a cafe.

Araucaria Ecotours: (07) 5544 1283;
www.learnaboutwildlife.com
Bushwacker Ecotours: 1300 559 355;
www.bushwacker-ecotours.com.au
Ferryman Cruises: (07) 3408 7124 or 0402 266 893;
www.ferryman.com.au
Redlands Indigiscapes Centre: (07) 3824 8611;
http://indigiscapes.redland.qld.gov.au

Lifesavers at Cylinder Beach, a patrolled family-friendly spot on North Stradbroke Island

Rock climbing on the cliffs at Kangaroo Point

South-east Queensland

According to folklore, it was the dairy-farming O'Reilly brothers who woke up to the beauty and tourism potential of this region, welcoming their first guests as early as 1915 and thereby starting one of the earliest, and longest-running, ecotourism ventures in this country, O'Reilly's. And any visitor to Lamington or Springbrook national parks will agree with the assessment of those early settlers. There are waterfalls and wompoo pigeons, towering Antarctic beech trees, massive carpet pythons, spiny blue Lamington crayfish, red-necked pademelons and parrots everywhere. It is no surprise that this region, extending south from the Sunshine Coast to the New South Wales border and including Toowoomba, is still an ecotourism hotspot, with great accommodation options, swimming and surfing on some of Australia's best known beaches, and challenging hikes in the Glass House Mountains.

A walking trail through the rainforest in the Binna Burra section of Lamington National Park

GREEN TRAVEL TIP Why wait for Clean Up Australia Day? If bushwalking, throw a small rubbish bag into your pack, not just for your own rubbish, but for any you find on the way.

Gold Coast and hinterland

WHERE TO STAY

Binna Burra Mountain Lodge

A long-running ecotourism operator, Binna Burra was the first private company in Australasia to achieve certification under the international Green Globe standards for ecological sustainability, and it has very thorough environmental policies publicly stated on its website and full eco-accreditation. Snuggled into a corner of Lamington National Park, it has plenty to protect. The rooms at the lodge have no TVs, clocks or telephones, in order to encourage guests to forget about the real world for a while. Some have private bathrooms and great views over the rainforest and mountains. There are also camping sites and permanent canvas safari-style tents.

Binna Burra Rd, Beechmont; (07) 5533 3622 or 1300 246 642; www.binnaburralodge.com.au

Cottages on the Creek

This 2-hectare establishment is managed as a Land for Wildlife property and the two, one-bedroom spa cottages have composting toilets, protecting Currumbin Creek with its turtles, catfish, platypus and yabbies.

1464 Currumbin Creek Rd, Currumbin Valley; (07) 5533 0449; www.cottagesonthecreek.com.au

Destiny Boonah

Set on 80 hectares of Land for Wildlife property, this self-contained three-bedroom cottage is solar- and wind-powered. You are encouraged to bring a mountain bike or go bushwalking on the property, which is located near Boonah (42 kilometres west of Beaudesert).

(07) 5463 2643; www.destinyboonah.com

Mt Barney Lodge Country Retreat

Almost surrounded by Mount Barney National Park, and with Queensland's fourth-highest peak overshadowing the 12-hectare Land for Wildlife property, this former farm hosts plenty of wildlife, including bandicoots, red-necked

Binna Burra Mountain Lodge in Lamington National Park

wallabies, frogs, geckoes, bats and phascogales, as well as growing habitat for the endangered glossy black-cockatoo. The spacious recycled farmhouses and cabins are more suited to large families or groups than couples, but there are also some safari tents and a camping area. The delightful owner–operators are keen to get you out exploring their local bit of paradise, offering rock climbing, bushwalking, children's night activities (leaving you in peace for a few hours) and an eco sunset tour.

1093 Upper Logan Rd, Barney View; (07) 5544 3233; www.mtbarneylodge.com.au

O'Reilly's Rainforest Retreat

One of the most recognised and long-running ecotourism ventures in the country, O'Reilly's has an excellent reputation. By planting more than 40 000 trees on their property, which is surrounded by Lamington National Park, they have turned the old dairy farm into a wildlife and ecotourism haven, with a strong emphasis on environmental education and an excellent discovery centre. Controversially, they feed the wildlife every day, resulting in abundant birds and pademelons around the place.

Lamington National Park Rd, via Canungra; (07) 5502 4911 or 1800 688 722; www.oreillys.com.au

The Mouses House, Springbrook

Set in a beautiful rainforest at more than 800 metres above sea level, this luxury resort has 11 self-contained chalets, hot tub, sauna, tennis court and bikes, a sensible environmental policy and eco-accreditation. It treats and returns all spring water that is used to the landscape, uses 100 per cent renewable energy, carbon offsets its gas use and takes care with the abundant wildlife on the property.

(07) 5533 5192; www.mouseshouse.com.au

The Tree Top Walk at O'Reilly's Rainforest Retreat

WHERE TO EAT

Songbirds in the Forest

At Songbirds the food is prepared using mainly organic and local produce. 'Organic ingredients are much more than a passing fad for the health conscious, they are simply a better way of doing things', says the chef at this restaurant in 20 hectares of rainforest in Mount Tamborine. (Accommodation is also available here in six luxury villas.)

Tamborine Mountain Rd; (07) 5545 2563; www.songbirds.com.au

ACTIVITIES

Girraween National Park

An 11 800-hectare sculpture garden of granite boulders in precarious poises, Girraween also has 17 kilometres of walking tracks, and two pleasant camping areas. Wildflowers colour the scenery among forests of red gum, stringybark and blackbutt. The two-hour return walks to the top of the Pyramid and Castle Rock are recommended, although the endings are not for the faint-hearted.

QPWS: (07) 4684 5157; www.epa.qld.gov.au

Kayaking

Go for a paddle, a snorkel and explore South Stradbroke Island, all in the one half-day tour with Australian Kayaking Adventures on Broadwater on the Gold Coast.

Australian Kayaking Adventures: 0412 940 135; www.australiankayakingadventures.com.au

Lamington National Park

One of this country's iconic parks, Lamington has lush, bird-filled subtropical rainforest on an extinct volcano. There are mossy Antarctic beech, elkhorns and staghorns, red-legged pademelons, a special endemic crayfish and more birds than you could hope to name. Understandably – as it is only two hours drive from Brisbane – the most popular Green Mountains section can get crowded on weekends and in school holidays, but the Binna Burra section of this 20 940-hectare park is usually quieter. Camping permits must be applied for in advance for all weekends and school holidays.

Among the 160 kilometres of walking tracks, there is bound to be something to suit everyone. Many people do the 21.4-kilometre Border Track, from Binna Burra to O'Reilly's (or the other way), staying a night and then returning. If you are doing that, make sure you walk the waterfall-filled Toolana Creek circuit at least one way (it is an extra couple of kilometres but a far more interesting walk).

Park rangers: Green Mountains (07) 5544 0634; Binna Burra (07) 5533 3584

QPWS: www.epa.qld.gov.au

Toonloona Creek in Lamington National Park

*Satin bowerbird (*Ptilonorhynchus violaceus*) and its bower in Lamington National Park*

Main Range National Park

This rugged 29 000-hectare national park near Warwick is great for bushwalking – with 14 tracks of all standards – and contains rainforest, spectacular eucalypt-covered mountain ranges and superb lookouts. The solid 12-kilometre-return Bare Rock Track and the exposed 10-kilometre Mount Mitchell Track are both recommended for their views. The park has a couple of pleasant camping areas with composting toilets.

Park ranger: (07) 4666 1133; www.epa.qld.gov.au

Springbrook National Park

Far enough away from the Gold Coast to avoid the screams from the theme parks, this beautiful, cool World Heritage–listed national park near the New South Wales border has rainforests, waterfalls and mountain streams to refresh the senses. It covers some 3425 hectares and has a series of superb short walks, including the iconic Natural Bridge, where a glow-worm-filled cave has a stunning waterfall coming down into it through basalt. There is one small campground.

Park ranger: (07) 5533 5147; www.epa.qld.gov.au

Surfing

Rather than lugging your own board, or paying in petrol by strapping it to a roof rack, you can rent a board from Gold Coast Surf Boards for the length of your stay. They will even drop it off for you. If you are not at that level, but want to learn on one of Australia's most well-known stretches of surf, there are plenty of places that will try to get you standing and paddling. Brad Holmes Surf Coaching teaches able-bodied and disabled surfers. Alternatively, try the well-respected Godfathers of the Ocean or Walkin' on Water Surf School and Surf Rentals. Surfing Australia has a current list of other surf schools on its website.

Gold Coast Surf Boards: 0432 742 560; www.goldcoastsurfboards.com.au
Brad Holmes Surf Coaching: (07) 5539 4068 or 0418 757 539; www.bradholmessurfcoaching.com
Godfathers of the Ocean: (07) 5593 5661; www.godfathersoftheocean.com
Walkin' on Water Surf School: (07 5534 1886 or 0418 780 311; www.walkinonwater.com
Surfing Australia: www.surfingaustralia.com

Tamborine Mountain Distillery

There is a multitude of chemical-free schnapps, gins and vodkas to try here, many of which come from the fruits grown on the farm. Try lemon myrtle vodka, the multifaceted choc'n'chili liqueur, forest peppermint vodka, macadamia nut liqueur or the zany Turkish delight liqueur. The distillery is on Beacon Road in North Tamborine.

(07) 5545 3452; www.tamborinemountaindistillery.com

*Carpet python (*Morelia spilota*) in Lamington National Park*

Whale-watching

This activity is relatively new to the Gold Coast compared to somewhere as established as Hervey Bay. However, it can provide a natural and refreshing break from the crowds and theme parks during the June–November season. Australian Whale Watching and Charters departs from Marina Mirage at Main Beach.

(07) 3630 2463; www.australianwhalewatching.com.au

Wildlife tours

Aries Tours runs advanced eco-certified tours from the Gold Coast to glow-worm caves in Springbrook National Park, generally with an Indigenous guide who provides information about the plants, animals and cultural history of the area. This long-running company also runs a night safari tour into the Currumbin Wildlife Sanctuary.

(07) 5594 9933; www.ariestours.com

Sunshine Coast and hinterland

WHERE TO STAY

Eumarella Shores Lakeside Cottages, Noosa

The eight, two-bedroom cottages here stand by Lake Weyba on a 20-hectare Land for Wildlife property and all have complimentary canoes. They have passive solar design, purify all wastewater, and no trees were removed in the construction of the cottages. There is a 20-minute bushwalk on the property, with interpretive signs, and you can hire bikes.

(07) 5449 1738; www.eumarellashores.com.au

Glass House Mountains Eco-Lodge

The simple, down-market rooms here include the use of old train carriages for a communal kitchen and group area. An old church has also been recycled, and all greywater and blackwater is used on site to irrigate the chemical-free orchard that guests are invited to raid. Guests are also encouraged to plant a tree and contribute to ongoing conservation projects such as the Richmond birdwing butterfly (*Ornithoptera richmondia*) recovery program.

198 Barrs Rd, Glasshouse Mountains; (07) 5493 0008; www.glasshouseecolodge.com

Stylish cabin at Glass on Glasshouse

Glass on Glasshouse

Very new, these three funky pads are great for couples that like the latest technology. The clean interior design includes clever louvres for cross-ventilation and floor-to-ceiling windows on the north side with views of the Glass House Mountains. Rainwater is collected, the fires are ethanol, the water solar-heated and wastewater from the spa goes into the garden, where eastern grey kangaroos graze. 'We aren't a purist eco-site, but we have tried to apply good eco principles wherever possible in the design of our cottages. We're light green rather than a dark green', says owner–operator Bill Rogers.

(07) 5496 9608 or 0431 101 208; www.glassonglasshouse.com.au

Heaven in the Hills, near Maleny

Generating all its own power through wind and solar technology, this 10-hectare retreat at Reesville has abundant wildlife and a range of accommodation, including a hundred-year-old train carriage.

(07) 5494 3359; www.heaveninthehills.com.au

Lyola, near Maleny

These very nice eco-certified pavilions are on a Land for Wildlife property. The place is involved in rainforest restoration, providing nesting boxes and habitat expansion for the Richmond birdwing butterfly species.

(07) 5429 6900; www.lyola.com.au

The 556-metre Mount Beerwah (left) and 377-metre Mount Coonowrin in Glass House Mountains National Park

ACTIVITIES

Bunya Mountains National Park

Those who make the drive up the winding roads to this 1100-metre-high mountain range near Kingaroy will discover the largest remaining area of towering bunya pines in the world as well as hoop pines, rainforest thickets, bottle trees and 35 kilometres of walking tracks, many of which feature great lookouts. The area is well known for king parrots, crimson rosellas, red-necked wallabies and great barred-frogs. There are three camping grounds, but only the one at Dandabah is suitable for caravans and trailers.

Park ranger: (07) 4668 3127; www.epa.qld.gov.au

Cycling

Join a half-day or longer guided bike tour with Bicycle Tours of Queensland, particularly the popular Sunshine Coast ride or Maleny to Glass House Mountains. A back-up bus is included if it all gets too much.

0400 019 059; www.bicycletoursqld.com.au

Glass House Mountains National Park

These 25-million-year-old cores of extinct volcanoes that give their name to the park pop sharply out of the landscape and are the perfect adventurer's playground. Have a half-day's rock climbing, bushwalking and abseiling with Pinnacle Sports, which includes a hike to the summit of Mount Ngungun. Alternatively, head out on your own on some of the spectacular walking tracks through open woodlands and heaths to panoramic lookouts and mountain summits. The Stony Creek day-use area in Bellthorpe Forest Reserve is an exceptionally good, forested picnic area with cascading creeks and a rockpool, and the view from the Glass House Mountains Lookout is a feast on its own, but goes well with a picnic. You can camp at nearby Coochin Creek.

QPWS: (07) 5494 3983; www.epa.qld.gov.au

Pinnacle Sports: (07) 3368 3335; www.pinnaclesports.com.au

Abseiling from the heights of Mount Beerwah

Cruising the tranquil waters of the Noosa Everglades

Kayaking and canoeing

Experience a bit of a different kayak tour with the eco-accredited Kayak Noosa, who for ten years have incorporated small sails on the front of their kayaks, giving you an extra 5 knots or so of speed. They have kayaks for hire and a range of tours, but the most popular is a day tour up the Noosa River and in Laguna Bay, looking for dolphins.

Noosa Ocean Kayak offers two quite different two-hour kayaking tours: one a more peaceful paddle up the Noosa River, where you are likely to see stingrays, bull sharks, crabs and a wide variety of birds; the other an ocean kayak around the Noosa National Park, among the waves, dolphins and turtles. The company also rents kayaks out if you want to go on your own. Former Australian surfing champion Merrick Davis also provides surfing lessons.

If you are keen to extend the adventure, rent a canoe and camping gear from Elanda Point and head out into the Cooloola section of Great Sandy National Park for a night or two. Or join the eco-accredited Tribal Travel on its three-day, two-night Noosa Everglades Canoe Safari, with all equipment supplied.

Blue Water Kayak tours at Caloundra runs a half-day kayak tour to Bribie Island, including a walk and possible swim on the island, and the chance to see animals such as wallabies, dingoes, kangaroos, honeyeaters, raptors, kingfishers, rays, dolphins and turtles. This operator also conducts a gentle two-hour twilight tour, which may be towards Bribie Island or up tranquil Bells Creek, depending on the weather.

Kayak Noosa: 0448 567 321; www.kayaknoosa.com
Noosa Ocean Kayak: 0418 787 577; www.noosakayaktours.com
Elanda Point: (07) 5485 3165; www.elanda.com.au
Tribal Travel: 1800 763 077; www.tribaltravel.com.au
Blue Water Kayak: (07) 5494 7789 or 0412 766 932; www.bluewaterkayaktours.com

Noosa Everglades Discovery

For three decades, this eco-certified company has been offering wildlife cruises along the Noosa River and also offers one- or two-day trips to Fraser Island.

(07) 5449 0393; www.noosaevergladesdiscovery.com.au
Noosa visitor centre: (07) 5447 4988; www.tourismnoosa.com.au

Noosa National Park

Several easy walking tracks lead through rainforest, open woodlands, coastal heath and pines, along this picturesque stretch of coast. Keep your eyes open and you may spy koalas, lace monitors, brush-turkeys and endangered ground parrots.

Park ranger: (07) 5447 3243; www.epa.qld.gov.au

Picnicking

Take your pick of picnic spots in this attractive region from any of the beaches or coastal parks, such as Bribie Island Recreation Area, through to rainforested parks in the hills with great views, such as Mary Cairncross Park at Maleny.

Sunshine Coast Hinterland Great Walk

Relatively new, this 58-kilometre, four-day walk along the Blackall Range links existing parks and reserves, and is perfect to stretch the legs for a couple of hours to take in a lookout or a 100-metre-high waterfall. Some sections run through agricultural areas, but there are also beautiful stretches through rainforests and woodlands.

QPWS: www.epa.qld.gov.au

Swimming

Obviously Queensland is known for its superb beaches, and the Sunshine Coast – although busy – rarely seems as overpopulated as the Gold Coast, south of Brisbane. Throw your towel down on virtually any patch of sand and enjoy the surrounds. The superb family-friendly Dicky and Kings beaches at Caloundra are particularly recommended.

*Lace monitor (*Varanus varius*) near Fig Tree Point on the Noosa River in the Cooloola section of Great Sandy National Park*

Wildlife cruises

Cruise Maroochy Eco was the first eco-certified operator on the Sunshine Coast and runs a variety of cruises on the Maroochy River. On the popular four-and-a-half-hour ecotour, you are likely to see kangaroos, wallabies, azure kingfishers and brahminy kites. The company does erosion monitoring, carries out all its wastewater, and also offers a cultural and bush-tucker tour.

0407 333 242 or 1800 333 242;
www.cruisemaroochyeco.com.au

*Flower of the Wallum banksia (*Banksia aemula*) in Noosa National Park*

*Quiet cove in Noosa National Park fringed with screw pine (*Pandanus tectorius*)*

Reef and islands

Some 2300 kilometres of reef stretch out along the north Queensland coast, providing habitat for an estimated 1500 fish species, 400 types of coral and more than 5000 mollusc species. Depending on the location, divers and snorkelling enthusiasts are confronted with a carpet of scales: parrotfish, silver bullseyes, coralfish, bannerfish, angelfish, wrasse and triggerfish, to name just a few. The 12 000-year-old reef will continue to adapt with climate change, but is likely to remain a very special area for ecotravellers.

Ecotourism in this region is as vibrant as the colours in the reef, and many operators have a focus on protecting this world treasure. But this is not just a place for water activities – there are also sublime rainforests and parks, birdwatching, and wildlife tours on land.

Sunset at Seventy Five Mile Beach on Fraser Island

GREEN TRAVEL TIP It is usually all too easy to encourage animals to come closer with a tasty titbit or two. However, most people who do this feed them inappropriate food, which can be damaging to all in the long term. For example, the familiarity with which campers treated dingoes on Fraser Island eventually led to a fatal encounter. Other animals, such as seagulls or cockatoos, can become a pest if fed regularly in the same spot. As a general rule, resist the urge to feed animals on holidays, and keep our animals wild.

Fraser Island and Hervey Bay

WHERE TO STAY

Emeraldene Inn and Eco-Lodge, Hervey Bay

The 14 hotel-style rooms here, including two disabled rooms, have solar hot water and an envirocycle treatment system so that all sewage and greywater is treated and reused on site. The lodge has a solid environmental policy and is endeavouring to make a difference with the little things. It has a kill switch for each room that turns everything off, including the refrigerators, if there are no guests booked in a room. There is a pool and two of the rooms have a full kitchen.

(07) 4124 5500; www.emeraldene.com.au

Kingfisher Bay Resort, Fraser Island

With 1000 beds, and a choice of pools, restaurants and bars, this is the largest accommodation place mentioned in this book, but it has a longstanding reputation as being a positive role model for large ecotourism developments. At the cutting edge of environmental management and design when it opened in 1993, this eco-accredited resort has an extensive environmental interpretation program run by one of the largest private ranger groups in Australia, with activities ranging from whale-watching to personalised 4WD tours with your own ranger. The on-site wastewater treatment plant feeds sludge to a worm farm, which is used to grow herbs and native plants for use in the restaurant, and the main, airy building has been designed to minimise power use, with natural heating and cooling.

(07) 4120 3333 or 1800 072 555; www.kingfisherbay.com

ACTIVITIES

Cycling

A very family-friendly, 18-kilometre ride goes along Hervey Bay's coastline from Point Vernon to the marina, all on a bike path, passing playgrounds, picnic areas and multiple cafes and ice-creameries. You can also ride out onto the 868-metre Urangan Pier. Rent mountain bikes, kids' bikes or surreys (with plenty of room for adults and children) from Beach Safaris on the Esplanade at Urangan.

(07) 4125 4585; www.beachsafaris.com.au

Dolphin tours

All year-round Blue Dolphin Marine Tours runs eco-tours to see the two species of dolphin in the area – the bottlenose, and the rare Indo-Pacific humpback dolphin. You have a 95 per cent chance of seeing the dolphins, and a fair chance of also spotting a dugong. The company is

Kingfisher Bay Resort

Seventy Five Mile Beach on Fraser Island is a popular 4WD route, allowing access to many of the sights

involved in research on the humpback dolphins, and also offers whale-watching in season and a sunset champagne tour completely under sail.
(07) 4124 9600; www.bluedolphintours.com.au

Four-wheel-drive tours

You will need a 4WD to see most of Fraser Island because it is largely made of sand. However, you do not need to bring one, as plenty of eco-certified companies will take care of the driving for you. Fraser Island Discovery has advanced eco-certification and uses small vehicles for personalised tours. Fraser Island Adventure Tours also has advanced eco-certification. Kingfisher Bay Resort offers either small, personalised tours with your own knowledgeable ranger, or larger group tours. The Fraser Island Company offers a range of guided tours and packages, including a three-day camping trip on the island.
Fraser Island Discovery: (07) 5449 0393;
www.fraserislanddiscovery.com.au
Fraser Island Adventure Tours: (07) 5444 6957;
www.fraserislandadventuretours.com.au
Kingfisher Bay Resort: (07) 4120 3333 or 1800 072 555;
www.kingfisherbay.com
Fraser Island Company: (07) 4125 3933 or 1800 063 933;
www.fraserislandco.com.au

Hiking

Fraser Island, with its 1653 square kilometres encompassing 200-metre-high sand dunes, 80 beautiful lakes and pockets of rainforest, is a delight for those prepared to put on a pack. Hikers can camp beside some of the lakes in areas where car campers are not allowed. There are many overnight or short options, but the ultimate hike on Fraser is the classic 90-kilometre, six-to-eight-day Fraser Island Great Walk from Happy Valley, which takes in many of the major natural attractions such as the Valley of the Giants, Lake McKenzie, Central Station, Lake Birrabeen and Lake Boomanjin, finishing at Dilli Village on Seventy Five Mile Beach. If it sounds like the spot for you, but you want the bulk of your camping gear and food carried for you, join a four- or five-day guided and supported walking tour with Footprints on Fraser. The entire island is protected within Great Sandy National Park.
Park ranger: (07) 4127 9191; www.epa.qld.gov.au
Footprints on Fraser: (07) 4125 6295 or 1300 765 636;
www.footprintsonfraser.com.au

Kayaking and canoeing

Freshwater Kayaking Tours operates two gentle kayaking tours from Hervey Bay – one up the Burrum River, which includes lunch, and a bay tour, which includes snorkelling.

On Fraser Island, Kingfisher Bay Resort has a short interpretive canoe tour along the beach and through mangroves.
Freshwater Kayaking Tours: 0406 161 940 or
1300 725 578; www.freshwaterkayaking.com.au
Kingfisher Bay Resort: (07) 4120 3333 or 1800 072 555;
www.kingfisherbay.com

NATURE WATCH Female humpbacks travel from Antarctic waters up the coasts of Australia to calve – and barely eat during the entire migration. When the calves are born, weighing nearly a tonne, the mothers supply some 600 litres of milk a day, primarily from their fat reserves.

*Humpback whale (*Megaptera novaeangliae*) in Hervey Bay*

Picnicking

The whole foreshore at Hervey Bay provides almost infinite places to picnic, but if you are after somewhere a little more secluded, try the Great Sandy Region Botanic Gardens near Urangan Harbour. The 26 hectares are home to turtles, birds and a huge variety of plants of the Wide Bay and Great Sandy regions. The gardens also have an orchid house, with an estimated 20000 orchids in the collection, a bush-tucker garden, picnic shelters and barbecues.

(07) 4125 9700; www.frasercoast.qld.gov.au

Whale-watching

Although there are plenty of places to see humpback whales on the east coast, few are as good as Hervey Bay. Many young calves and their mothers rest up here between August and the start of November, before heading south. The waters are generally calm, and the whales are unafraid – even curious – about the whale-watching boats, approaching within metres on nearly every whale-watching trip. The calves can be as playful as puppies, jumping clean out of the water or splashing around. If you do boat-based whale-watching in only one place in Australia, do it here.

Not surprisingly, there are plenty of operators who will take you out. Quick Cat is the longest running, has advanced eco-certification and is one of the best set up, with two vessels operating half-day and full-day tours. On board there are hydrophones to listen to the whale song and other marine sounds, underwater cameras to keep an eye on the whales even underwater, and the boats are wheelchair accessible. The company has sensible environmental policies, including no Styrofoam cups on board.

Other recommended operators include Kingfisher Bay Resort and the eco-certified Whalesong Cruises.

Quick Cat: (07) 4128 9611 or (07) 4128 9387 or 1800 671 977; www.herveybaywhalewatch.com.au

Kingfisher Bay Resort: (07) 4120 3333 or 1800 072 555; www.kingfisherbay.com

Whalesong Cruises: 1800 689 610; www.whalesong.com.au

Kayaking through mangroves at Kingfisher Bay Resort

Bundaberg to Rockhampton

WHERE TO STAY

Lady Musgrave Island

This 14-hectare island has a vast coral lagoon suitable for snorkelling novices. Like North West below, it has no facilities except composting toilets, but feels less remote as it is regularly visited by daytrippers. It has space for 40 campers. You can travel to the island – for camping or a day tour – through Lady Musgrave Cruises.

(07) 4974 9077 or 1800 631 770; www.lmcruises.com.au

North West Island

The second largest coral cay on the Great Barrier Reef, after Yorke (Masig) Island, this wildlife paradise 75 kilometres off Gladstone has no facilities bar three composting toilets, from which the waste is carted off the island. There is camping for up to 150 people, but you need to bring your own drinking water and everything else. It is home to the largest pisonia forest in Australia and some of the largest nesting populations of wedge-tailed shearwaters (an estimated 800 000), black noddies (some 500 000) and green turtles (the island is closed from Australia Day to Easter to protect the turtle hatchlings). Although some of the coral in the lagoon is dead, it has superb snorkelling off the edge of the reef. Well-prepared campers will love this piece of secluded paradise, safely away from the daytrippers. Curtis Ferry Services operates barges out to the island and supplies 5 litres of water per person, per day.

Camp bookings: 13 1304; www.qld.gov.au/camping

Curtis Ferry Services: (07) 4972 6990; www.curtisferryservices.com.au

Wilson Island

Only six couples are allowed at a time on this tiny 2-hectare coral cay, staying in minimal-impact luxury tents with wooden floors. All power is provided by solar power and batteries, and the eco-accredited resort uses rainwater and bottled water. The island is closed during February to help protect the multitude of nesting birds.

(02) 8296 8010 or 1300 134 044; www.wilsonisland.com

ACTIVITIES

Bushwalking

Aside from the plentiful beaches, there are quite a few places to stretch the legs on this section of coast. A very short walk up to Ganoonga Noonga Lookout in Eurimbula National Park, near Agnes Water, provides views over Bustard Bay, swamplands, heath and mountains.

Alternatively, take your pick of walks in the dramatic sandstone gorges of Cania Gorge National Park, inland from Gladstone, including the interesting 5.6-kilometre circular walk to Fern Tree Pool and Giants Chair. There are caves to explore, rare palm trees, platypus in the creeks and Aboriginal paintings.

Tondoon Botanic Gardens, 6 kilometres from the centre of Gladstone itself, is surprisingly beautiful, with tracks through 104 hectares of forest, with turtles, abundant birdlife and plenty of spots for a picnic.

QPWS: www.epa.qld.gov.au

Tondoon Botanic Gardens: (07) 4971 4444

Kayaking and canoeing

The company 1770 Liquid Adventures at Agnes Waters operates a two-and-a-half-hour sunset kayaking and dolphin-spotting tour, and a three-and-a-half-hour daytime tour in which you will not only get a chance to see turtles, rays and other marine life, but also to catch some waves. In addition, the company hires canoes and kayaks, runs a drop-off service if required, and can supply kayaks if you are heading to Lady Musgrave Island for the day.

0428 956 630; www.1770liquidadventures.com.au

Snorkelling and diving

One of the best new operators on this stretch of coast is 1770 Reef Explorers, operating out of the town of Seventeen Seventy. It takes no more than 12 people at a time for boat-based snorkelling trips to parts of the reef that few visit. Guests can take part in coral research in between their snorkelling and donate to reef-protection programs. Every detail of the operation has been thought of in terms of its environmental impact, from the organic ingredients and locally grown salad items in the food, through to the fact that each trip generates no new rubbish and no anchors are used.

Diving companies are always great sources of information for possible shore dives and snorkelling, but the best diving and snorkelling in this area is out at the reef, which is one to two hours away on most boats. In Seventeen Seventy, try 1770 Undersea Adventures.

1770 Reef Explorers: 0422 216 922

1770 Undersea Adventures: 1300 553 889; www.1770underseaadventures.com.au

Turtle-watching

Marine turtles are abundant throughout this area and Mon Repos (pronounced 'mon repoe'), near Bundaberg, supports the largest concentration of nesting marine turtles on the eastern Australian mainland. It is also the largest loggerhead turtle rookery in the South Pacific Ocean. Between November and early February, the female turtles lug themselves above the high-tide mark at night to lay their eggs and the tiny hatchlings emerge from mid-January to late March. Access to the park is restricted at these times.

To protect the turtles, the Queensland Environmental Protection Agency has implemented ticketed beach access and runs inexpensive guided talks and tours nearly every night during this period. A tour starts at the visitor centre at 7pm, while rangers check the beach to see if there are any turtles about. If there are, people will be split into groups and taken down to the beach. If it is a slow night, rangers are prepared to wait until after midnight to see if any turtles turn up.

The EPA emphasises, however, that the turtles are wild, and sightings cannot be guaranteed. Bookings must be made through Bundaberg Region Tourism.

QPWS: www.epa.qld.gov.au

Bundaberg Region Tourism: (07) 4153 8888 or 1800 308 888; www.bundabergregion.info

Loggerhead turtle (Caretta caretta) *hatchling at Mon Repos Conservation Park*

Lady Musgrave Island

Rockhampton to Townsville

WHERE TO STAY

Broken River Mountain Resort, Eungella

This large eco-accredited resort has two-bedroom cabins, one-bedroom units and motel-style accommodation. It has an advanced sewage treatment system, much appreciated by the platypus in the creek alongside the resort. Interpretive tours are offered in and around Eungella National Park, including birdwatching, guided walks and nocturnal-spotlighting tours.

(07) 4958 4000; www.brokenrivermr.com.au

Cape Gloucester Eco Resort, near Bowen

This small resort between Airlie Beach and Bowen has ten cabins, a solid environmental policy and is a member of Land for Wildlife.

(07) 4945 7242; www.capegloucester.com

Paradise Bay Eco Escape

The eight waterfront, island-style bungalows here are reliant on solar power, natural gas and a biodiesel generator, have solar hot water, passive cooling, rainwater and a biocycle waste treatment system. All the company cars are Toyota Prius, and they do carbon offsetting through revegetating other properties owned by the company and through plantation forest.

(07) 4946 9777; www.paradisebay.com.au

Platypus Bush Camp, Finch Hatton Gorge

If you are after an authentic, old-school ecotourism experience, this could be the place. There is no electricity, and hot water – when needed – is made with a donkey boiler. Almost everything is open air, from the bush kitchen to the three sleeping huts positioned beside a pool with platypus. There are flushing toilets draining into a septic trench system and about ten campsites.

(07) 4958 3204; www.bushcamp.net

ACTIVITIES

Camping

If you want to camp on one of the Whitsunday Islands but do not want to kayak and do not own a boat, Camping Whitsundays and Island Camping Connections run a drop-off and pick-up service, supply camping gear and food if you need it, and will help you determine the best campsite for your holiday. Top options include Naris Beach on the 109-square-kilometre Whitsunday Island, and Boat Port on the 8-square-kilometre Lindeman Island, which has masses of butterflies in summer and a walking track up the 212-metre Mount Oldfield for views over some of the other islands.

Keppel Islands National Park also has seven camping areas, the largest on North Keppel, with composting toilets and space for 75 people. You can get a water taxi to any of the camping areas.

Camping Whitsundays: (07) 4948 0933 or 1800 550 751; www.campingwhitsundays.com

Island Camping Connections: (07) 4948 2201; www.whitsundaybookings.com.au

QPWS: (07) 4936 0511; www.epa.qld.gov.au

Water taxi: (07) 4939 8655 or 1800 180 235

Cape Hillsborough National Park

This small rainforested national park near Seaforth touches the coastline and is known for its tropical butterflies, 150 bird species, kangaroos and wallabies. You can also spy whales and turtles from the beaches. Walking tracks wander through eucalypt forests, mangroves, ferns and hoop pines. There are picnic areas with gas barbecues and a basic camping area.

QPWS: (07) 4944 7800; www.epa.qld.gov.au

Canoeing in Eungella National Park

Caving

Escape the sunshine for a while with an hour-long, eco-certified tour of Capricorn Caves, 23 kilometres north of Rockhampton. These caves feature intricately sculpted formations and the tour includes an optional candlelight section. Budding cavers can also do a two-hour adventure cave trip, with obstacles carrying titles such as 'fat man's misery', and the chance of seeing some of the bent-wing bats that inhabit the cave system. Camping and cabins are available.

(07) 4934 2883; www.capricorncaves.com.au

Eungella National Park

One of Queensland's most ecologically diverse parks, Eungella (pronounced 'Young-g'lah') has mist-shrouded hills that hold more than 860 plant species. The creeks contain platypus, turtles, eels and endangered frogs, and more than 225 bird species inhabit the area, including the spectacular buff-breasted paradise-kingfisher and the endemic Eungella honeyeater. Tracks to suit walkers of all persuasions wind through the forests and gorges, but serious hikers should consider the 56-kilometre, three-to-five-day Mackay Highlands Great Walk, which takes in rainforests, cliffs, mountains and rural areas. Walkers who make it down the steep 2.1-kilometre track from the Finch Hatton Gorge picnic area to the Wheel of Fire cascades, can swim or paddle before walking back.

QPWS: (07) 4958 4753; www.epa.qld.gov.au

Hiking

In the past few years a 30-kilometre walking track – the Whitsundays Great Walk – has been established, from Brandy Creek to Airlie Beach, through Conway State Forest. The two main camps, Repulse Creek and Bloodwood, have toilets and drinking water. If you just want to experience a fraction of the walk, weaving through tulip oaks and strangler figs while brilliantly coloured Ulysses butterflies flit around, try the 2-kilometre Kingfisher Circuit from the Brandy Creek carpark.

QPWS: (07) 4946 7022; www.epa.qld.gov.au

Picnicking

There is plenty of shade to go around at Mullers Lagoon in Bowen, a 24-hectare parkland with botanic gardens, wetlands, a bird hide and free barbecues. The lush Botanic Gardens at Mackay are also recommended.

Sailing

Sailing through the Whitsundays is simply glorious. By day there are more than 90 islands to explore, most of which are national parks, and such iconic places as Whitehaven Beach. At night you can anchor in sheltered bays, surrounded by coral bommies, and sleep on the deck under a million stars. There are bareboating charters, where you and your 'crew' of mates sail off on your own, but you will need to go through a thorough briefing and a trial run, and some companies insist that you have previous sailing experience. Alternatively you can hire a skipper and crew to take care of all the hard work. There is no shortage of yachting companies in and around Airlie Beach. Charter Yachts Australia and Queensland Yacht Charters are both eco-certified. All yachters need to be extremely careful when anchoring, so as not to damage the fragile corals.

The eco-certified Tall Ship Adventure Sailing operates two-night sailing adventures through the Whitsundays on its classic tall ships, where you will help hoist the sails and have discussions on the environment while relaxing with a drink or two. Oz Adventure Sailing holds a two-night sailing eco-safari, with an emphasis on snorkelling and the natural environment.

If you just want a day's sailing trip, with some snorkelling or diving thrown in, or want to have a picnic on Whitehaven Beach, try *Maxi Ragamuffin*, a 24-metre yacht that won the Sydney to Hobart race three times, and carries advanced eco-certification.

Charter Yachts Australia: (07) 4946 6666 or 1800 639 520; www.charteryachtsaustralia.com.au
Queensland Yacht Charters: 1800 075 013; www.yachtcharters.com.au
Tall Ship Adventure Sailing : (07) 4946 7124 or 1800 334 773; www.tallshipadventures.com.au
Oz Adventure Sailing: (07) 4948 2352 or 1300 653 100; www.ozsailing.com
Maxi Ragamuffin: (07) 4946 7777 or 1800 454 777; www.maxiaction.com.au

Sea-kayaking

The Whitsundays are increasingly becoming known as one of the best spots for multi-day sea-kayaking, camping on isolated islands at night and paddling, snorkelling and exploring during the day. There are more than 30 camping areas, most for no more than a dozen people. Some have composting toilets and picnic tables, but you will need to bring your own fresh water. If you have little to no experience in sea-kayaking, join an overnight or six-day tour with Salty Dog Sea Kayaking, who will provide everything, including tents, food and camping permits, and guide you through this tropical paradise. You will cover about 20 kilometres a day, which is about

Sailing the Whitsundays, with Cid Island (right)

Ulysses buttefly (Papilio ulysses)

Clown anemonefish (Amphiprion percula)*, one of the colourful marine species that inhabit the reef*

three to four hours of paddling. The company will also hire kayaks, provide safety gear and hire camping equipment if you want to head out on your own for a few hours, days or even weeks, but with this option you will need to secure your own camping permits with the Environmental Protection Authority (EPA). Salty Dog Sea Kayaking also runs popular half-day and full-day kayaking tours out of Shute Harbour.

Hamilton Island has its own eco-certified sea-kayaking company, Sea Kayaking Whitsundays, which offers day tours (with snorkelling), a sunset tour and a full-moon tour.

Salty Dog Sea Kayaking: (07) 4946 1388; www.saltydog.com.au

QPWS: www.epa.qld.gov.au

Sea Kayaking Whitsundays: (07) 4946 8305 or 0439 665 695; www.kayakwhitsunday.com

Snorkelling and diving

Capricorn Reef Diving in North Rockhampton focuses on diving tours and some snorkelling in Keppel Bay Islands National Park, highlighting Egg Rock as one of the greatest little-known dive sites in Australia, with rich anemones, coral trout, clownfish and coral gardens.

Bowen is one of the few areas where you can snorkel straight off the mainland, and has some lovely reefs just a few metres offshore. Usually calm, it is a great place to teach snorkelling to kids among the parrotfish, coral trout, blue tangs, wrasse, eels and humbugs. Horseshoe and Murray bays are recommended, but check with the Bowen Visitor Centre for other spots that are favoured by locals.

In the Whitsunday area, Odyssey H2O at Cannonvale near Airlie Beach offers a double-dive and snorkelling trip.

Capricorn Reef Diving: (07) 4922 7720 or 0419 764 779; www.capricornreefdiving.com

Bowen: (07) 4786 2208; www.tourismbowen.com.au

Odyssey: (07) 4948 1207; www.odysseyh2o.com; www.islandive.com

Swimming

Safe, sheltered beaches are prominent in the area, particularly around Bowen, but Harbour Beach at Mackay is one of the most popular and is patrolled year-round. Near Yeppoon try Main, Lammermoor or Kemp beaches. At Cedar Creek Falls, 19 kilometres south-west of Proserpine, you can enjoy a freshwater swimming hole under a waterfall.

Wildlife tours

Proserpine River Eco Tours runs an eco-accredited all-day wildlife safari in which you have a fairly good chance of seeing saltwater crocodiles, agile wallabies, mud crabs and frill-necked lizards. The tour combines a wetland wagon ride, a boat cruise on the Proserpine River and a hearty barbecue lunch.

Waterpark Eco Tours at Byfield combines a cruise through tropical rainforest in an electric-motor boat, with a tour of its organic tea-tree farm by horse-drawn wagon.

Proserpine River Eco Tours: (07) 4948 3310; www.crocodilesafari.com.au

Waterpark Eco Tours: (07) 4935 1171; www.waterparkecotours.com

Magnetic Island

Taking in the view on the Forts Walk

WHERE TO STAY

Bungalow Bay Koala Village

Declared Australia's best backpacker accommodation, this low-key eco-accredited resort, with pool and family-style restaurant, has 2.8 hectares of camping area and 30 A-frame bungalows, 25 of which are doubles/twins. The others are dormitories. The young enthusiastic owners started one of the first recycling programs on the island, have revegetated a creek that runs through the area, and revegetated public land across the road. They help care for injured and orphaned wildlife, and have a focus on protecting and preserving the cultural and natural values of the area. You can do tours of the resort's small wildlife park, where the emphasis is on teaching people about the environment and their impact on it, a guided bushwalk into the pandanus and melaleuca forest, or have a champagne and bush-tucker breakfast with

A 20-minute ferry trip from Townsville with Sunsea Ferries, this island is a top spot for the ecotourist, with koalas in the trees, birds and butterflies everywhere, quiet beaches and a range of bushwalks. There is a regular bus service stopping at key points around the island, and you can hire bikes and innovative electric-powered bikes at Magnetic Island Bike Hire at Arcadia so you do not need to hire a car.

The island is a key part of the Solar Cities program as a satellite suburb to Townsville. There is a Smart Lifestyle Centre at Horseshoe Bay with an energy efficiency information centre and interpretive displays about solar power. As part of the Solar Cities plan, some 500 solar-power units are being established on the island and energy use here is expected to be cut by about 25 per cent.

Sunsea Ferries: (07) 4726 0800 or 1800 447 333; www.sunferries.com.au

Magnetic Island Bike Hire: (07) 4758 1333; www.magneticinformer.com.au

www.environment.gov.au

Beachscape at Horseshoe Bay

Short-beaked echidna (Tachyglossus aculeatus) at Bungalow Bay resort's wildlife park

native bush tomatoes, rosella jam, native honeycomb and green-ant tea.
(07) 4778 5577 or 1800 285 577;
www.bungalowbay.com.au

ACTIVITIES

Bushwalking

Magnetic Island has about 25 kilometres of walking tracks, many with outstanding views of the coast, or ending at isolated beaches. Do not miss the 2-kilometre Forts Walk, with a good chance of seeing a koala or two, and catching some superb views along the way.
QPWS: www.epa.qld.gov.au

Diving

Some of the dive sites at Magnetic have easy walk-in entry from sheltered beaches, but more experienced divers would probably want to head out with Adrenaline Dive in Townsville, Pleasure Divers on the island, or one of the other boat-dive operators. Adrenaline has two main dive sites:

The remains of a World War II defence installation marks the end of the Forts Walk

Wheeler Reef, which is very pretty and has lots of coral; and the SS *Yongala*, known as one of the best dive sites in Australia, with coral and lots of big fish. The wreck is in about 30 metres of water and seas can be rough so this site is recommended for experienced divers only.
Adrenaline Dive: 1300 664 600;
www.adrenalinedive.com.au
Pleasure Divers: (07) 4778 5788 or 1800 797 797;
www.magnetic-island.com.au

Sailing

Several sailing charters will take you on short or long trips around the island, including the three-hour Blue Parrot Sunset Cruise, departing from Horseshoe Bay.
(07) 4758 1336 or 0448 581 330;
www.magneticislandhomes.com

Sea-kayaking

The eco-accredited Magnetic Island Sea Kayaks runs a four-hour morning trip in which you will see raptors and hopefully sea turtles, while learning about the ecology and history of the island. The company also does a sunset tour and hires kayaks and safety gear to experienced kayakers who want to travel around the island.
(07) 4778 5424; www.seakayak.com.au

Snorkelling

With sheltered beaches, and coral reefs generally just a short swim away, Magnetic Island is well set up for snorkelling, although windy or rough conditions will probably stir up too much sand. Try Florence, Alma, Arthur or Geoffrey bays, or go with a marine biologist as a guide. He will not only take you to the best spots but will also increase your knowledge about what you see. Sites are usually no more than 50–100 metres offshore, and suitable for beginners.
Reef Ecotours: 0419 712 579; www.reefecotours.com

Townsville to Cairns

Heading off for a day walk on Hinchinbrook Island

WHERE TO STAY

Hidden Valley Cabins, Hidden Valley

Acclaimed as being Australia's first completely solar-powered resort, with a restaurant, pool and room for 31 guests, this serious environmental resort is in secluded dry forest well off the Bruce Highway. It is powered by 90 (130-watt) solar panels, and offsets gas and fuel used, making it completely carbon neutral. Guests receive a certificate for 'having a sustainable experience'. From the resort you can take a platypus-watching tour, in which you will also see eastern long-necked turtles, and night-spotlighting tours to see pretty-faced wallabies, allied rock-wallabies, rufous bettongs and gliders if you are lucky. The rustic cabins are primarily built from recycled or salvaged timber, but are a little on the poky side.

(07) 4770 8088 or 1800 466 509; www.hiddenvalleycabins.com.au

Hinchinbrook Island Wilderness Lodge

Revolutionary in terms of minimal-impact tourism when it was first established in 1974, this classy resort has no more than a toehold on the 393-square-kilometre Hinchinbrook Island, and you can hardly see the treetop cabins and beach bungalows for the trees. On-site sewage treatment returns water to a potable level, and the raised cabins and walkways are designed to minimise the number of trees cut down, prevent compaction of the forest floor and allow animals such as goannas to wander underneath – some of the eco-design features that have since been adopted elsewhere. There is a guest library and lounge area, an excellent restaurant, free wireless internet, and snorkelling equipment and canoes for guest use. Walking tracks head out through the thickly forested national park to isolated coral-strewn beaches. The resort is closed from mid-January to Easter.

(07) 4066 8270; www.hinchinbrookresort.com.au

Jabiru Safari Lodge, Mareeba Wetlands

By staying in one of the five safari tents here, you will be contributing to wildlife conservation at the Mareeba Tropical Savanna and Wetland Reserve. Run by a non-profit trust that includes the Wildlife Conservancy of Tropical North Queensland, the 2000-hectare reserve has eight lagoons full of birds and is

Treetop cabin at Hinchinbrook Island Wilderness Lodge and Resort

Blue-faced honeyeater (Entomyzon cyanotis) collecting nectar from a grevillea bloom

Late afternoon on Clancy's Lagoon at Mareeba wetlands

now one of the most important crane-roosting sites in Queensland. Two of the safari tents have solar power and gas appliances, and the others are on mains power. Barbecue packs and breakfast are provided, and there is a shared outdoor spa in the bush.

(07) 4093 2514; www.mareebawetlands.com

Possum Valley Rainforest Cottages

Near Millaa Millaa, the two secluded bush cabins here, on 62 hectares of bushland and rainforest, can sleep up to eight people each, and are completely powered by solar technology and a small water turbine in Possum Creek.

(07) 4097 8177; www.bnbnq.com.au

Rose Gums Wilderness Retreat

By renting out nine elegant eco-accredited treehouses (near Malanda), the owners have funded a massive weed-clearing and revegetation program – including planting 20 000 trees – on their 92-hectare property, which was previously degraded farmland. There are 9 kilometres of walking tracks through the forest and the owners support various local environmental projects. For a small fee, you can offset your carbon footprint by planting a rainforest tree while there. The tree houses take two to six guests.

(07) 4096 8360; www.rosegums.com.au

Sanctuary Retreat, Mission Beach

This eclectic resort was set up to fund the protection of 20 hectares of some of the best cassowary rainforest habitat left in the world, and cassowaries are seen there almost every day. About 95 per cent of the property has been placed under a registered conservation covenant so no one can clear the land in the future. It has two quite different types of accommodation – inexpensive adult cubbyhouses with shared amenities and use of a communal kitchen, and seven excellent secluded cabins, with ensuites and showers with full-glass views of the outside vine jungle. There is a very good restaurant, with an emphasis on local seafood, fruit and vegetables, and a communal area with candlelight and cushions, beads and bare feet. All wastewater is treated to a potable standard and reused on site.

(07) 4088 6064; http://sanctuaryretreat.com.au

Mareeba wetland residents: (left) comb-crested jacana (Irediparra gallinacea), and delicately coloured dragonfly

The Canopy, near Malanda

Located at Tarzali, this place comprises six beautiful glass and timber treehouses set in 40 hectares of rainforest that has never been logged, with Lumholtz tree-kangaroos creeping around, green ringtail possums, sawshell turtles in the Ithaca River and a healthy population of Victoria's riflebirds. The whole place runs on renewable energy and you can take part in a revegetation scheme on a neighbouring property.

(07) 4096 5364; www.canopytreehouses.com.au

A termite mound beside a walking track through Mareeba wetland reserve

ACTIVITIES

Birdwatching

You do not need to be a bird nerd to appreciate Tyto Wetlands near Ingham. It is a beautiful, peaceful spot for a picnic, a pleasant walk or a pre-dinner drink. But if you stop at one of the benches or bird hides and stay still for a couple of minutes, you will no doubt spot more than a dozen avian species. The wetlands, with bright fuchsia and mauve waterlilies, have been created over 90 hectares to attract a wide range of wildlife, so as well as spotting some of the 230 bird species found there, you have a good chance of seeing agile wallabies and a snake or two.

Mareeba Tropical Savanna and Wetland Reserve is another outstanding spot for birdwatchers. The eight lagoons and their surrounds are teeming with birds: jabirus, pheasant coucals, red-backed fairy-wrens, wandering whistling-ducks, Gouldian finches and emus. You can explore the tracks on your own, but it is best to join one of the excellent, informative tours with Chook Crawford. On the morning three-hour tour, Chook guarantees you will see 50 bird species, and probably mammals such as northern spotted quolls, tree-rats, agile wallabies and pretty-faced wallabies. The sunset wildlife tour is also excellent, beginning with a tour on Clancy's Lagoon in a silent, electric-motor boat, and finishing with wine and cheese at sunset.

Mount Hypipamee and Crater Lakes national parks near Malanda are excellent for seeing rainforest birds, including spotted catbirds and orange-footed scrubfowl.

Further south, try the 3245 hectares of wetlands in Townsville Town Common Conservation Park, which has abundant numbers of brolgas, cisticolas and magpie geese. Ross River Dam is another favoured spot, with more than 220 bird species recorded. It also has picnic facilities.

Tyto Wetlands: (07) 4776 5211;
www.tytowetlands.com.au
Mareeba reserve: (07) 4093 2514;
www.mareebawetlands.com

Bushwalking

This entire region offers great delights to bushwalkers, although you are likely to get damp, either from the humidity or from a tropical shower (it is not called 'rainforest' for nothing). The Rainforest and Reef Information

Taking the last steps on the Thorsborne Trail, which ends at Ramsay Bay

Centre at Cardwell is an interesting starting point to plan your next hike.

In the lowland rainforests and vine forests of the Mission Beach area, you have a reasonable chance of spying an endangered southern cassowary. Pick up walking-track maps from the Mission Beach visitor centre or try the 6-kilometre Musgravea track through the thick fan-palm forest in Tam O'Shanter National Park. Nearby, the 4-kilometre circuit up Bicton Hill provides some excellent views of the coast.

Barron Gorge National Park near Cairns has a wide range of tracks, from the 1.1-kilometre wheelchair-accessible boardwalk to Barron Falls lookouts and the 10-minute climb to Glacier Rock and its panoramic views, to long day walks and overnight hikes on the historic Douglas and Smiths tracks.

Rainforests in the highlands are generally cooler, and can offer quite different, and often expansive views over the hinterland. Paluma Range National Park, at around 1000 metres, has great views from the end of the 1.5-kilometre Witts Lookout Track (if you can ignore the powerlines), and the area is known for visitations from the beautiful blue riflebird. If you are quiet, you are bound to see plenty of other birds – such as chowchillas (the female has the rich rufous breast) – hidden among the paperbark satinash, figs and ironwood. If you are very keen on seeing a golden bowerbird, try the Birthday Creek Falls Track.

*Female chowchilla (*Orthonyx spaldingii*) in her nest, Paluma Range National Park*

Girringun National Park, near Ingham, provides access to an extensive 110 kilometres of walking tracks, several of which start from the spectacular Wallaman Falls, reportedly the largest single-drop waterfalls in Australia (although most have not been properly measured). Really keen hikers can start the superb, eight-day Wet Tropics Great Walk from this location.

Cardwell centre: (07) 4066 8601;
www.greatgreenwaytourism.com
Tam O'Shanter National Park: (07) 4066 8601
QPWS (Wallaman Falls walks): www.epa.qld.gov.au

Cheese-tasting

In the lush highlands of Millaa Millaa, overlooking Mount Bartle Frere, the certified biodynamic Mungalli Creek Dairy has a superb range of organic cheeses and yoghurts for sale and tastings. You can watch the delectable items being made while enjoying a cuppa or lunch. Five minutes down the road visit Mungalli Falls for a short walk and a chance to see Ulysses butterflies.

(07) 4097 2232; www.mungallifalls.com

Hiking the Thorsborne Trail

The 32-kilometre Thorsborne Trail is a classic tropical bushwalk that weaves along the east coast of the 393-square-kilometre Hinchinbrook Island National Park. There is a maximum of 40 people allowed on the track at a time, and the campsites are restricted to six people. You will walk along coral-strewn beaches fringed by lime rainforest and coconut palms, see sea-turtles and sweat profusely as you hike up steep hills in the humid conditions. Although the distances are not long, the EPA recommends a minimum of three nights and four days. The northern end of the track is Ramsay Bay, serviced by the ferry at Hinchinbrook Island Wilderness Lodge and Resort. The ferry does not run from mid-January to Easter. For ferries to and from the southern end, contact Hinchinbrook Wilderness Safaris. For mainland buses between Lucinda and Port Hinchinbrook, contact Ingham Travel.

QPWS: (07) 4776 5211; www.epa.qld.gov.au
Resort: (07) 4066 8270; www.hinchinbrookresort.com.au
Hinchinbrook Wilderness Safaris: (07) 4777 8307;
www.hinchinbrookwildernesssafaris.com.au
Ingham Travel: (07) 4776 5666

Indigenous tour

During the Aboriginal-owned-and-operated, two-hour tour at Mungalla Station, you will have the chance to throw a boomerang and hear the history of the Nywaigi people. Mungalla is 12 kilometres from Ingham.

(07) 4776 2355; www.mungallaaboriginaltours.com.au

Reef HQ, Townsville

This eco-accredited, non-profit aquarium is a great spot to go before or after you visit the reef itself, as it will introduce you to some of the main characters out there and give you lots of

The living coral reef at Reef HQ in Townsville

great information about them. Staffed mainly by volunteers, the aquarium changes 750 000 litres of water every ten days and has a wave machine and currents, which has enabled the growth of the world's largest living coral reef aquarium. Do not miss the 'deep and dark' section at the back, with bizarre nautilus and glowing onefin flashlight fish.

(07) 4750 0800; www.reefhq.com.au

Sea-kayaking

Several companies are running seven-day sea-kayaking trips around Hinchinbrook Island, with chances of encountering dugong, dolphins, sea-turtles, crocodiles and copious other wildlife. You will camp on the island and have the chance to snorkel, bushwalk and explore. Try World Expeditions or Coral Sea Kayaking. The latter also offers three-day tours of the Family Islands and one-day kayak tours of Dunk Island, from Mission Beach.

World Expeditions: 1300 720 000; www.worldexpeditions.com/au/

Coral Sea Kayaking: (07) 4068 9154 or 0419 782 453; www.coralseakayaking.com

Snorkelling and diving

As with elsewhere in this region, there is no shortage of operators to take you out to the reef for a snorkel, a dive or a look around in a glass-bottomed boat. All operators work under strict environmental guidelines, but some are better than others. Most tourists seem to prefer smaller boats, with less people on board, although they might not get out to the reef as fast. Eco-certified operators include the Cairns Dive Centre, which has day trips and two- and three-day, live-aboard trips, and Passions of Paradise, which runs tours on a 25-metre catamaran to Michaelmas Cay and Paradise Reef. Big Cat Green Island Cruises was one of the first recipients of the gold 'Leader' Climate Action Program certificate, and is carbon-neutral. It operates day tours to Green Island out of Cairns.

A bushfood demonstration at Tjapukai Aboriginal Cultural Park

Cairns Dive Centre: (07) 4051 0294; www.cairnsdive.com.au

Passions of Paradise: (07) 4041 1600 or 1800 111 346; www.passions.com.au

Big Cat Green Island Cruises: (07) 4051 0444; www.bigcat-cruises.com.au

Swimming

Not far from Townsville there are a couple of popular swimming holes: Big Crystal Creek near Mutarnee, the icy Little Crystal Creek on the road to Paluma, and under the Rollingstone Bridge. Near Tully, you can cool off in the crystal clear rockpools at the base of the 30-metre-high Murray Falls.

Closer to Cairns, join the locals at a not-so-secret swimming hole, Crystal Cascades, in tropical rainforest about 10 kilometres from the suburb of Redlynch. There are picnic tables and barbecues.

The swimming hole at Babinda Boulders near Mount Bartle Frere and Josephine Falls in Wooroonooran National Park are both good spots for a dip from April to October, but are not considered safe in the wet season or after heavy rain.

Tjapukai Aboriginal Cultural Park

Almost like a theme park in scope, this award-winning, 10-hectare living cultural centre showcases Tjapukai culture, with multiple ways to get involved. During the day there are didgeridoo demonstrations, dances, theatre productions, spear- and boomerang-throwing lessons and bushfood tours, as well as a museum, gallery and restaurant to visit. At night you can attend a food and cultural evening, with traditional dances, music and story telling. The park is at Smithfield, some 13 kilometres north of Cairns.

(07) 4042 9900; www.tjapukai.com.au

Whitewater rafting

The Cairns area is a bit of a hotspot for rafting, with tours ranging from half-day introductions to multi-day camping adventures. RnR White Water Rafting is eco-accredited, has a popular one-day trip on the Tully River, a half-day on the Barron and an exciting four-day trip down the North Johnstone, including grade five rapids.

Foaming Fury runs a pick-up service from Cairns and Port Douglas, and does a half-day introduction to rafting in Barron Gorge National Park, or a full-day adventure on the Russell River. Raging Thunder also has half-day rafting trips on the Barron River and full-day trips on the Tully.

RnR: (07) 4041 9444; www.raft.com.au

Foaming Fury: (07) 4031 3460 or 1800 801 540; www.foamingfury.com.au

Raging Thunder: (07) 4030 7990; www.ragingthunder.com.au

Wildlife experience

Combine several of the Cairns area's main wildlife attractions into one seamless day out: the Kuranda Scenic Railway, Skyrail, Kuranda Koala Gardens, Birdworld and the Australian Butterfly Sanctuary. Book through Kuranda Scenic Railway.

(07) 4036 9333; www.ksr.com.au.

Wine-tasting

The Murdering Point Winery at Silkwood East sells tropical fruit wines from its cellar door, with all fruit grown within 100 kilometres of the winery and many bushfoods incorporated in the production process. On offer are mango, lychee, passionfruit, lemon aspen and Davidson plum wines and a very more-ish port made from black sapote, the so-called chocolate-pudding fruit. The vineyard takes it name from an 1878 massacre of shipwreck survivors by a local Indigenous group.

(07) 4065 2327; www.murderingpointwinery.com.au

Whitewater rafting on the Tully River

Far North Queensland

Cape York Peninsula stretches northwards from Cairns in the east and Karumba in the west. Within easy reach of Cairns is the Daintree River, where hibiscus flowers float on the mirror-calm water and white-rumped swiftlets zip through the ylang-ylang trees and matchbox beans. In the early morning, green tree snakes seem to drip off the branches and you may see Papuan frogmouths sleeping huddled together, bright yellow figbirds and sunbirds, and spectacular azure kingfishers keeping a close eye on the water.

Beyond the Daintree, the legendary Cape York Peninsula beckons invitingly to those keen to explore some real Australian wilderness. Past Cooktown, facilities are few and far between, and generally only for the well prepared, but the initial stretch from Cairns to Cape Tribulation and around the Daintree River is an ecotourism hotspot, with a great range of accommodation and tours. Dip your toe into the region, or plunge right in and explore the rich cultural and environmental treasures that it holds.

Cape Tribulation, Daintree River National Park

*The green python (*Chondropython viridis*) inhabits the Daintree River area*

Cairns to Cape Tribulation

WHERE TO STAY

Daintree Eco Lodge and Spa

If you are in need of some pampering, this is the place to go. With strong and proud links to the Aboriginal heritage of the site – a women's healing place – the Eco Lodge has 15 sumptuous villas set over a creek in a secluded rainforest valley. The operators describe 'borrowing' the healing waters from the creek, using it in the unique spa treatments, for drinking, and in the resort, then treating it through a biocycle system and returning it through the soil.

(07) 4098 6100 or 1800 808 010;
www.daintree-ecolodge.com.au

Daintree Rainforest Retreat, near Cow Bay

When the owners here decided to reduce their carbon footprint by installing 48 solar panels, the generator's monthly diesel consumption changed from 1600 litres to 200 litres. By revegetating a rainforest on their own block of land they offset all the remaining carbon debt, so are completely

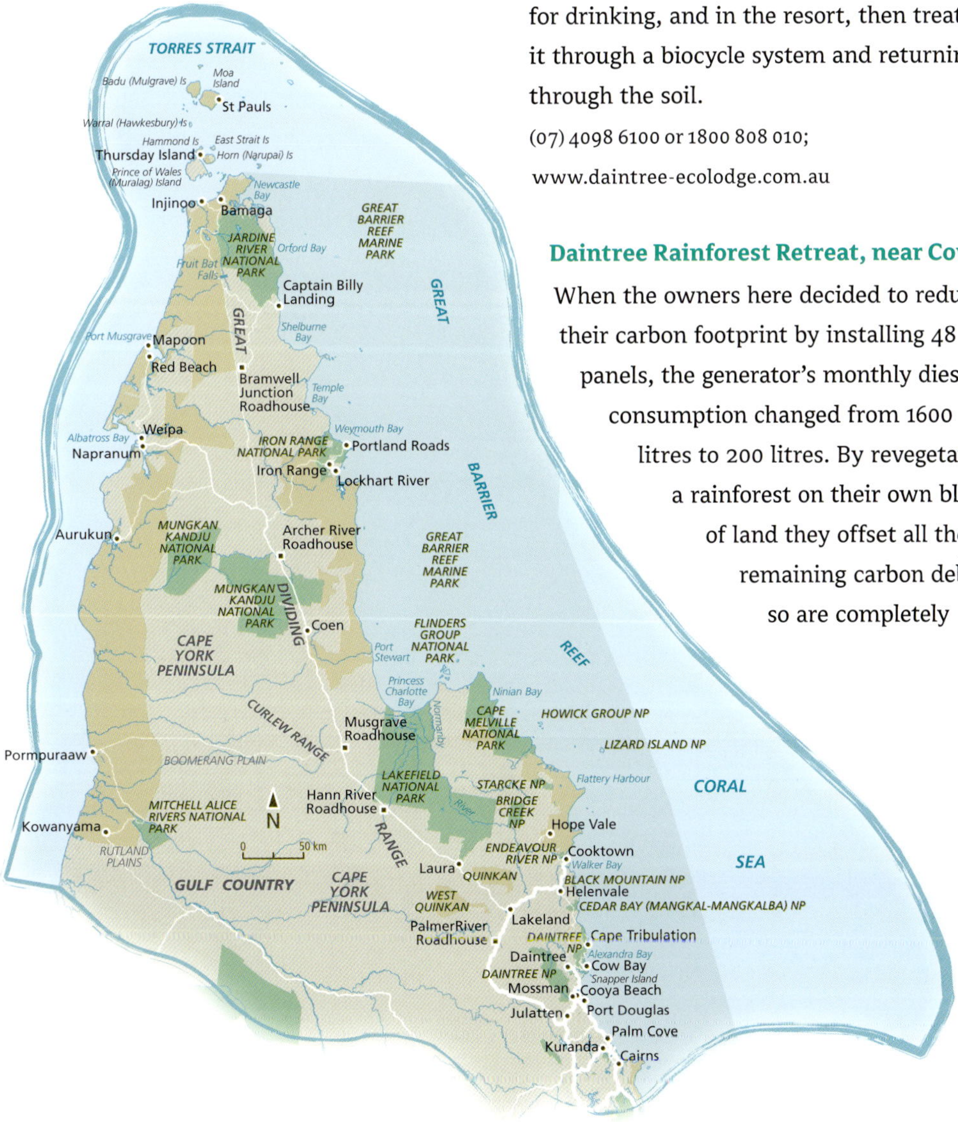

GREEN TRAVEL TIP Wilderness hikers rarely need detergent to wash up – even so-called biodegradable detergents are foreign to the environment. Grab a handful of sand or grit and clean grease off pans and plates with that instead.

carbon neutral. The retreat, near Cow Bay, has ten rooms, some with a kitchenette, and is described as a 'cross between a house and a mini-resort'.

(07) 4098 9101; www.daintreeretreat.com.au

Daintree Wilderness Lodge, Alexandra Bay

Set in fan-palm rainforest, the eight bungalows here, accessed by raised boardwalks to protect the forest floor, are partially solar-powered by 20 solar panels, and a biocycle system breaks down all waste on site. As well as providing education about the surroundings, the organisation supports the Cassowary Care Group.

(07) 4098 9105; www.daintreewildernesslodge.com.au

Kingfisher Park Birdwatcher's Lodge

Guaranteed to get keen birdwatchers excited, this eco-accredited establishment at Julatten is renowned as one of the best birdwatching spots north of Cairns, with rare endemic species seen around the pool.

White-lipped tree frog sighted along the Bloomfield Track

For six months of the year, one of the sexiest birds in Australia, the buff-breasted paradise-kingfisher, can be seen nesting in the termite mounds on the 5-hectare property. One of the owners is an ornithological consultant and upon arrival at the lodge you will be given up-to-date information on possible places to find particular bird species, a comprehensive bird list for the area and maps of the local birding hotspots. Accommodation includes self-contained units, camping or a bunkhouse.

(07) 4094 1263; www.birdwatchers.com.au

ACTIVITIES

Bushwalking

Join a guided day or night bushwalk in the privately owned Cooper Creek Wilderness, to discover the incredible natural riches of this

Accommodation at Daintree Wilderness Lodge

Papuan frogmouth (Podargus papuensis), Daintree River

area. Back Country Bliss Adventures also runs gentle, guided half-day bushwalks to Hidden Valley and Spring Creek Falls.

Cooper Creek Wilderness: (07) 4098 9126; www.ccwild.com

Back Country Bliss Adventures: (07) 4099 3677 or 0420 101 757; www.backcountryblissadventures.com.au

Cape Tribulation Wilderness Cruises

This eco-accredited, six-hour experience includes a cruise up pristine Cooper Creek looking for saltwater crocodiles, a two-hour guided bushwalk through ancient, untouched rainforest, a great lunch in the rainforest and even a swim if the conditions are right. There are shorter cruise options too.

(07) 4033 2052; www.capetribcruises.com

Daintree Discovery Centre

This multi-award-winning ecotourism centre is a great place to learn about the legendary Daintree rainforest. There are elevated boardwalks, an aerial walkway, a canopy tower and a large interpretive display centre with information on everything from stinging trees to butterflies. The private venture has a rigorous carbon-offset program. It is justifiably the premier tourism facility in the Daintree.

(07) 4098 9171; www.daintree-rec.com.au

Daintree National Park

Perhaps the most well-known rainforest in Australia, this area was inscribed on the World Heritage List in 1988. Its secrets are hard to decode though, and some travellers leave this national park disappointed, as many of the best areas are difficult to access. A guided 4WD or walking tour will provide insights that you might not gain on your own. The Cape Tribulation section has steep mountain ranges, quiet beaches, rocky headlands, crocodiles, tree-kangaroos, cassowaries and rich birdlife,

Searching the mangroves for bush tucker on a Kuku Yalanji Cultural Habitat Tour

as well as camping and walking tracks. The Mossman Gorge section has a 2-kilometre rainforest circuit track, a suspension bridge, a lookout over the Mossman River and picnic areas, but camping is not permitted there.

QPWS: (07) 4098 0052; www.epa.qld.gov.au

Four-wheel-drive tours

Reef and Rainforest Connections is eco-certified, has an extensive green policy, and is one of several 4WD companies that offer full day tours in small groups from Port Douglas through the Daintree World Heritage Area.

Although the roads on Cape York Peninsula are being improved all the time, a 4WD is still needed to get to many of the key spots and is vital after wet-season rains. Various companies offer 4WD tours up the Peninsula, with either camping or accommodation options. The eco-certified company Wilderness Challenge offers trips from three to 14 days, to the Peninsula and further afield. Their trips often involve tree-planting and support of organisations such as the Australian Rainforest Foundation and the Wilderness Society.

Oz Tours, another eco-accredited company, has a 12-day Cape York trip that includes

The impressive Bloomfield Falls near Cape Tribulation

travelling on a cargo ship from Cairns to the Torres Strait, through the Great Barrier Reef Marine Park, then 4WD back to Cairns. There are also options to visit the Torres Strait Islands. On Thursday Island, make sure you visit the Gabi Titui Cultural Centre.

Reef and Rainforest Connections: (07) 4099 5333; www.reefandrainforest.com.au
Wilderness Challenge: (07) 4035 4488 or 1800 354 486; www.wilderness-challenge.com.au
Oz Tours: (07) 4055 9535 or 1800 079 006; www.oztours.com.au
Gabi Titui Cultural Centre: (07) 4090 2130; www.tsra.gov.au

Indigenous tours

Go out on a hunt with two young Aboriginal men, gathering traditional foods and using traditional methods, such as spearing, on Cooya Beach, north of Port Douglas, and in mangroves and mudflats. Learn to throw a spear properly, and participate in the hunt as much or as little as you like. Towards the end of the two-to-three-hour Kuku Yalanji Cultural Habitat Tour, you will be shown artefacts, and have a feed with some fresh damper and some of the tucker you caught.

The short Indigenous Guided Rainforest Walk of 240 metres, to a women's healing site at the base of a waterfall, takes more than an hour, because the Kuku Yalanji guide provides so much ancient wisdom about traditional uses for plants, animals and ochres along the way. You will smell, touch and taste during this sensual experience that finishes in the Daintree Eco Lodge's restaurant where there are some amazing artefacts, such as 30-year-old woven dilly bags and a heavy ironwood sword. Wear cool, long clothes, as the mosquitoes in the rainforest are ferocious.

On a 30-minute guided walk to the 40-metre-high Bloomfield Falls, near Cape Tribulation, Walker Family Tours will introduce you to some of the local Yalanji women, who will share a number of the ancient secrets of this beautiful spot – its bush tucker and medicines, stories and significance.

Adventure North offers one- and two-day tours, from Cairns, that combine several of the great Aboriginal experiences on offer.

Masons Tours runs a 4WD tour on the famous Bloomfield Track to Aboriginal sites or a night or day walking tour on private tracks abutting Daintree National Park near Cape Tribulation. As well as providing great natural history and cultural information, this company supports Amnesty International.

Kuku Yalanji tour: (07) 4098 3437 or 0403 403 528; www.bamaway.com.au

Daintree Eco Lodge: (07) 4098 6100 or 1800 808 010; www.daintree-ecolodge.com.au

Walker Family Tours: (07) 4060 8069 or (07) 4060 8139; www.walkerfamilytours.com

Adventure North: (07) 4053 7001; www.adventurenorthaustralia.com

Masons Tours: (07) 4098 0070; www.masonstours.com.au

Reef tours

As with elsewhere on the reef, there is the luxury of choice for diving or snorkelling trips, particularly from Port Douglas. However, remember the reef is not just offshore and involves a boat trip. Among the eco-accredited operators are Calypso, Sailaway Port Douglas, Haba Great Barrier Reef Adventure, Poseidon's day trip to three spots on the Agincourt Outer Reefs and the beautiful schooner *Malaita*. The vessel *Wavelength* offers trips for snorkellers only, which take in three outer reef sites in a day, and has a marine biologist as an informative guide.

On the trip with Sailaway Port Douglas, a maximum of 33 people are taken out to the Low Isles, a coral cay with a sheltered lagoon. Here snorkellers can explore the underwater gardens, comprising 150 hard coral species and 15 soft coral species. A trip on a glass-bottom boat is also provided, with the chance to see green turtles and a wide variety of reef fish including the colourful clown anemonefish.

Shark-watching from the back of a tour boat

Calypso: (07) 4099 3377; www.barrierreefaustralia.com/port-douglas/

Sailaway Port Douglas: (07) 4099 4772; www.sailawayportdouglas.com

Haba Great Barrier Reef Adventure: (07) 4098 5000; www.habadive.com.au

Poseidon: (07) 4099 4772; www.poseidon-cruises.com.au

Malaita: (07) 4099 5064; www.malaita.com.au

Wavelength: (07) 4099 5031; www.wavelength.com.au

*Swimming with a green turtle (*Chelonia mydas*) on a snorkelling trip with Sailaway Port Douglas*

Sea kayaks on the beach at Cow Bay, the starting point for tours south to Snapper Island

Sea-kayaking

Paddle out to Snapper Island just south-east of Cape Kimberley and within Hope Islands National Park, 2 kilometres from the mouth of the Daintree River, and stay the night, enjoying gourmet food, great snorkelling and isolated camping, with just your group of 12 or less on the whole tropical island (the four campsites have toilet facilities). You will paddle back again the next day, all under the watchful eye of a guide. The company, Crocodylus Village, also offers a four-hour sunrise paddle, with snorkelling and breakfast thrown in, and a legendary night walk at Cape Tribulation in which you will be introduced to a huge diversity of wildlife.

Back Country Bliss Adventures offers a one-day kayaking trip out to Snapper Island and other four-hour trips along the coast from Port Douglas or Cairns. Paddletrek Cape Tribulation also runs eco-accredited guided kayaking trips every morning and afternoon.

Crocodylus Village: (07) 4098 9166; www.crocodyluscapetrib.com
Back Country Bliss Adventures: (07) 4099 3677 or 0420 101 757; www.backcountryblissadventures.com.au
Paddletrek Cape Tribulation: (07) 4098 0131; www.capetribpaddletrek.com.au

Treat your tastebuds

The organically certified Cape Trib Exotic Fruit Farm has a huge range of tropical fruits available, many of which you may not have even heard, such as soursop, jackfruit, dragonfruit, black sapote and pommelo. At 2pm, Monday to Friday, you can treat your tastebuds to at least ten different fruits in a tasting session.

(07) 4098 0057; www.capetrib.com.au

Wildlife tour

For a wildlife tour with a difference, don a wetsuit and snorkel and float down the pristine Mossman River, with a fish-eye view of jungle perch, freshwater prawns, Pacific blue eyes, catfish, turtles and occasionally a platypus. Above, azure kingfishers and Ulysses butterflies flit around the strangler figs and rainforest. The company that runs this unique tour, Back Country Bliss Adventures, has a solid environmental policy and runs a wide variety of sustainable outdoor activities, including half-day and full-day mountain-biking tours from Port Douglas.

The endangered southern cassowary (Casuarius casuarius)

Jungle Adventures Cape Tribulation runs a night tour with guides who are all biologists, in which you may encounter fireflies, bandicoots, cassowaries, goannas and amethyst pythons.

Back Country Bliss: (07) 4099 3677 or 0420 101 757; www.backcountryblissadventures.com.au

Jungle Adventures: (07) 4098 0043; www.junglesurfingcanopytours.com.au

Cooktown to Cape York

ACTIVITIES

Aurukun Wetland Charters

Explore one of Australia's largest wetland areas, the 11 000-square-kilometre Aurukun Wetlands on the west coast of the Peninsula, with guides from the proud Wik and Wik Way people. In a three-night tour, you will stay each night on the comfortable twin-hulled *Pikkuw*, and spend days meeting a range of local Aboriginal experts in different subjects – story-telling, basket-weaving, art and carving, bush tucker, spear-making and hunting. You will experience it all in a setting surrounded by thousands of birds, crocodiles, flood plains, lagoons and thick and towering vine forest.

(07) 4058 1441; www.aurukunwetlandcharters.com

Cape York Turtle Rescue

Join an extraordinary three- or five-day program tagging, rescuing and studying four species of sea turtle – green, olive ridley, hawksbill and flatback – on the remote western coast of Cape York Peninsula at Mapoon. You may be involved in counting and measuring eggs, removing drift nets to stop turtle entanglement, and hands on participation, including tagging and measuring turtles. The

*A pair of white-bellied sea-eagles (*Haliaeetus leucogaster*) at Aurukun Wetlands*

programs run June to October and you will work alongside the Mapoon people, and stay in semi-permanent, spacious two-person tents. This is an incredible opportunity to get up close to some endangered animals and contribute to their long-term survival.

(07) 4069 9978; www.capeyorkturtlerescue.com

Indigenous tours

Guurrbi Tours offers an award-winning tour with Willie Gordon, Nugal-warra elder, Guugu Yimithirr speaker and author, on which you will visit a series of sacred rock-art sites that you otherwise cannot see. There are self-drive and full-tour options from Cooktown, and Willie is bound to blow you away with his passion and knowledge about his culture and spirituality. You will learn the stories and lore behind the art.

Maaramaka Walkabout near Hopevale includes information on Indigenous culture, history, bushfoods, medicine and the story of the giant Marramaka (fig) tree. You can drive out to the tour or be picked up from Cooktown.

Learn about the area's Indigenous, European and Chinese cultural heritage at the Quinkan and Regional Cultural Centre at Laura. (The area to the south-east of town is known as Quinkan country after the Aboriginal spirits depicted at the rock-art sites there.) You can also book for a two- or three-hour Aboriginal-led tour of the extensive art at Mushroom Rock and Giant Horse. Tours can be tag-along or transport may be provided. The three renowned art galleries at Split Rock can be viewed without a guide, and a 4WD is not necessary in the dry season.

A range of rock-art tours is on offer at Jowalbinna Rock Art Safari Camp, including the giant wallaroo and emu dreaming. Most people who come stay at the campground or in the simple cabins, which have low-powered fluorescent lights run on rechargeable batteries.

Guurrbi Tours: (07) 4069 6043; www.guurrbitours.com
Maaramaka Walkabout: (07) 4069 5381; irenehammett@hotmail.com
Quinkan centre: (07) 4060 3457; www.quinkancc.com.au
Jowalbinna: (07) 4035 4488

Iron Range National Park

This birdwatching mecca preserves the largest surviving area of lowland rainforest jungle in the country, with at least 1500 plant species and wildlife like that in New Guinea, including more than 200 species of butterfly. Keep your eyes open and you may see palm cockatoos, eclectus parrots, magnificent riflebirds and even the secretive spotted cuscus. There are four camping areas, but the only toilets are at Chili Beach and Cooks Hut.

QPWS: (07) 4060 7170; www.epa.qld.gov.au

Aboriginal women demonstrating basket-weaving techniques

Jardine River National Park

If you reach this national park, way up north, you are probably ready for a swim, and some say there is no place better for a soak than Fruit Bat Falls on Eliot Creek. There is camping and a few short walks from the Eliot Falls campsite.

QPWS: (07) 4046 6600; www.epa.qld.gov.au
Park ranger: (07) 4060 3241

Lakefield National Park

If you are keen to see crocodiles, this could be the park for you, particularly around Kalpowar Crossing on the Normanby River, where there is a 4-kilometre bushwalk. Dominated by

Discovering bushfoods on an Indigenous tour with Adventure North

Aurukun Wetland Charters

Willie Gordon explaining the intricacies of rock art at the sacred Jiliburu Cave

tropical savannah sprinkled liberally with termite mounds, this national park, the second largest in Queensland, has grassy eucalypt and paperbark woodlands that turn into vast wetlands during the wet season. About 8 kilometres north of the ranger station are two special billabongs: Red Lily Lagoon, dominated by red lotus lilies; and White Lily Lagoon where only white lilies are found. There are plenty of great campsites, but you will need to be completely self-sufficient. Kalpowar Crossing has toilets and showers.

Park ranger: (07) 4060 3271 or (07) 4060 3260; www.epa.qld.gov.au

*A pair of stately brolgas (*Grus rubicundus*) dances beside dense vine forests in the Aurukun Wetlands*

Savannah and outback

Encompassing the Gulf Savannah country and the huge areas of central and western Queensland, this region is as diverse as it is large. Travel by heritage train to a vast labyrinth of tunnels below the western slopes of the Great Dividing Range, 300 kilometres south-west of Cairns, or follow in the footsteps of the dinosaurs in central Queensland. In the far west, the remote dunes of the Simpson Desert beckon those with a taste for adventure.

The region also protects some unique treasures. Epping Forest National Park in central Queensland provides habitat for one of the most rare large mammals in the world, the northern hairy-nosed wombat. There are less than 150 of these creatures left on the planet – all living in this national park. It is a reminder that for all its space and vast tracts of agricultural land, outback Queensland is indeed a special place for wildlife. The natural wonders here might be widespread, but those who seek them out will be richly rewarded.

Aboriginal stencil art at Carnarvon Gorge

Carnarvon National Park

The Gulflander crossing the grasslands of the Gulf country

West of Brisbane

WHERE TO STAY

Kilcowera station

This organically run cattle and sheep station on the border of Currawinya National Park touches Lake Wyara, and is home to 160 bird species. Accommodation is in shearer's quarters, with plenty of camping and caravan sites too.

(07) 4655 4960; www.kilcowera.com.au

ACTIVITIES

Currawinya National Park

This remote national park has rivers, lakes and wetlands that make it ideal for birdwatching. It is also the focus of the Save the Bilby Fund's bilby reintroduction program, with a large feral-free area in the mulga. There is camping, but very limited facilities.

QPWS: (07) 4655 4001; www.epa.qld.gov.au

Thargomindah's hydro power plant

This little town was the first in Australia to produce hydro-electric power for street lighting. In 1898, generators were linked to water pouring out of a bore to produce the power. Amazingly the system still functions and runs every afternoon at 4.30 (except in summer).

(07) 4655 3399; thargo.info@bigpond.com

Westlander

Take the overnight train ride from Brisbane to Charleville or Quilpie, travelling over the Great Dividing Range and through some of Queensland's rich farming areas.

(07) 3235 1122 or 1300 131 722; www.traveltrain.com.au

Around Charleville

ACTIVITIES

Bilby experience

As the home of the Save the Bilby Fund, Charleville is the spot to learn about the greater bilby, which has disappeared from nearly 90 per cent of its former range in Queensland. Learn about the habits and habitat of these small, rabbit-like animals then, as night falls, see these cute creatures up close. Bookings can be made through the visitor centre.

Charleville visitor centre: (07) 4654 3057

Charleville Cosmos Centre

During the day at this centre you can view the sun through special telescopes, play with the interactive displays and watch films on astronomy. Come at night to explore the stars, planets, moons and galaxies with an expert guide, using telescopes.

(07) 4654 7771; www.cosmoscentre.com

The bore at Thargomindah

Cabin accommodation at Carnarvon Gorge Wilderness Lodge

Around Emerald

ACTIVITIES

Carnarvon Gorge National Park

Do not let the long drive in or the 20 kilometres of gravel road (impassable to 2WDs in the Wet) put you off this priceless national park. It has remnant rainforest, cabbage tree palms, ancient cycads, rare king ferns, moss gardens, countless eucalypts, Aboriginal art, towering multi-coloured cliffs, and some of the best bushwalking in the state. Camping is permitted in the Carnarvon Gorge day-use area during the Easter, winter and spring Queensland school holidays. Big Bend camping area, reached by a 10-kilometre walk, is open all year (for bookings, *see* below). The two closest accommodation options, just outside the park, are the eco-accredited Carnarvon Gorge Wilderness Lodge and Takarakka Bush Resort, which both have simple cabins. They also offer guided walking tours.

QPWS: (07) 4984 4505; www.epa.qld.gov.au
Camp bookings: 13 1304; www.epa.qld.gov.au
Carnarvon Gorge Wilderness Lodge: (07) 4984 4503; www.carnarvon-gorge.com
Takarakka Bush Resort: (07) 4984 4535; www.takaru.com.au

Walkers crossing a creek in Carnarvon National Park

Emerald Botanic Garden

Pack a picnic and explore the 42-hectare Emerald Botanic Garden on the banks of the Nagoa River. It has 6 kilometres of walks, and gardens representing major plant communities in central Queensland (with 90 per cent of plants labelled), as well as playgrounds, a melaleuca maze, bush chapel and barbecues.

Visitor centre: (07) 4982 4142; www.emerald.qld.gov.au

When planning your holiday around Emerald, drop in to the Emerald visitor centre, which is made from environmentally friendly straw bales.
Visitor centre: Clermont St; (07) 4982 4142; www.emerald.qld.gov.au

Expedition National Park

Like Carnarvon, this park features sheer sandstone cliffs and gorges, rainforests and wildflowers. There are a couple of campgrounds and a range of walks, including an exciting 10-kilometre round trip from Starkvale camping area across Shepherds Peak to Cattle Dip.

QPWS: (07) 4627 3358; www.epa.qld.gov.au

Crossing the dunes in the Simpson Desert

Far west

ACTIVITIES

Simpson Desert National Park

Queensland's biggest national park is also one of the most inaccessible, only suitable for well-prepared four-wheel drivers. The terrain is dominated by large dunes, spaced about a kilometre apart, with gibber plains, spinifex, claypans and open shrublands. There are no walking tracks and you are recommended to stay near your car, but the rewards include 180 species of bird, mulgaras, numerous lizards and snakes, mobs of red kangaroos – and isolated desert camping.

QPWS: (07) 4656 3272; www.epa.qld.gov.au

Central Queensland

ACTIVITIES

Dinosaur Discovery Weeks

Go out on a real dinosaur dig in the heart of Australia's dinosaur territory for a week with palaeontologists who will school you in everything you need to know. The Dinosaur Discovery Weeks, run by the Australian Age of Dinosaurs Museum at Winton, operate in August and September and only have places for a dozen people, so get in quickly for this experience. Accommodation is usually in shearer's quarters. Due to open in 2009 is the long-awaited Australian Age of Dinosaurs Museum, on 1400 hectares out of Winton, which will include a preparation and collection laboratory, dinosaur remains and information on the natural and cultural heritage of the area.

(07) 4657 0414; www.australianageofdinosaurs.com

Looking at dinosaur footprints at Lark Quarry Conservation Park

Kronosaurus Korner, Richmond

This dinosaur museum in the heart of Australian dinosaur territory focuses on ancient native creatures. It has one of the country's best preserved dinosaur skeletons.

(07) 4741 3429; www.kronosauruskorner.com.au

Lark Quarry Conservation Park

Situated 110 kilometres south-west of Winton, some 4000 fossilised footprints here tell the only known story of a dinosaur stampede that took place an estimated 95 million years ago. Access to the trackways is only with a tour at 10am, 12noon or 2pm, but there are also picnic facilities and a short walk through spinifex jump-up country. The drive to the park may be inaccessible to 2WD vehicles after rain.

(07) 4657 1188; www.dinosaurtrackways.com.au

Porcupine Gorge National Park

Little known, this national park has towering cliffs of vibrantly coloured sandstone, a spectacular gorge known as the Little Grand Canyon, thick vine forest and a small campground at the Pyramid, but you will need to bring your own drinking water.

QPWS Hughenden: (07) 4741 1113; www.epa.qld.gov.au

Wombat caretaker

You can have the priceless task of caring for the only remaining population of northern hairy-nosed wombat – one of the most rare large mammals in the world – by becoming a caretaker at Epping Forest National Park (Scientific). For a month, you will check the feed and water stations and the feral-proof fence, and contribute to the ongoing conservation of the creature's remnant habitat with feeding programs. Accommodation in your own homestead is provided free of charge. Call ranger Andrew Dinwoodie. The park is located north-west of Emerald.

(07) 4936 0549 or (07) 4936 0511

Canoeing through Lawn Hill Gorge in Boodjamulla National Park

North and north-west

ACTIVITIES

Birdwatching

Take your binoculars to the 9000-hectare Mutton Hole Wetlands, between Karumba and Normanton, which are of international significance as a breeding, feeding, moulting and drought refuge for birds. You will find a variety of waterbirds, including whistling-ducks, sarus cranes, brolgas and waders.

Boodjamulla (Lawn Hill) National Park

As well as containing the World Heritage–listed Riversleigh fossil sites, Boodjamulla is widely known as one of Queensland's most scenic national parks. It has spectacular gorges with great opportunities for swimming, hiking and just sitting around enjoying it all, among pandanus and freshwater crocodiles.

You can hire canoes by the hour from the Lawn Hill Gorge campsite, which has toilets and showers. Bookings are required from Easter to October and will usually need to be made well in advance, online or by phone (*see* below).

Many travellers prefer to camp at Adels Grove, which has shady campsites, some permanent tents and rooms, hot showers and a restaurant. Activities include swimming, canoeing, and half-day interpretive tours of the Riversleigh fossil sites, where you will see fossils in situ.

Lawn Hill Gorge: 13 1304; www.epa.qld.gov.au

Adels Grove: (07) 4748 5502; www.adelsgrove.com.au

Chillagoe–Mungana National Park

As well as a few short walks, Aboriginal rock art and an abundance of wallaroos, birds and agile wallabies, this national park's main features are its unusual rock towers and more than 700 documented limestone caves. Rangers

conduct guided tours in three of them, but you will need to book through the Chillagoe Hub visitor centre, which also has displays of some of the fossils found on nearby properties. The park lies some 210 kilometres west of Cairns.
(07) 4094 7111; www.chillagoehub.com.au

Chillagoe Observatory and Eco Lodges

Join a guided tour of the heavens, with close-up views of nebulas and star clusters from two large telescopes. There is camping and cabin accommodation here as well.
(07) 4094 7155; www.coel.com.au

Gulflander

Jokingly referred to as the train from nowhere to nowhere, the *Gulflander* runs 150 kilometres between Normanton and Croydon, along a track that has never been linked to the main Queensland rail system. It is a great way to see some of the most remote and inaccessible countryside in Queensland, with landscapes from wetlands and grasslands to arid savannah. With stops, it takes about five hours each way.
(07) 4036 9333; www.kurandascenicrailway.com.au

Riversleigh Fossils Interpretive Centre

Situated in Mount Isa and considerably easier to get to than the fossil fields of Riversleigh, which are a three-to-four-hour drive away, this centre has palaeontologists working on site on weekdays, and offers a half-hour laboratory tour. You can browse through the other displays in about half an hour.
(07) 4749 1555 or 1300 659 660

Savannahlander

This small two- or three-carriage train heads out across the savannah country from Cairns to Forsayth on a four-day round trip, allowing you to get off at towns and see key places, such as Undara, along the way. You can sit next to the train driver, who will even stop the train for you if you want to get out and have a look at something. There are fully catered four-day options, with tours, meals and accommodation included, or cheaper options where you bring your own tent. Book well ahead for the trips with accommodation.
(07) 4053 6848 or 1800 793 848;
www.savannahlander.com.au

Undara Volcanic National Park

Although there are a few bushwalks leading to lookouts here, the main reason people come is to see the world's longest lava tubes, created when a volcano erupted about 200 000 years ago. The tubes are not open to the public without a guide. Undara Experience offers two-to-eight-hour tours with trained savannah guides. Accommodation at Undara Experience ranges from refurbished historic railway carriages to permanent tents, dormitories and campsites.
(07) 4097 1900 or 1800 990 992; www.undara.com.au

The long-extinct Dickson's thylacine, a close relative of the Tasmanian thylacine, is depicted in a diorama at Riversleigh Fossils Interpretive Centre

Standing in one of the huge lava tubes at Undara Volcanic National Park

Western Australia

Tourism in Western Australia has long been nature-focused, but it is only in recent years that greater emphasis has been placed on looking after its natural treasures. In the past, for instance, tourists at Monkey Mia could feed the dolphins all sorts of food, with no regard for their welfare. Gradually better safeguards and controls have been put in place – limited feeding and touching of the dolphins, and educational talks.

Western Australia seems to be accelerating its ecotourism development, which is good news because it has the most to protect. By far Australia's largest state, it has a huge diversity of wild landscapes, and the amazing natural experiences range from wandering among multicoloured rock formations in the Kimberley and coming face to face with whale sharks at Ningaloo Reef, to climbing into the canopy of towering forest in the South-west and bunking down at Eyre Bird Observatory, one of the most remote birdwatching spots in Australia.

THE KIMBERLEY, although one of the most remote parts of the country, has some superb ecotourism options, including tours taking in the regional highlights.

PERTH TO PORT HEDLAND is the area perhaps best known for interactions with whale sharks and dolphins, but also has gorges, reefs, waterholes and mountain ranges to explore.

SOUTHERN WESTERN AUSTRALIA is an ecotourism hotspot, with plenty to experience around the Margaret River and Capes area, from spectacular caves and towering forests to pristine, sand-rimmed coastlines.

Western Australian Visitor Centre: Albert Facey House, Cnr Forrest Pl and Wellington St, Perth; (08) 9483 1111 or 1300 361 351; www.westernaustralia.com

Department of Environment and Conservation (DEC)*: The Atrium, 168 St Georges Tce, Perth; (08) 6467 5000; www.dec.wa.gov.au

*The DEC has replaced the Department of Conservation and Land Management (CALM), but the latter name is still often used in regional areas.

TOP TEN

1 Swim alongside whale sharks, the world's biggest fish, and manta rays at Ningaloo Reef on the state's outback coast

2 Spend a night holding back the tide of cane toads from the Kimberley, on a toad-busting trip out of Kununurra

3 Learn to surf on the legendary breaks near Margaret River

4 Meditate on Australia's most amazing rock-art collection on the Burrup Peninsula, near Karratha in the Pilbara, or at one of the many mysterious spots in the Kimberley

5 Sample organic wines and produce in the South-west region

6 Hike among swirling winds and maybe even snow in Stirling Ranges National Park, north of Albany

7 Try to spot a rare Gouldian finch in the wild while staying at Mornington Wilderness Camp in the Kimberley, run by the Australian Wildlife Conservancy

8 Swim, slide and hike through the beautiful gorges of Karijini National Park in the Pilbara

9 Set aside a day to explore the rich diversity of Kings Park and Botanic Garden in Perth

10 Cycle around the quokkas of Rottnest Island, with views of the turquoise waters and white sands rimming the coastline

GREEN TRAVEL TIP If driving in Western Australia's desert country, keep a close eye on the road for thorny devils. Smaller than your hand, they tend to 'freeze' on the road, rather than run away, and too many are squashed by careless drivers. Although they can look frightening they merely eat ants, and can easily be picked up and gently moved off the road.

Perth

Central Perth is a great city to walk and cycle around. Grassy stretches of parkland fringe the Swan River and to the west lies the Indian Ocean, providing a string of waterfront suburbs with great beaches. Accommodation options for ecotourists, however, are not great here.

WHERE TO STAY

Camping

For accommodation with minimal impact on the environment, the best choice in Perth is under canvas, a little out of the city. There are excellent and very popular camping facilities at Mundaring National Park, with hot showers, a camp kitchen and a refrigerator. The park is near Mundaring Weir, 40 kilometres east of the city. You can also camp in Walyunga National Park, 40 kilometres north-east of Perth, where the Avon River becomes the Swan River.

DEC Perth Hills: (08) 9295 2244; www.dec.wa.gov.au
Walyunga park ranger: (08) 9571 1371

WHERE TO EAT

The Sandcastle

The Sandcastle is an up-market option in South Fremantle, with beautiful food, much of which comes from sustainable resources, and organic wines and beers. As well as stocking organic vegetables, grains and meats, the owners investigate the origins of all their ingredients, going for minimum distance travelled, as well as specialities such as chemical-free spirits.

11/396 South Tce, South Fremantle; (08) 9335 2445;
www.sandcastleorganic.com.au

ACTIVITIES

Cycling

Perth is a great city to cycle around, with more than 400 kilometres of linked, flat bike paths, including along the Swan River and the 25 kilometres to Fremantle, as well as through Kings Park and Botanic Garden. One of the most popular shorter rides goes around the river and crosses the Narrows and Causeway bridges. There are plenty of places to hire bikes. About Bike Hire at Point Fraser Reserve also hires caboose child trailers and inline skates. You can download maps and guides from the Department for Planning and Infrastructure (DPI) website.

DPI: 441 Murray St, Perth; (08) 9216 8313;
www.dpi.wa.gov.au
About Bike Hire: (08) 9221 2665;
http://aboutbikehire.com.au

Diving

There are some shore dives in and around Fremantle and Perth, and plenty of great boat dives to Rottnest Island and further afield. Dolphin Dive Fremantle is an eco-accredited dive shop with a large boat, and will rent gear and give you more information.

(08) 9336 6286; www.dolphindiveshop.com

Picnicking at Walyunga National Park, north-east of Perth

Kayaking

The Swan River may not be the most interesting place to kayak in terms of natural beauty, but a pod of dolphins often interacts with kayakers around Heirisson Island, and there are plenty of little bays with great birdlife. You can hire kayaks from About Bike Hire (*see* Cycling above).

Kings Park and Botanic Garden

Arguably the most scenic botanic gardens in the country, Kings Park and Botanic Garden, with its hilltop location, offers great views over the city and beyond, and has plenty of space for picnicking, cycling and walking. The park extends over 400 hectares, of which 267 hectares is natural bushland. The garden primarily focuses on Western Australian plants, with about 3000 on display. There is a tree canopy walk, some really interesting playgrounds, free guided walks and free electric barbecues.

Parks Authority: Fraser Ave; (08) 9480 3600; www.bgpa.wa.gov.au

Perth Zoo

You can certainly while away a few hours at this excellent zoo, which is involved in conservation and has a breeding program for native endangered species, including the western swamp tortoise, Shark Bay mouse and chuditch (western quoll).

20 Labouchere Rd, South Perth; (08) 9474 3551 or (08) 9474 0444; www.perthzoo.wa.gov.au

Swimming

Locals know that beaches near Perth are some of the most underrated in the country, and rarely have crowds. Scarborough is one of the most popular patrolled beaches, and, when calm, Cottesloe can be perfect for a dip with a mask and snorkel. Floreat and City beaches are also recommended.

Whale-watching

Although there are probably more whales and a greater variety of species further south, whale-watchers on trips leaving from Perth get the bonus of a cruise down the Swan River during the short September–November humpback season. Alternatively, you can leave from Fremantle. Operators include Oceanic Cruises and Rottnest Fast Ferries.

Oceanic Cruises: Barrack St Jetty, Perth; also B Shed, Victoria Quay, Fremantle; (08) 9325 1191; www.oceaniccruises.com.au

Rottnest Fast Ferries booking office: Shop 56, Southside Dr, Hillarys Boat Harbour, Hillarys; (08) 9246 1039; www.rottnestfastferries.com.au

Southern Western Australia

At Point Ann in Fitzgerald River National Park, a world biosphere reserve with more plant diversity than anywhere else in Australia, colourful wildflowers bloom everywhere in season – grevilleas, hakeas, eucalypts, peas, bottlebrushes and the endemic crimson qualup bells. The lucky visitor may also see southern right whales cruising quietly up and down the bay beside the pristine beach or a pod of dolphins surfing the waves. To those who know where to look, wild experiences like this are common in south-western Australia, which has some of the finest natural landscapes in the country. Thankfully ecotourism ventures here are on the rise, although primarily centred on the area between Perth and Albany. There are organic wines to sip, tracks to walk, forests to explore and rivers to paddle.

Eagle Bay on Rottnest Island

Rottnest Island

WHERE TO STAY

The Rottnest Island Authority (RIA) holiday units on Rottnest use green power from the 69-metre-high, 600-kilowatt wind turbine that provides up to 37 per cent of the power on the island. There is limited camping and you can also stay in dorm rooms in the old barracks, cottages or other accommodation, but it is recommended that you book.

Central reservations: (08) 9432 9111 or 1800 111 111; www.rottnestisland.com

ACTIVITIES

Cycling

You can hire a bike before you get to Rottnest, and take it on the ferry, or hire on the island at Rottnest Island Bike Hire (located behind the Quokka Arms Hotel). The company has tandems, child seats, trailers and electric buggies for the elderly and disabled, but does not take bookings. In around five hours, cyclists can tour the whole island, stopping at points

Nature lovers should not miss this 1900-hectare paradise, just a 30-minute ferry ride from Fremantle. It is one of the only places where you can see quokkas bouncing around, and has superb swimming and snorkelling. The Rottnest Island Authority plants about 40 000 native trees on the island and recycles greywater onto the oval.

Cars are virtually non-existent, so the only way around the island is walking, cycling or by the bus that travels the main 24-kilometre loop. Many people do a day trip only, but for the best chance to see quokkas you should take your time and stay longer.

Ferries to Rottnest leave from Perth, Hillarys or Fremantle. The ferry companies may be able to arrange tours, bike hire and accommodation. Rottnest Air Taxi has had a carbon neutral policy since 2005, and return flights, in a four- or six-seater aircraft, are probably cheaper than you would expect.

Rottnest Air Taxi: (08) 9292 5027, 0411 264 547 or 1800 500 006; www.rottnest.de

Ferry information:

Rottnest Express: 1300 467 688; www.rottnestexpress.com.au

Rottnest Fast Ferries: (08) 9246 1039; www.rottnestfastferries.com.au

Oceanic Cruises: (08) 9325 1191; www.oceaniccruises.com.au

*A quokka (*Setonix brachyurus*) on Rottnest Island*

of interest; alternatively, a leisurely three-hour ride will take in the salt lakes, lighthouse and the east end of the island.

Rottnest Island Bike Hire: (08) 9292 5105; www.rottnestisland.com

Snorkelling

Snorkel in the turquoise waters of the Basin to see some of the 100-odd species of tropical fish pushed here by the warm Leeuwin Current, or head to the snorkelling trail at Little Salmon Bay. Other top snorkelling spots include Parakeet and Little Parakeet, with some substantial coral reefs and around 360 species of fish. You can pick up a snorkelling guide from Rottnest Island Bike Hire (*see* above).

Perth to Bunbury

ACTIVITIES

Dolphin Discovery Centre

This non-profit organisation is committed to education, conservation and research about dolphins, but also provides extraordinary opportunities to interact with these creatures. About 90 wild bottlenose dolphins live in Koombana Bay at Bunbury and visit the shallow waters in front of the centre most mornings. Under strict guidelines, you can stand in the water with the dolphins as they are fed small amounts of fish. You can also join a snorkelling tour to swim with the dolphins in the bay. The discovery centre has detailed displays and information on dolphins and other marine life, and also offers a short cultural tour, where you will learn about the spiritual relationship between dolphins and the Wardandi people, as well as cultural activities such as campsite construction, tool-making, bush tucker and fire-lighting.

447 Koombana Dr, Bunbury; (08) 9791 3088; http://dolphins.mysouthwest.com.au

Bathers in the Basin below Bathurst Point Lighthouse on Rottnest Island

Dryandra Woodland, near Narrogin

Although it may not look like much to the casual observer, this forest of white-barked wandoo and powderbark is one of the last vestiges of woodland in a landscape of cleared farmland, and is home to some incredible animals and a wildlife breeding enclosure that has seen the revival of several important species. The numbat is probably Dryandra's best-known inhabitant, but there are woylies, tammar wallabies, brushtail possums and tawny frogmouths, and the thickets of rock she-oak provide habitat for red-tailed phascogales and other rare species. More than 100 bird species have been recorded here, including the mound-building mallee fowl. Dryandra Woodland is around 164 kilometres south-east of Perth, and 22 kilometres north-west of Narrogin. You will need to stay overnight in the basic cottages, dormitories or campground to see many of the animals, or join the night tour in the animal sanctuary, but during the day there are cycling tracks and walks to explore – including one to an Aboriginal ochre pit.

DEC Narrogin: (08) 9881 9200; www.dec.wa.gov.au

Mountain-biking

One of the world's premier off-road biking tracks, the Munda Biddi Trail is being established through the forests of south-western Australia. Currently stretching from Mundaring to Nannup, it will eventually run for 900 kilometres (to Albany), and is great for day rides, overnighters or longer excursions of a week or more. Purpose-built, cycle-friendly campsites have been built every 35–40 kilometres between towns, with composting toilets, water tanks, picnic tables, an undercover bike-storage facility, sleeping quarters for 25–30 people and cleared tent sites. No campfires are allowed, so you will need to take a stove. The Munda Biddi Trail Foundation is a great source of knowledge and maps on this brilliant ecotourism venture.

*Little penguin (*Eudyptula minor*) near its burrow in Shoalwater Islands Marine Park*

Several operators will help you with either guided tours or bike hire for the Munda Biddi and other tracks. Daktari Mountain Biking is an environmentally focused company that will hire gear and help you get out on the trail, with either supported or unsupported trips. Pedal Oz hires bikes, panniers, repair equipment and so on and offers transfers to get you on and off the track.

Munda Biddi Trail Foundation: (08) 9481 2483; www.mundabiddi.org.au

Daktari Mountain Biking: (08) 9524 1671 or 0428 888 184

Pedal Oz: 1300 784 864 or 0425 200 958; www.pedaloz.com.au

Sea-kayaking

Along the coast at Rockingham, less than 45 minutes drive south from Perth, you can kayak to the Shoalwater Islands Marine Park just offshore, which harbours a host of wildlife. There are Australian sea-lions on Seal Island, and little penguins on Penguin Island (including some being cared for in the Penguin Discovery Centre – they are fed three times a day). The eco-accredited company Rockingham Wild Encounters will hire gear and advise you on great places to paddle to, or you can join one of their wildlife tours, including one in which you will hopefully get to swim with dolphins.

Rockingham Wild Encounters: (08) 9591 1333; www.rockinghamwildencounters.com.au

Short walks

Leschenault Inlet, near Koombana Bay at Bunbury, holds the southernmost white mangroves in Western Australia. A short boardwalk winds through the mangroves, where you may see some of the 60 waterbird species found here. There are also several short walks at Big Swamp Reserve, which has a bird hide, and Maidens Reserve, one of the few natural tuart forests left in the state.

Bunbury Visitor Centre: (08) 9792 7205; www.visitbunbury.com.au

Swimming

There is almost no limit to the number of particularly fine beaches along this stretch of coast for swimming, surfing and snorkelling, and you will have no trouble finding a spot to lay out your towel and dip a toe or ten in the water. Backbeach and Koombana Bay at Bunbury, and Biningup Beach some 37 kilometres to the north, are all highly recommended for swimming.

Whitewater rafting

Dwellingup Adventures has a one-day rafting trip on the Murray River suitable for novices and children from ten years and upwards. This operator also hire canoes, kayaks, rafts and mountain bikes and, for self-guided tours, will drop your craft in the water and pick it up again later.

(08) 9538 1127; www.dwellingupadventures.com.au

Busselton to Augusta

WHERE TO STAY

Burnside Bungalows

At Margaret River you can stay on this certified organic and biodynamic farm that produces mulberries, apricots, nectarines, peaches, avocados and olives. The accommodation is in cottages made with rammed earth and recycled and salvaged timbers. Rainwater is collected to supply the bungalows and all wastewater is treated in an on-site sewage plant and recycled onto the gardens.

(08) 9757 2139; www.burnsidebungalows.com.au

Yallingup Strawbale Retreat

The two retreats here have walls built of straw. You can collect eggs for your breakfast, or see what is in season in the orchard.

(08) 9755 2009; www.yallingupstrawbaleretreat.com.au

Fresh plums produced on the farm at Burnside Bungalows

Rammed earth cottage at Burnside Bungalows

Yelverton Brook Eco Spa Retreat

Set in a 40-hectare conservation reserve protected from feral predators, with woylies, bandicoots and other animals roaming around, the self-contained chalets here have everything you could want, including local free-range eggs and other produce. Some chalets are made with mud bricks and have a passive solar design, and much of the furniture is made from salvaged or recycled timbers. The owners have been pioneers in trying to develop sustainable tourism practices and support wildlife carers in the area. They offer a two-day eco package, including a choice of eco-friendly towels and sheets (some made with hemp) and a meal at Bay Organics in Busselton (*see* Wine and food tasting, page 154).

(08) 9755 7579; www.yelvertonbrook.com.au

ACTIVITIES

Birdwatching

Keen birdwatchers should not miss the Ramsar-listed Vasse–Wonnerup Wetlands east of Busselton, where up to 33 000 waterbirds have been recorded at a time. There is a walking trail and a bird hide hidden amid the paperbarks.

CALM Busselton: (08) 9752 1677; www.dec.wa.gov.au

Canoe tour

Bushtucker River and Winery Tours will take you canoeing down the quiet Margaret River, with opportunities to see kangaroos, bush-tucker-bearing plants and heritage sites on a guided four-hour excursion. There is time for swimming, a cave adventure and a bushwalk, and lunch is a native foods experience including kangaroo, emu and wild turkey.

Bushtucker River and Winery Tours: (08) 9757 9084 or 0419 911 971; www.bushtuckertours.com

Caving

Six limestone caves in the Capes region are open to the public and there are self-guided and adventure-caving options. Jewel Cave is the largest of Western Australia's tourist caves and has beautiful formations including a 'frozen' waterfall and one of the world's longest straw stalactites. Lake Cave is also stunning, with formations reflected in a beautiful underground lake. If there, spend some time at CaveWorks, which is an interesting interpretive centre.

Ngilgi Cave has the most exciting cave tours for novices. If you are over 15, and prepared to get a bit dirty and squeeze through tight gaps underground, you can join the Crystal Crawl Tour or the Ultimate Ngilgi Adventure, accessing some of the deepest, most beautiful, and hard-to-reach spots in the cave system. For the less

*Splendid fairy wren (*Malurus splendens*) in breeding plumage at Cape Naturaliste*

Exploring the caves near Margaret River

adventurous, there are other options, including a tour conducted by candle and torch light.

Tour information: (08) 9755 2152; www.geographebay.com

Leeuwin–Naturaliste National Park/CALM Busselton: (08) 9752 1677; www.dec.wa.gov.au

Cycle tour

You can explore this scenic region at your own pace, including wineries, karri forests, caves and beaches on a bike. Dirty Detours hires bikes in Margaret River and runs a one-day, off-road Sip and Cycle tour, while Pedal Oz offers a three-to-seven-day, self-guided tour, with bus transfers, maps, itineraries and accommodation.

Dirty Detours: 0417 998 816; www.dirtydetours.com

Pedal Oz: 1300 784 864 or 0425 200 958; www.pedaloz.com.au

Hiking

One of Western Australia's brilliant long-distance walks, the Cape to Cape Walk covers 135 kilometres between Cape Naturaliste and Cape Leeuwin, going through coastal heath, wildflowers, jarrah–marri forest and past rugged granite headlands and plunging cliffs. The trail mostly follows the coast, but there are some inland loops. Walkers often spot western grey kangaroos in the bush, and dolphins offshore, and, in the second half of the year, migrating whales are sometime seen. It takes about seven days to do the entire track, but there are plenty of options for shorter walks. You can camp all the way along, or stay in a variety of accommodation just off the track.

Coastal scene at Cape Leeuwin – at one end of the Cape to Cape Walk

The best source for all information on the walk is the Friends of the Cape to Cape Track website. It lists several operators that offer guided walks, including fully supported walks.

Friends of the Cape to Cape Track: www.capetocapetrack.com.au

Snorkelling and diving

The marine life growing off and feeding near the historic 1841-metre Busselton Jetty makes it one of the easiest and best snorkelling and dive sites in Western Australia. The Underwater Observatory (*see* entry below) at the seaward end of the jetty will give a preview of the marine world that awaits you. Meelup Beach, between Dunsborough and Eagle Bay, and Canal Rocks, just south of Yallingup, are other recommended spots for a shore dive or snorkel. The crew at the Dive Shed in Busselton will give advice, hire gear, run diving courses and offer a changing schedule of boat dives.

(08) 9754 1615; www.diveshed.com.au

Surfing

Well known as holding some of the best surfing breaks in the country, beaches near Margaret River also provide a great venue to learn to surf, with plenty of teachers to help you start and a variety of surf conditions. Escape Safaris for Women has surfing holidays for women only, in which you can do as little or as much surfing as you want. Blue Spirit Retreats also has women-only options, but plenty of mixed and family learn-to-surf holidays as well. The Margaret River Surf School runs two-hour group lessons, and offers private lessons as well.

Escape Safaris for Women: (08) 9755 2488; www.escapesafaris.com.au

Blue Spirit Retreats: (08) 9757 9284; www.bluespiritretreats.com.au

Margaret River Surf School: (08) 9757 1111; www.margaretriversurfschool.com

Snorkelling amid the marine life near the Busselton Jetty

Tuart Forest National Park

Although small, this treasure of a national park, 15 kilometres north-east of Busselton, contains the largest remaining tuart forest in the world, with a vast number of 300-year-old trees. It has great picnic spots, a bird hide and a few walking tracks, including a 1.5-kilometre trail marked with reflectors for a night-spotlighting walk.

CALM Busselton: (08) 9752 1677; www.dec.wa.gov.au

Underwater Observatory

Near the end of the almost 2-kilometre-long Busselton Jetty is an interpretive centre and observatory 8 metres under the water's surface, where you can see brightly coloured corals, sponges, fish and invertebrates without getting wet. You will need to book as the observatory can only fit 40 people at a time.

(08) 9754 0900; www.busseltonjetty.com.au

Enoplosus armatus sighted from Busselton Jetty's Underwater Observatory; the common name of the species, old wife, derives from the grating sound emitted by the fish when stressed

Wardan Aboriginal Centre

The cultural centre for the Wardandi people, this rammed-earth building in Yallingup has Aboriginal art displays, guided tours, tool-making and spear-throwing workshops and dance demonstrations.

(08) 9756 6566; www.wardan.com.au

Whale-watching

The south-west corner of the continent is a famous vantage spot to see southern right whales, humpbacks, blue whales and minkes as they migrate up and down the coastline. To make the most of this natural spectacle, Naturaliste Charters operates three-hour, whale-watching tours out of Augusta in the first part of the season (June–September) and then out of Dunsborough for the second half of the season (September–December). Of course, there are plenty of excellent vantage points to spy them from the shore as well, including purpose-built whale-watching platforms at Cape Naturaliste.

Naturaliste Charters: (08) 9755 2276; www.whales-australia.com

Wine and food tasting

Well known for its wine and foods, the Margaret River region has an increasing number of organic and environmentally friendly food producers.

Wineries The multi-award-winning Settlers Ridge at Cowaramup was the first internationally certified organic winery in the country and

Hand-picking grapes at Cullen Wines at Cowaramup

it is well worth treating your tastebuds to its offerings. Random Valley Organics not only has award-winning organic wines, but also a unique and unusual cellar-door building made of water-filled wine bottles, providing insulation, heating and cooling. Cullen Wines at Cowaramup is an organic winery that is Certified A Grade Biodynamic with the Biological Farmers Association (and their wines are magnificent). You can stay in homestead accommodation here.

Foodstuffs Once a month, the local producers put on a farmer's market in Margaret River, where you can taste and buy a range of organic delights. Cullen Wines at Cowaramup has a restaurant in which all food is prepared using fresh, biodynamic and organic produce sourced from its own garden and local producers. In Busselton, Bay Organics sells organic fruit, vegetables and other produce, and also has a cafe stocked with only organic foods, coffees and teas.

Settlers Ridge: (08) 9755 5883; www.settlersridge.com.au
Random Valley Organics: (08) 9758 6707; www.randomvalley.com
Cullen Wines: (08) 9755 5277; www.cullenwines.com.au
Farmer's market: www.margaretriver.asn.au
Bay Organics: (08) 9751 1315

Augusta to Albany

WHERE TO STAY

Watermark Kilns

For something completely different, stay in one of two ex-tobacco kilns, converted into comfortable, low-key accommodation. The double kiln (suitable for large families or bigger groups) has recycled timbers, water is captured rainwater, and guests can help themselves to eggs, fruit and vegetables from the permaculture garden. The property, located in Karri Hill Road between Northcliffe and Pemberton, is also a marron farm, and you can buy the scrumptious crustaceans direct at wholesale prices.

(08) 9776 7349; www.watermarkkilns.com.au

Windrose B&B

With a philosophy of minimising their environmental footprint, the owners of Windrose B&B near Denmark have developed a cosy, environmentally helpful four-room B&B. They have 24 solar panels and solar hot water, and they invest in carbon offsets for all other CO_2 emissions, such as car travel. They buy only fair-trade coffee, tea and chocolate, local fruit and vegetables and donate to projects of the Denmark Environment Centre.

(08) 9848 3502; www.windrose.com.au

ACTIVITIES

Boat tour

In Walpole–Nornalup National Park you can relax on a cruise then walk to a secluded beach on the Southern Ocean. The two-and-a-half-hour cruise includes entertaining interpretation of science, nature and culture from a national eco-guide award winner. Wow Wilderness contributes directly to natural and cultural conservation efforts and is currently involved in fire research, dieback management and an eco-education project at Walpole Primary School.

Wow Wilderness: (08) 9840 1036; www.wowwilderness.com.au
CALM Walpole: (08) 9840 1027; www.dec.wa.gov.au

Canoeing

For a pleasant afternoon canoeing through old-growth forests in Warren National Park (9 kilometres south west of Pemberton), join a

A guided walk of the Bibbulmun Track with Out Of Sight! Tours takes in these mysterious limestone-encrusted forms at William Bay National Park near Denmark

tour with Pemberton Hiking and Canoeing. This environmentally aware company offers a range of tours from four hours to five days, travelling through ancient forests, lakes, rivers and dune systems. There are night walks and a great summer option of floating down the Warren River in tyre tubes.

(08) 9776 1559; http://hikingandcanoeing.com.au

Cycling tours

Denmark Bike Adventures hires bikes and recommends a couple of cycling tours, including a hike–bike combination in which you can walk a section of the Bibbulmun Track (*see* Hiking below), then hop on a bike to cycle back to Denmark.

(08) 9848 3300; www.denmarkbluewren.com.au

D'Entrecasteaux National Park

In this national park, a 350-metre walk follows the clifftops around Point D'Entrecasteaux, with four lookouts offering dramatic views over the Southern Ocean, and prime vantage points to see whales during winter and spring. The 1700-square-kilometre park is great for four-wheel driving and camping.

CALM Pemberton: (08) 9776 1207; www.dec.wa.gov.au

Four-wheel-drive tours

Pemberton Discovery Tours is a carbon-neutral business that runs 4WD and tag-along tours through the great karri forests, along beaches and through dune systems, with a particular focus on environmental impact. There are regular evening frog and bug walks and the company is involved in Clean-up Australia Day, teaching the local school to make biodiesel fuel, and replanting to counter rising salinity in the South-West region.

With an emphasis on low-impact practices, Out Of Sight! Tours runs small-group, educative 4WD tours through places such as West Cape Howe National Park and the Walpole Wilderness, and guided walks on the Bibbulmun Track (see Hiking below). Although there is no formal carbon-offsetting scheme, the operator is involved in tree planting and revegetating a property.

Pemberton Discovery Tours: (08) 9776 0484; www.pembertondiscoverytours.com.au

Out Of Sight! Tours: (08) 9848 2814 or 0427 234 388; www.denmarkecotours.com

CALM Albany: (08) 9842 4500; www.dec.wa.gov.au

Hiking

You do not need to dedicate six to eight weeks to walk the superb 965-kilometre Bibbulmun Track in order to enjoy it. There are plenty of places to get on and off the track, so you can stretch the legs for a few hours, take a series of overnight walks staying in B&Bs, or strap on a load and immerse yourself in a section. The track cuts across the south-west corner of the state, from Kalamunda on the outskirts of Perth, to Albany on the south coast, travelling through a range of Western Australian landscapes – towering karri forests, waterfalls on granite cliffs, valleys of pine, carpets of wildflowers and 200 kilometres of coast. There are simple hiking huts every 15–20 kilometres and plenty of places to pick up supplies along or just off the route, but because you cannot book the huts, overnight walkers have to carry a tent. Particularly recommended sections are the spectacular coastal views through the Albany wind farm and Conspicuous Cliffs near Walpole, karri forests around Pemberton, and the wildflower-rich jarrah and marri forests near Collie.

The Bibbulmun Track Foundation, as well as helping maintain the trail and providing the most comprehensive information on it, offers a wide range of experiences along the way, including walks staying in comfortable beds each night, birdwatching walks and overnight introductions to the track. A variety of independent operators also offer guided walks. These are generally 'highlights' packages, which offer transport between sections. Most of the best operators are listed on the Bibbulmun Track Foundation website.

Bibbulmun Track Foundation: (08) 9481 0551; www.bibbulmuntrack.org.au

Tree-climbing

This activity seems a strange thing to put in an ecotourism guide, considering that metal spikes and pegs have been hammered into the trunks of these magnificent karri trees in order to scale them (originally for fire lookouts), but surprisingly the spikes do not seem to have affected the trees, and climbing them gives you an incredible perspective of the majesty of these forest kings. Even if you think you are not afraid of heights, it is very daunting, and do not expect to take children up more than a few rungs. The 61-metre Gloucester Tree just south of Pemberton is the most commonly climbed, but the 75-metre Dave Evans Bicentennial Tree in Warren National Park (*see* Canoeing above) is in a more scenic location.

Pemberton Visitor Centre: (08) 9776 1133 or 1800 671 133

CALM Pemberton: (08) 9776 1207; www.dec.wa.gov.au

Walpole–Nornalup National Park

In its 200 square kilometres this lovely park has towering karri and red tingle forests, coastal

Climbing up the metal spikes of the Gloucester Tree

Boardwalk through the Ancient Empire in the Valley of the Giants, Walpole–Nornalup National Park

heath, wetlands, beaches and rivers. It has around 700 known plant species, including more than 100 orchids. There are plenty of great walks, picnic areas and scenic locations, but the most visited part of the park is the Valley of the Giants, where you can walk at the base of the red tingles, yellow tingles, marri and karri trees – some of which are 80 metres high – or get on the famous 600-metre canopy walk, which takes you 40 metres off the ground.

DEC Walpole: (08) 9840 0400; www.dec.wa.gov.au

Beyond Albany

WHERE TO STAY

Munglinup Beach Park

With advanced eco-accreditation and a quiet location to die for, this caravan park east of Hopetoun is a little special. It has wind generators and solar power providing nearly all the electricity, rotary composting toilets and an organic vegetable garden that you are allowed to raid if there is enough of something in season. There is a range of self-contained cabins and vans on site, as well as camping.

(08) 9075 1155; www.munglinupbeach.com.au

ACTIVITIES

Beach and wetland walks

There is no shortage of great beaches to walk on around Esperance, and during the winter–spring whale-watching season you are likely to see one or two of these large marine mammals. But for a walk with a different feel, head to Kepwari Wetland, on the outskirts of Esperance, where a 3.6-kilometre track has interpretive panels and a couple of bird hides.

Cape Arid National Park

Very scenic, with white beaches, granite headlands and stunning turquoise water, this national park, around 120 kilometres east of Esperance, is generally very quiet. There are some good walks that will take a couple of hours, as well as excellent camping spots, but you will need to bring your own drinking water.

Park ranger: (08) 9075 0055

CALM Esperance: (08) 9071 3733; www.dec.wa.gov.au

Cape Le Grand National Park

Located some 50 kilometres south-east of Esperance and with similar terrain to the above, this excellent national park has kangaroos on the beach at Lucky Bay, freshwater pools, rocky outcrops and stunning beaches. The Coastal Trail (15 kilometres each way) is magnificent, and you can do sections of it if you are not up for the six-hour haul. The 3-kilometre-return walk to Frenchmans Peak is also recommended.

Park ranger: (08) 9075 9072

CALM Esperance: (08) 9071 3733; www.dec.wa.gov.au

Cruising

MacKenzies Island Cruises is a long-standing tourist operator in this area with, justifiably, a great reputation for nature-based tourism. On a half- or full-day cruise, the company will take you out around the more than 100 islands of the Recherche Archipelago, where you will see

New Zealand fur-seals, white-bellied sea-eagles, dolphins and other wildlife. Cruises include a stop at Woody Island, where you can choose to stay in the huts and tents, enjoying the snorkel trail, bushwalks, swimming and skinny dipping in this special spot. About 70 per cent of the power needs on the island come from solar power, there are waterless composting toilets, and rainwater is collected for use.

(08) 9071 5757; www.woodyisland.com.au

Eyre Bird Observatory

Nestled within Nuytsland Nature Reserve (*see* below), this non-profit, self-funding facility way out on the Nullarbor coast is for education and research on everything from dune stabilisation to reptiles. If you have your own linen, you can stay in shared rooms here, benefiting from the experience of expert birdwatchers in one of the most remote dedicated birdwatching spots in Australia. The observatory runs on solar power. You need a 4WD for the last 12 kilometres, or alternatively arrange to be picked up by the caretakers. A better option still is to have an extended experience out here, by becoming a volunteer caretaker for a month or two, with free food and accommodation.

Accommodation bookings: (08) 9039 3450; www.eyrebirds.org

CALM Esperance: (08) 9071 3733; www.dec.wa.gov.au

Fitzgerald River National Park

Situated some 180 kilometres north-east of Albany, Fitzgerald River National Park straddles the coast between the towns of Bremer Bay and Hopetoun. Not as commonly visited as many of Western Australia's other national parks, this is a world biosphere because of its incredible plant life – it contains more than 20 per cent of Western Australia's plants, some 1900 species, and over 100 are found only in the park and its immediate surrounds. There are some easy walking trails, and excellent vantage points to see southern right whales along the coast. Other attractions are the great camping, picnic and barbecue spots, but you will have to bring your own drinking water.

Park ranger: (08) 9835 5043

CALM Albany: (08) 9841 7133; www.dec.wa.gov.au

Indigenous tour

Kepa Kurl is an Aboriginal-owned-and-run business providing personalised and informative cultural tours of the Esperance region, including bushfoods and cultural history. Its sister company, Esperance Eco-Discovery Tours, offers 4WD tours to places such as Lucky Bay (*see* Cape Le Grand National Park above) – voted one of Australia's best beaches – and a two-hour introduction to the area.

(08) 9072 1688 or 0418 913 414; www.kepakurl.com.au

Lucky Bay in Cape Le Grand National Park

*Camping in Fitzgerald River National Park amid western grey kangaroos (*Macropus fuliginosus*)*

Nuytsland Nature Reserve

Running along the Great Australian Bight, this reserve comprises a narrow 400 000-hectare strip of isolated terrain, stretching from Cape Arid National Park to Red Rocks Point – only 140 kilometres from the South Australian border. Reputedly boasting some of the best, most undiscovered coastline in the country, this wild and untamed area is for committed, well-prepared four-wheel drivers only. Eyre Bird Observatory (*see* above) lies within the reserve.

Cape Arid park office: (08) 9075 0055

CALM Esperance: (08) 9071 3733; www.dec.wa.gov.au

Porongurup National Park

Situated 40 kilometres north of Albany, this 2621-hectare park is smaller and less spectacular than its neighbour, Stirling Range National Park (*see* below), but is still worth more than a passing visit. Porongurup's rounded granite domes reach a height of 670 metres, and are home to more than 700 plant species, including sheltered 60-metre-high karri forests and fern gullies. There are walks past balancing rocks and other features, some of which will get pulses racing as you scale the sloping summits.

Park ranger: (08) 9853 1095; www.dec.wa.gov.au

Porongurup Shop: (08) 9853 1110

Stirling Range National Park

One of the only places in Western Australia where it snows, this spectacular 1159-square-kilometre national park should definitely be on your list of places to go in Western Australia. The rugged sandstone and shale cliffs include the highest point in the state – Bluff Knoll at 1095 metres – and shelter 1500 types of plant, including nearly a hundred that are not found anywhere else. Bushwalking in the park is exciting and liberating, with dramatic changes in temperature, windy conditions, mists and fogs, and incredible views along knife-edge ridges. The 6-kilometre-return climb up Bluff Knoll takes three to four hours, but any of the other medium-length walks, such as the hike up the 1052-metre Toolbrunup Peak, are also highly recommended. You can camp at Moingup Springs.

Park ranger: (08) 9841 7133

CALM Albany: (08) 9842 4500; www.dec.wa.gov.au

Wildflower tour

The Banksia Farm at Mount Barker has the world's only arboretum of all 77 banksia species and nearly all the dryandras as well. Join a tour around the farm to hear fascinating yarns about how banksias were used in the past by Aboriginal people and early settlers, along with information about plant evolution and ecology.

(08) 9851 1770; www.banksiafarm.com.au

The distinctive peak of Bluff Knoll in Stirling Range National Park

Yongergnow Australian Malleefowl Centre

This not-for-profit venture at Ongerup (around 140 kilometres north of Albany) is housed in a $2 million, purpose-built centre. Staffed by volunteers and including a cafe and gallery that has nature-based photography and art, it aims to provide education about and help conserve endangered mallee fowl – the plump ground-dwelling birds that build massive mounds in which they lay eggs. There is an aviary with mallee fowl, and an interpretation centre describing all facets of their lifecycle.

(08) 9828 2325; www.yongergnow.com.au

Near Kalgoorlie

WHERE TO STAY

Camping

The Western Australian goldfields region is not the easiest area for the ecotraveller, but there are a few recommended natural attractions and campsites around Kalgoorlie. To the north is an ex-cattle station, Goongarrie, which has been destocked and made into a national park. It has some good camping among the mulga.

Goldfields Woodlands National Park, south-west of Coolgardie, also has plenty of spots to camp among the saltbush, salt lakes, salmon gums, she-oaks and mallee. Victoria Rock, in the south-east of the park, is recommended.

Kalgoorlie Visitor Centre: (08) 9021 1966 or 1800 004 653; www.kalgoorlietourism.com

CALM Kalgoorlie: (08) 9021 2677; www.dec.wa.gov.au

ACTIVITIES

Birdwatching

Rowles Lagoon Conservation Park is a 2-kilometre wide, semi-permanent freshwater lake that provides habitat for more species of waterbird than any other arid zone wetland south of the Kimberley. It also provides habitat for local waterskiers.

www.birdswa.com.au

CALM Kalgoorlie: (08) 9021 2677; www.dec.wa.gov.au

Kalgoorlie Visitor Centre: (08) 9021 1966 or 1800 004 653; www.kalgoorlietourism.com

Bushwalking

On the outskirts of Kalgoorlie, in Riverina Way, is the Karlkurla Bushland Park, with 4 kilometres of walking tracks, masses of wildflowers, and native bananas. It is a great example of natural regrowth, demonstrating what can be done in this area.

www.about-australia.com

CALM Kalgoorlie: (08) 9021 2677; www.dec.wa.gov.au

Kalgoorlie Visitor Centre: (08) 9021 1966 or 1800 004 653; www.kalgoorlietourism.com

Wildflowers in Goldfields Woodlands National Park

Perth to Port Hedland

Australia's lesser known great reef, Ningaloo, comes so close to sections of the coast that you can snorkel straight from the shore to enter this marine marvel of more than 200 coral and 500 fish species. Nature lovers swim beside the world's largest fish, the whale sharks, and among graceful manta rays. There are dugong and dolphins, and, if you can ever get out of the water, the terrestrial wonders are endless, with awesome gorges, rugged ranges resplendent in spinifex and snappy gums, and the world's largest Aboriginal art gallery. Ecotourism here now caters for every accommodation level, from deluxe and expensive eco safaris, to camping under the stars.

Early morning light captures the striking colours of this beachscape in Francois Peron National Park

NATURE WATCH Emus roam throughout the majority of mainland Australia and are most commonly seen in Western Australia. Occasionally they are found in large mobs of more than 15 – particularly if they are looking for water – but they usually move in pairs or alone. Very curious, they are often attracted by sparkling objects. The male bird is solely responsible for looking after the nest and the chicks, and during the 56 days he sits on the large avocado-like eggs, he does not eat or drink, and loses about a third of his bodyweight.

Perth to Geraldton

WHERE TO STAY

Hi Vallee Farm, Badgingarra

One-fifth of this 2000-hectare sheep and wheat farm, located around 200 kilometres north of Perth, has been left untouched, and contains some of the greatest botanical diversity in the world. There are some simple camping facilities with chemical toilets, and you can take a birdwatching or wildflower tour with local experts.

(08) 9652 3035

ACTIVITIES

Badgingarra National Park

This 13 000-hectare park has primarily been set aside to protect the abundant wildflowers in the area. Take the 2-kilometre Badgingarra Nature Trail to see black kangaroo paws, purple starflowers and the world's largest eucalypt flowers.

(08) 9652 7043; www.dec.wa.gov.au

Geraldton Meteorological Office

For something different, you can learn how modern weather-forecasting works and the measuring instruments involved, in a 40-minute midday tour of the Geraldton

Meteorological Office that culminates in the release of one of the huge weather balloons.

Tour information: (08) 9923 3671

Geraldton visitor centre: (08) 9921 3999 or 1800 818 881

Indigenous tour

Take the Yamatji Cultural Trail to see the Geraldton area through the eyes of the Yamatji people, visiting some fascinating sites, including the old gaol. You can listen to creation stories at significant sites and try your hand at throwing a boomerang.

Geraldton–Greenough Visitor Centre: (08) 9921 3999; www.geraldtontourist.com.au

LedaSwan Organic Wines

In Baskerville at the top of the Swan Valley, only half an hour's drive out of Perth, this organic winery has a focus on sustainable production, and uses a minimum of electricity to produce its range of organic wines. Small groups can head out on a morning walk through the vineyard with the winemaker, discussing winemaking techniques and philosophy, before tasting several wines.

LedaSwan Wines: (08) 9296 0216; www.ledaswan.com.au

The strange limestone formations of the Pinnacles Desert in Nambung National Park

Nambung National Park

This park is best known for the Pinnacles, thousands of limestone pillars up to 4 metres tall. The stacks formed underground some 15 000–80 000 years ago, and have been exposed by wind erosion so that they now stand like tombstones in yellow sand. About three hours drive from Perth, Nambung also has great beaches, wildflowers and picnic areas with gas barbecues, but there is no camping.

Turquoise Coast Enviro Tours runs highly informative tours of the Pinnacles and the surrounding area with an environmentally aware guide who spent nearly 20 years as a park ranger and prides himself on providing the most accurate information available.

CALM Jurien: (08) 9652 1911; www.dec.wa.gov.au

Turquoise Coast Enviro Tours: (08) 9652 7047; www.thepinnacles.com.au

Snorkelling and diving

You can snorkel face-to-face with sea-lions in Jurien Bay Marine Park, or join a boat tour to see them up close. Jurien Charters in Jurien Bay also offers diving on rock walls with lionfish, butterflyfish and wrasse. Sealion Charters operates out of Green Head, and guarantees interaction with the sea-lions.

In Geraldton, the Batavia Coast Dive Academy will set you up with gear for snorkelling and diving, and point you in the direction of snorkelling spots at Drummonds Beach or shore dives at Point Moore. The company also has plenty of boat dives available, including to the beautiful coral reefs of the Abrolhos Islands.

Jurien Charters: (08) 9652 1109; www.juriencharters.com

Sealion Charters: (08) 9953 1012 or 0427 931 012; http://sealioncharters.biz

Batavia Coast Dive Academy: (08) 9921 4229; www.bcda.com.au

Geraldton to Carnarvon

WHERE TO STAY

Monkey Mia Dolphin Resort

The Dolphin Resort is the only accommodation operator in Monkey Mia but it offers numerous choices, from beachside villas and units to backpacker rooms and tent sites. The resort has supported Monkey Mia dolphin research for more than a decade. It has an extensive wastewater recycling facility, is plastic-bag free and converts its cooking oils into biodiesel that is used on the site.

(08) 9948 1320 or 1800 653 611; www.monkeymia.com.au

Riverside Sanctuary, Ajana

More than ten years ago, the owners of this sheep and wheat farm, inland from Kalbarri, noticed the environmental degradation on their property from many years of soil tillage compounded by erosion and compaction from sheep. The health of many areas of remnant vegetation was also declining. They began revegetating and removed all livestock, and the property has now won Landcare awards for its efforts and the wildlife has returned in abundance. There is a wide range of farmstay options here, from self-contained cottages to shearer's quarters and camping. The sanctuary also offers a variety of tours of the property, taking in its Aboriginal sites, plants, animals and explanations of modern farming methods.

(08) 9936 1021; http://riversidesanctuary.com.au

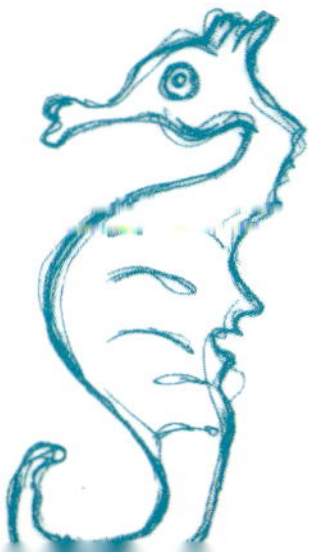

Relaxing on the deck of a beachfront villa at Monkey Mia Dolphin Resort

ACTIVITIES

Beachcombing

If you are searching for solitude, examine the countless billions of tiny shells that make up the 110-kilometre Shell Beach near Denham, a great place for a contemplative meander.

Canoeing

A couple of companies offer canoe safaris down the Murchison River, with transport by 4WD. Try Kalbarri Adventure Tours or Kalbarri Boat Hire and Canoe Safaris, which also hires out canoes and paddleboats.

Kalbarri Adventure Tours: (08) 9937 1677 or 0427 371 677, www.kalbarritours.com.au

Kalbarri Boat Hire and Canoe Safaris: (08) 9937 1245; www.kalbarriboathire.com

Dolphin-feeding

Almost without fail, the famous wild bottlenose dolphins visit the beach in front of the Monkey Mia Dolphin Resort several times a day, year-round. Under the watchful gaze of national parks rangers, who provide a 20-minute talk about the dolphins, you can stand in the water

*Feeding a wild bottlenose dolphin (*Tursiops truncatus*) at Monkey Mia*

with these marine creatures, and some lucky people will be picked from the crowd to hand-feed them small amounts of fish. The dolphins are fed the first three times they come in each day, anytime between 8am and noon. Although there are other spots in the country to get up close to wild dolphins, this place offers the most reliable experience, and the most famous.

Four-wheel driving in Francois Peron National Park

The resort is in the Monkey Mia Reserve, and there is a fee to enter the reserve, but no fee for the dolphin experience.

DEC Monkey Mia: (08) 9948 1366; www.sharkbay.org

Francois Peron National Park

From the top of the rust-red sand dunes here, you will not just see azure blue water and white sand beaches. You are also likely to see dugong, dolphins, manta rays, sharks and turtles in the clear waters of the Shark Bay World Heritage Area. The 52 500-hectare national park is home to some of the most endangered animals in Western Australia, but you will need a high-clearance 4WD to travel across the terrain or to reach the camping areas. Of course, you can join a 4WD tour with a focus on the seasonal wildlife and wildflowers in the park, with the eco-accredited Monkey Mia Wildsights.

Monkey Mia Wildsights: (08) 9948 1481 or 1800 241 481; www.monkeymiawildsights.com.au

DEC Denham: (08) 9948 1208; www.dec.wa.gov.au; www.sharkbay.org

Indigenous tour

To discover the rich cultural heritage of the Shark Bay area, visitors can embark on an award-winning Wula Guda Nyinda morning, afternoon or night tour. There are creation stories, bush-tucker tastings and demonstrations of traditional tools and activities, all in a setting of spectacular sand-dune country inhabited by abundant wildlife.

0429 708 847; http://wulaguda.ixwebhouse.com.au

Kalbarri National Park

The most spectacular feature in this park is the lower reaches of the Murchison River, where the waterway has cut magnificent red and white banded gorges, up to 150 metres high, for 80 kilometres. Check out the Z-Bend, just a 500-metre walk from the carpark. With more than 1800 square kilometres of protected land, the park also has plenty of other features, including coastal cliffs with humpback whales cavorting in the waters at their base, rock stacks and bridges, sand plains, wildflowers from June to November, walking tracks, lookouts and picnic spots. There are no camping areas and no drinking water.

DEC Geraldton: (08) 9921 5955; www.dec.wa.gov.au

Snorkelling

Near Kalbarri there are several top snorkelling spots, including the protected Blue Holes, Red Bluff and Chinamans Beach.

Wildlife cruises

You have the opportunity to see dugong, dolphins and other marine animals up close on a three-hour sailing cruise that uses less than 2 litres of fuel (just to get the boat to and from the jetty).

The 18-metre-long catamaran, *Shotover*, is one of the fastest vessels of its kind in the world, and uses solar and wind power for its electrics, and the eco-accredited company that runs it, Monkey Mia Wildsights, has a great cruise guarantee: 'Love it or it's free'. There is a shorter sunset cruise as well.

The eco-accredited Monkey Mia Yacht Cruises also has a vast array of different cruises on offer, during which you are also likely to see marine animals such as dugong and bottlenose dolphins.

Monkey Mia Wildsights: (08) 9948 1481 or 1800 241 481; www.monkeymiawildsights.com.au

Monkey Mia Yacht Cruises: 1800 030 427; www.monkey-mia.net

Learning about the environment on a Wula Guda Nyinda tour

Carnarvon to Port Hedland

WHERE TO STAY

Karijini Eco-retreat

Solar panels provide the majority of power for the 50 permanent safari tents in this eco-accredited retreat, which is owned by the Gumala Aboriginal Corporation and Gumala Enterprises Pty Ltd. Most of the tents have ensuites. There are also plenty of campsites.

(08) 9425 5591; www.karijiniecoretreat.com.au

Red Bluff, Quobba Station

This beautiful spot 140 kilometres north of Carnarvon, on the southern tip of Ningaloo Reef, has secluded eco-friendly ocean-view retreats, and seascape bungalows with Natureloo composting toilets, solar power and rainwater. All have private decks, and bungalows share a facility-rich camp kitchen. There are also some palm-frond humpies and camping sites if your budget does not quite stretch to the bungalows or retreats.

(08) 9948 5001; www.quobba.com.au

Sal Salis, Ningaloo Reef

Luxurious but sensitive, this establishment comprising five deluxe safari tents with ensuites is set in sand dunes just 50 metres from the water's edge, around an hour's drive south of Exmouth. Wildlife wanders through the dunes and you can snorkel straight off the shore. Sal Salis has Natureloo composting toilets, solar power and raised boardwalks, and imposes daily water restrictions on their guests.

(02) 9571 6399 or 1300 790 561; www.salsalis.com.au

Luxury safari-tent accommodation at Sal Salis

ACTIVITIES

Cape Range National Park

This 50 000-hectare national park has 50 kilometres of great beaches and plenty of bush camping (some sites with toilets), but is also an excellent spot for wildlife-watching. There is a bird hide and fauna hide at Mangrove Bay, and if you come in the early morning or late afternoon you are likely to spot red kangaroos and euros as well as a wide variety of waders and other birds.

At Yardie Creek, keep an eye on the gorge walls for black-footed rock-wallabies. For a one-day tour of the best parts of this rugged national park, including time for snorkelling and a boat trip up Yardie Creek, contact the eco-accredited Ningaloo Safari Tours.

CALM Exmouth: (08) 9949 1676; www.dec.wa.gov.au
Ningaloo Safari Tours: (08) 9949 1550; www.ningaloosafari.com
Milyering Visitor Centre: (08) 9949 2808

Indigenous tours

With an Outback Coast Safaris Aboriginal heritage or dreaming tour you can learn about the Indigenous culture of the Gascoyne region. You will sample bush tucker and bush medicine, watch your guide hunting for lunch, and listen to stories of the Dreamtime. The Carnarvon-based company also runs overnight tours wider afield, including to Mount Augustus.

Quobba Station's retreats and bungalows overlook this beautiful bay at Red Bluff

On the Burrup Peninsula, those with time to explore can view the most extensive art gallery in Australia, with thousands of petroglyphs estimated to be 6000 to 20 000 years old. This incredibly important site near Karratha, irrevocably changed by industrial developments in the area, is poorly marked and signposted, and its past and future management is controversial. You could spend hours looking at the many different markings here, which include animals such as thylacines (extinct on mainland Australia for 3000 years), spirit figures, tools and humans. There are very occasional tours of the area, but mostly you will just experience this extraordinary place on your own.

Outback Coast Safaris: (08) 9941 3448 or 0417 335 504; www.outbackcoastsafaris.com.au
www.burrup.org.au

Karijini National Park

The second-largest park in Western Australia, Karijini is one of the country's most beautiful. Carved deeply into the semi-arid Pilbara landscape are 15 multi-hued gorges, with sheer cliffs, waterfalls, freezing swimming holes and caves. There are walks around the top of some canyons and short walks into them, but if you are keen on really getting intimate with Karijini's canyons – with a combination of abseiling, jumping, swimming, rafting and sliding down narrow chutes and waterfalls – look no further than West Oz Active. The company offers a range of different tours, or you can sign up for multi-day packages.

The park has an exceptional visitor centre, abundant wildlife – particularly birds, lizards and snakes – and wildflowers can carpet the area in the middle of the year or in the weeks after heavy rain. Karijini is one of Western Australia's must-see national parks.

West Oz Active: 0438 913 713; www.westozactive.com.au
CALM Pilbara: (08) 9143 1488; www.dec.wa.gov.au
Park ranger: (08) 9189 8157
Park visitor centre: (08) 9189 8121

Millstream–Chichester National Park

With beautiful swimming holes fringed by palms and paperbarks, this seeming oasis in the desert has popular camping spots, but you will need to boil the water for drinking, or bring your own. On short- and medium-length walks through the landscape you will encounter spinifex and Sturt desert peas, white gums and wildlife, or just wait by the water and watch the rainbow bee-eaters, budgerigars, bats and reptiles come to you.

Park ranger: (08) 9184 5144

CALM Karratha: (08) 9143 1488; www.dec.wa.gov.au

Mount Augustus National Park

Despite popular belief, the largest rock in Australia is not Uluṟu, but the much less visited Mount Augustus, which at 8 kilometres long is about twice the size of Uluṟu and has its own national park. After winter rains, its red rocky flanks are clothed in purple mulla mulla and other flowers, and you can climb to its summit on a solid 12-kilometre walk, getting more than 700 metres above the surrounding plain. It is a great place to spot emus, bustards and other birds. There are several shorter walking tracks – some leading to Indigenous engraving sites – and Emu Hill Lookout is a top location for sunset, when you can watch the big monocline change colour. There is no camping in the park, but the Mount Augustus Outback Tourist Resort is nearby.

DEC Denham: (08) 9948 1208; www.dec.wa.gov.au

Mount Augustus Outback Tourist Resort:

(08) 9943 0527; www.mtaugustusresort.com.au

Touring near Mount Augustus with Outback Coast Safaris

Sea-kayaking

Operating around Rottnest Island in the summer, Capricorn Seakayaking offers one-, two- and five-day sea-kayaking tours out of Exmouth during the middle of the year, with regular sightings of dugong, turtles, whales, osprey, manta rays and all manner of other wildlife. Kayakers take regular breaks, jumping in the water with snorkels and masks to enjoy the reef, often in places that only kayaks can reach. The five-day trip in particular explores Cape Range National Park and includes sleeping in swags or tents and optional walks.

The eco-accredited Ningaloo Kayak Adventures in Coral Bay also runs tours and hires glass-bottom kayaks, see-through boogie boards and other items to get you out paddling and seeing the reef.

Capricorn Seakayaking: (08) 6267 8059; www.capricornseakayaking.com.au

Ningaloo Kayak Adventures: (08) 9948 5034; www.ningalookayakadventures.com

Snorkelling and diving

Coral reefs are found just off the beaches around Coral Bay, providing excellent, easy-access snorkelling in some spectacular sites, and a safe lagoon between the reefs and the shore. There are around 500 species of fish and more than 200 species of brightly coloured coral in the reef system, as well as golden sea snakes, starfish, clams, turtles and manta rays. Bundegi Beach, north of Exmouth, can also be a great snorkelling and swimming location. Shore divers can have difficulty getting over the fringing reef if there is a

Snorkelling in Ningaloo Reef Marine Park

swell, but there are plenty of opportunities for boat snorkelling and dive trips to very special spots. To hire or buy gear and walk straight in off the shore, see Exmouth Diving Centre or Village Dive Shop.

Exmouth Diving Centre: (08) 9949 1201;
www.exmouthdiving.com.au

Village Dive Shop: (08) 9949 1116 or 1800 224 060;
www.villagedive.com.au

Swimming with manta rays

Unlike whale sharks, giant manta rays glide gracefully around the waters near Exmouth year-round, particularly congregating in the latter half of the year to breed. Although you are most likely to see mantas smaller than 3 metres wide, they can grow up to 9 metres across, weighing up to 1.5 tonnes. Manta rays can reach speeds of more than 20 kilometres per hour, but they are often seen hardly moving at underwater 'cleaning stations' being preened by wrasse. Coral Bay Adventures and the eco-accredited operators listed below (*see* Swimming with whale sharks) run snorkelling cruises to see mantas, but will also endeavour to get you in the water with turtles, dolphins and the huge variety of other marine life in the spectacular Ningaloo Marine Park.

Coral Bay Adventures: (08) 9942 5955;
www.coralbayadventures.com.au

Swimming with whale sharks

Swimming with the largest fish in the ocean, the gentle filter-feeding whale sharks, has to be high on any nature-lover's list. They are usually 5–12 metres long, but grow up to 18 metres. They congregate near Coral Bay from late March to June, and several operators will get you out there swimming and snorkelling beside them. There are lots of good operators but, unfortunately, the best way for them to work out where the whale sharks are is by spotter plane, which adds to the carbon cost of the trip. Recommended eco-accredited tours include those listed below.

Ningaloo Reef Dreaming: (08) 9949 4777 or
1800 994 210; www.ningaloodreaming.com

King's Ningaloo Reef Tours: (08) 9949 1764;
www.kingsningalooreeftours.com.au

Three Island Marine Charters: (08) 9949 1994;
www.whalesharkdive.com

Ningaloo Experience: (08) 9942 5877;
www.ningalooexperience.com

*Swimming with a whale shark (*Rhincodon typus*) near Coral Bay*

The Kimberley

Resplendent and regal, the Kimberley wears its coat of many colours with pride. From the turquoise Indian Ocean surging against fiery red rocks in the west, to the orange-and-black-striped Bungle Bungles in Purnululu National Park, its palette is bold and bright and its natural treasures gleam.

Most tourism in this area is nature-based and as efforts have been made in recent years to reduce the environmental impact, ecotourism is growing rapidly, particularly along the coast north of Broome. An increasing number of Aboriginal communities are also recognising the value of tourism and are endeavouring to set up activities and accommodation services for tourists, adding to the range of cultural experiences on offer.

The Kimberley coast's Prince Frederick Harbour, rimmed by Mitchell River National Park

Kimberley tours

As with other areas where distances and remote travel may trouble some ecotourists, you can reduce your carbon footprint by joining a tour. One of the most complete tours of the Kimberley – from the Mitchell Plateau to the Bungle Bungles – is the eco-accredited 13-day trip with APT Wilderness Adventures, primarily staying in their own eco camps, with solar power and high environmental standards. The company also offers a wide range of other eco-accredited tours and self-drive stays at its four eco camps at Mitchell Falls, on the Gibb River Road, the Mitchell Plateau and in Purnululu National Park.

Kimberley Specialists adds an environment and research levy onto their prices, which facilitates and sponsors significant Landcare and research projects in the Kimberley. Several of the tours on offer focus on Bradshaw art, led by one of the best experts in the area on these mysterious works.

Uptuyu Tours offers tag-along 4WD trips, with an Aboriginal guide. While learning about the Indigenous history and culture of the Kimberley, you can join in spear-making, food gathering and other activities.

Learning the art of spearfishing with Uptuyu Tours

APT Wilderness Adventures:
(03) 9277 8444 or 1300 656 985;
www.kimberleywilderness.com.au
Kimberley Specialists:
(08) 9168 2576 or (08) 9161 4345;
www.kimberleyspecialists.com
Uptuyu Tours: 0400 878 898;
www.uptuyu.com.au

Ju Ju Wilson explains the meaning of ancient figures depicted on stone, during an Indigenous rock-art tour at Faraway Bay

Kimberley cruises

The pristine Kimberley coast, with its dramatic colours, is a growing cruise destination for all manner of cruise boats, including large vessels with their own helicopters. Unfortunately, the coastline's remoteness and large distances usually means that wastewater on board goes directly into the sea, and some companies are currently trying to address this. The Kimberley Cruise Centre is a central booking agency for all cruises and can recommend the right trip for you, but you should particularly consider the eco-accredited One Tide Charters, which includes camping on land; *Kimberley Quest II*, which has a range of cruises that focus on the unique Indigenous art of the area; and the catamaran run by Red Sky Cruises.

Kimberley Cruise Centre: 1800 677 830

One Tide Charters: (08) 9193 1358; www.onetide.com

Kimberley Quest II: (08) 9193 6131; www.kimberleyquest.com.au

Red Sky Cruises: 0407 739 738; www.redsky.com.au

*Making the steep climb to the Wandjina art shelter at Raft Point, at the southern entrance to Doubtful Bay (*Kimberley Quest II *tour)*

Around Broome

WHERE TO STAY

Coco Eco Nature Retreat

This B&B with ocean views won architectural awards for its sustainable design that uses recycled and plantation timbers, captures breezes and requires no air-conditioning, which is pretty extraordinary in these parts. It is partially solar-powered, all grey and black water is recycled on site, and there are free-range eggs and organic vegetables available. It is closed from October to May.

(08) 9192 3103 or 0408 921454; www.cocoeco.com.au

Eco Beach

After being wiped out by a cyclone, this new eco-resort south of Broome was still being built as this book was compiled, but is set to feature award-winning environmentally sustainable designs of 25 villas and 30 tents, built by Eco Constructions, and run on 50 per cent solar power.

(08) 9193 8015; www.ecobeach.com.au

ACTIVITIES

Birdwatching

Dedicated to the conservation of migratory shorebirds, the Broome Bird Observatory receives visits from an estimated 150 000 birds each year and is one of the best spots in the world to see some of these well-travelled species. The track out to the observatory can be corrugated, but most 2WDs should be able to make it during the dry season. There is a great range of half-day and full-day wildlife tours, including one specially to see the yellow chat. You can camp or stay in cabins at the observatory, or just go out for the day.

(08) 9193 5600; www.broomebirdobservatory.com

Hiking

The 72-kilometre Lurujarri Heritage Trail goes from Coulomb Point to Gantheaume Point, and has seven accessible starting points if you want to do day walks, or you can walk the whole trail end to end, passing old Aboriginal camping grounds, burial sites and some of the most beautiful coastline in the country. In July each year, there is a guided walk telling the story of the trail for around 35 lucky walkers, with many Indigenous people joining the walk to participate in their part of the story.

Heritage Council of WA, Perth: (08) 9221 4177 or 1800 644 177; http://tourism.heritage.wa.gov.au

Sailing and diving

For a major diving adventure, head out to Rowley Shoals, 300 kilometres off Broome, to dive in swimming-pool-like coral gardens, as well as canyons, sheer vertical walls and high-speed

Eco-friendly tents at APT's Imintji Wilderness Camp on the Gibb River Road

King George Falls, where the King River drops 80 metres off the Kimberley plateau

drifts. The eco-accredited Odyssey Expeditions will get you there, or to other dive sites in the Abrolhos Islands or Monte Bello Islands. You can also head out to Rowley Shoals with the eco-accredited schooner *Pindan*.

Odyssey Expeditions: 1300 683 255;
www.odysseyexpeditions.com.au

Pindan: 0429 884 440; www.pindansailing.com

Walking

Broome has some great walking options, including the 22-kilometre stretch of Cable Beach. Nearby Minyirr Park has 22 kilometres of colour-coded walking trails through bright green spinifex (after the Wet) and fiery red soil, and some surprisingly cool and lush areas of monsoon vine thickets and woodland. At Gantheaume Point, where the red cliffs meet the turquoise Indian Ocean, low tide reveals ancient dinosaur footprints more than 120 million years old. There is a replica of a print on the headland if you visit at high tide.

Dampier Peninsula

WHERE TO STAY

Goombaragin Eco Retreat

Built high on a clifftop overlooking Pender Bay, 160 kilometres north of Broome, this Aboriginal-owned-and-run resort has eco tents built on platforms and new chalets, primarily run on solar power and with greywater recycling. You can take on-site bushwalking cultural tours, discovering local bushfoods, creation stories and Aboriginal connections to the country.

(08) 9192 4717 or 0429 696 180;
www.goombaragin.com.au

Kooljaman at Cape Leveque

Aboriginal owned, this resort sits in a sensational spot on the tip of the Dampier Peninsula, 220 kilometres from Broome. It offers accommodation from beach shelters with sand floors, to comfortable safari tents with ensuites and kitchens, and the resort is about 75 per cent solar-powered. The safari tents are on raised platforms to minimise damage to the environment, stocked with soaps made by local schoolchildren, and are constructed of recycled timbers. You can swim and snorkel here year-round – they have not yet had a problem with crocodiles or stingers.

(08) 9192 4970; www.kooljaman.com.au

ACTIVITIES

Indigenous tours

Swan Point Tag-Along Tours offers half-day tours departing from Kooljaman through spectacular scenic areas off-limits to the general public.

Replica of a dinosaur footprint on the cliff at Gantheaume Point

Safari tent at Kooljaman, below the Cape Leveque Lighthouse

GIDW

Picturesque Gladstone Lake, dotted with waterlilies, at Mornington Wilderness Camp

The guides provide information about plants, animals and local history, and take you to some spots where you can swim and snorkel and then cook any fish you catch on coals. Lombadina Aboriginal Adventures, 200 kilometres from Broome, has intimate local tours, including a bushwalk focusing on bushfoods and medicines, and a kayak and snorkelling tour.

Swan Point Tag-Along Tours: (08) 9192 4970; www.kooljaman.com.au

Lombadina Aboriginal Adventures: (08) 9192 4936; www.lombadina.com.au

Central Kimberley

WHERE TO STAY

Mornington Wilderness Camp

All proceeds from this comfortable camp go to the Australian Wildlife Conservancy. The site is primarily solar-powered and on a 3000 square kilometre private wildlife sanctuary that includes some of the best remaining habitat for the endangered and stunningly beautiful Gouldian finch. There are ten spacious safari tents with ensuites and balconies, as well as a great camping ground limited to 50 people. Tucked away in the King Leopold Ranges, the camp lies 90 kilometres south-east of the Gibb River Road. Imintji, on this road, is the nearest town, while Broome to the west and Kununurra to the north-east are both some 550 kilometres away. The camp is open from May to October.

1800 631 946; www.australianwildlife.org

ACTIVITIES

Geikie Gorge National Park

In this park you can explore the spectacular gorge cut by the Fitzroy River on a Darngku Heritage cruise conducted by the Banuba people. As well as cruising the placid waters surrounded by 30-metre-high weathered cliffs, you will hear Indigenous stories of the area, look for bushfoods, probably see an archerfish or two and have lunch beside the Fitzroy River. You need to book this tour at the Fitzroy Crossing Visitor Centre. The Department of Conservation and Land Management (CALM) also runs an hour-long cruise in the gorge on a first-come basis.

Fitzroy Crossing Visitor Centre: (08) 9191 5355

CALM Broome: (08) 9192 1036

Indigenous tour

An hour from Fitzroy Crossing you can take a three-hour guided tour with the traditional owners of Mimbi Cave. You will see fossils of ancient creatures and rock art on this recently developed tourism venture. Bookings are taken at the Fitzroy Crossing Visitor Centre (*see* above).

Mitchell River National Park

With its dramatic waterfalls plunging off the Kimberley escarpment, this park is probably best seen from the air, but there is a rugged 4WD track for the well-prepared. You need to obtain permits from the Kununurra Visitor Centre to enter Aboriginal land.

Kununurra Visitor Centre: (08) 9168 1177

Windjana Gorge National Park

At Windjana you can walk the 7-kilometre-return length of the gorge along the Lennard River, which becomes a series of pools in the dry season. Watch out for bats, crocodiles and birds aplenty. You can camp in this peaceful spot, with toilets and water available.

CALM Broome: (08) 9192 1036; www.dec.wa.gov.au

Around Kununurra

WHERE TO STAY

Faraway Bay

This luxurious resort is only accessible by sea or by air from Kununurra. Eco features include the use of recycled timbers from the Wyndham Wharf and solar hot water, and the resort sponsors and supports environmental and archaeological research.

(08) 9169 1214 or 0417 986 614; www.farawaybay.com.au

ACTIVITIES

Birdwatching

With up to 20 000 birds on the billabongs at a time, Parry Lagoons Nature Reserve, an hour's drive north-west of Kununurra, is a top spot for birding. There are brolgas, jabirus, magpie geese, whistling-ducks and egrets in abundance as well as migratory species that have flown from as far away as Siberia.

Boating

Diversion Cruises and Hire has craft to take out on Diversion Dam north of Kununurra, from small pedal-powered boats and vessels with electric motors, to large houseboats (with solar panels) that contain all sullage (greywater and blackwater), pumping it into the town's sewerage system on your return.

(08) 9168 3333

Verging on decadence at Faraway Bay

Outdoor shower at Faraway Bay

Canoeing

For those ecotourists seeking a little Kimberley adventure, canoe down the Ord River for one to three days with Go Wild Adventure Tours, staying at camps with ecotoilets and seeing crocodiles, waterfalls, Aboriginal art and incredible birdlife. The eco-accredited company also offers abseiling, canyoning and rock-climbing excursions.

1300 663 369; www.gowild.com.au

Purnululu National Park

With its iconic rock formations – rounded domes gaudily striped orange and black – Purnululu is one of Australia's must-see national parks. Many people only view it from the air, catching a scenic flight from Kununurra, but from the ground the landscape comes alive with Mertens monitors and frisky rockhole frogs swimming through waterholes, and myriad birds such as red-backed fairy wrens. Visitors to this World Heritage area are restricted to just a few special walks, but if you do not mind carrying a pack, head off for a few days up Piccaninny Gorge. There are no facilities up the gorge but you can explore the canyons, swim in beautiful, remote waterholes and marvel at the natural wonders of this special place. Access to Purnululu is by 4WD or plane and there are two public camping areas.

One of the nicest safari-camp-style places you can stay anywhere, with great food and facilities, is APT's Bungle Bungle Wilderness Camp. Some tents have their own ensuites (with flushing toilets) and the camp runs on solar power. The Victorian-based APT can organise your flights and tours into Purnululu as well.

Just across the road from APT's camp is the Bungle Bungle Bushcamp, run by East Kimberley Tours, the first major tour operator in the area. This camp also has strict environmental policies.

APT: (03) 9277 8444 or 1300 656 985;
www.kimberleywilderness.com.au
East Kimberley Tours: (08) 9168 2213;
www.eastkimberleytours.com.au
CALM Kununurra: (08) 9168 4200; www.dec.wa.gov.au

Toad busting

In this region, you can do some real hands-on work in the fight against one of Australia's worst introduced pests, the cane toad. Every week, Kimberley Toad Busters runs toad-busting trips at the cane-toad front, in an effort to stop these poisonous animals invading the Kimberley. You will spend a night catching, documenting and disposing of the creatures, up to 400 kilometres from Kununurra. The trips are free, but donations are greatly appreciated, and it is best to give about a week's notice that you are coming.

(08) 9168 2576; www.canetoads.com.au

Walking

If you stretch your legs in Mirima National Park, just 2 kilometres from Kununurra, you will be rewarded with a taste of the Kimberley landscapes. There are some small rock features similar to the Bungle Bungles in Purnululu, boab trees and spinifex country. Keep your eyes and ears open to the many birds, reptiles, dingoes and agile wallabies that also inhabit this park.

CALM Kununurra: (08) 9168 4200; www.dec.wa.gov.au

Victoria

While Melbourne loudly proclaims its attractions to visitors, the rest of the state seems simply to whisper its secrets. If you have not explored much outside the capital, tune in to those whispers. Victoria's natural landscapes cover everything from snow-capped peaks to lush rainforests, from mallee country to dramatic coastal scenery, and wildlife seems to be everywhere, from seals, dolphins and whales offshore, to endangered mallee fowl, koalas and kangaroos.

Ecotourism here also seems to keep a low profile but there are some groundbreaking ventures, particularly along the coast and in the High Country. One of the most exciting changes in the past few years has been the transformation of many old rail trails into cycling routes. Built for trains, the trails generally have low gradients and many travel through beautiful terrain, so are great for hiking and cycling.

WESTERN VICTORIA does not offer the range of ecotourism ventures common in the rest of the state, but there are some special opportunities for rock climbing, hiking, canoeing and four-wheel driving.

EASTERN VICTORIA encompasses a plethora of national parks and the beautiful Victorian High Country, with a vast terrain in which to stretch your legs with some serious hiking or cross-country skiing.

COASTAL VICTORIA is the place for wildlife encounters, great snorkelling, diving and surfing in clear waters, and long walks on wild and dramatic stretches of coastline.

Melbourne Visitor Information Centre: Federation Square, Cnr Flinders St and St Kilda Rd; (03) 9658 9658; www.visitmelbourne.com.au

Parks Victoria (PV): 13 1963; www.parkweb.vic.gov.au

TOP TEN

1 Stay in a lightkeeper's cottage on Gabo Island, site of the world's largest little penguin colony

2 Cycle the Murray to the Mountains Rail Trail

3 Join a tour of the wildflower-rich Little Desert National Park in the far west of the state, with a chance to see the endangered mallee fowl

4 Swim with dolphins, seals and weedy sea dragons off the Mornington Peninsula, only an hour away from Melbourne

5 Strap on a pack and hike to Refuge Cove or one of the other special, secluded bays in Wilsons Promontory

6 Go for a ranger-guided snowshoe tour in Mount Buffalo National Park

7 Sample the fine range of wines and food produce available throughout the state, which has been made using organic principles

8 Camp by the unusual Pink Lakes in Murray–Sunset National Park

9 Catch a glimpse of the world's largest creature, the blue whale, near Portland

10 Face your fear of heights on a rock face in Mount Arapiles–Tooan State Park in the state's far west

GREEN TRAVEL TIP When camping along the Murray River or many of the other scenic waterways in Australia, do not set up camp below a river red gum, no matter how attractive the site looks. They can drop their massive limbs in any weather – not just on windy days.

Melbourne

Melbourne's heartland of cafes and culture is certainly not a barren wasteland when it comes to ecotourism. The city surrounds are rich in wildlife – particularly around Port Phillip to the south and the picturesque ranges to the east – and the cycling community has helped establish some great bike routes. In addition to this, there are some excellent opportunities, right in the centre of Melbourne, to experience the traditional culture and lifestyle of the local Indigenous people.

The Yarra River is the focal point for many of the city's ecotourism activities, with canoeing upstream and cycling paths along the banks

WHERE TO STAY

Alto Hotel on Bourke

Although it is not doing anything radical, this plush hotel on Bourke Street is one of the most ecologically aware in Melbourne, and should be commended for its power-saving measures, garbage sorting, supply of pump-action dispensers rather than individual bottles, installing insulation, and more.

636 Bourke St, Melbourne; (03) 8608 5500 or 1800 135 123; www.altohotel.com.au

Melbourne Oasis YHA

Like many hostels, this North Melbourne hostel is in an older building that was not originally designed with the environment in mind. However, the keen staff and managers are doing their best to be environmentally sound. There is solar hot water, rainwater tanks, worm farms and recycling programs, and a choice of dorm rooms, twins or doubles.

76 Chapman St, North Melbourne; (03) 9328 3595; www.yha.com.au

WHERE TO EAT

Tjanabi

For an authentic Australian eating experience, with an emphasis on foods produced and harvested by sustainable means, try Tjanabi (a word that means 'celebrate') at Federation Square, a restaurant owned by a Boonwurrung elder. Meals usually combine wild-harvested bushfoods such as kangaroo, wallaby and native fruits with produce from the Gippsland region, particularly organic, free-range and other ingredients chosen on strict environmental criteria. All the wooden tables in the restaurant have been crafted from recycled timber that may otherwise have been burned or chipped.

The Atrium, Federation Square, Flinders St, Melbourne; (03) 9662 1225; www.tjanabi.com.au

Stylish bush tucker served at Tjanabi

ACTIVITIES

Cycling

Melbourne has an active cycling community that has helped develop and establish some great routes and a network of cycle paths. One of the best sources of information is Bicycle Victoria. One option is to hop on the Main Yarra Trail at Southbank and follow the Yarra River for 35 kilometres, through tranquil bushland and open paddocks, until it meets up with the Mullum Mullum Creek Trail in Templestowe. Hire A Bicycle in the city centre is one of many companies that will get you twirling the pedals. Bike Now is located in South Melbourne near bike paths linking with the Royal Botanic Gardens and Albert Park Lake.

St Kilda is another popular spot for a cycle. You can just take a short ride along the waterfront trail or travel the 30 kilometres to Brighton and back. St Kilda Cycles will set you up and get you on your way. The company also offers guided bike tours along the beaches or the Yarra Trail.

Bicycle Victoria: Level 10, 446 Collins St, Melbourne; (03) 8636 8888 or 1800 639 634; www.bv.com.au

Hire A Bicycle: Vault 14, Federation Square, Princes Walk, Melbourne; (03) 9654 2762

Bike Now: Cnr Park St and Kings Way, South Melbourne; (03) 9696 8588; www.bikenow.com.au

St Kilda Cycles: 150 Barkly St, St Kilda; (03) 9534 3074; www.stkildacycles.com.au

Cycling through the tall eucalypt forests of Dandenong Ranges National Park

Dandenong Ranges National Park

About an hour's drive out of Melbourne, some 35 kilometres east of the city, this park has forests of towering mountain ash and lush, damp fern gullies. Around 300 kilometres of walking tracks crisscross the park, including several great short and medium walks such as the popular Fern Gully trail and the Sherbrooke Forest loop. There are also plenty of pleasant picnic spots, including Grants and Valley picnic areas. The best access is from Mount Dandenong Tourist Road.

PV: 13 1963; www.parkweb.vic.gov.au

Echidna Walkabout wildlife tour

On a full day trip, with great opportunities to see koalas, kangaroos and other wildlife, the eco-accredited Echidna Walkabout will take you to two locations on the Werribee Plains – Serendip Sanctuary (*see also* Melbourne to Cape Otway/Birdwatching), and either You Yangs Regional Park (*see also* Melbourne to Cape Otway/Mountain-biking) or Brisbane Ranges National Park (*see* The Goldfields/Activities) – and explain the great significance of the plains region for the local Indigenous people. The company runs other longer wildlife-focused trips as well, including a three-day Fur and Feathers tour from Melbourne.

PO Box 370, Port Melbourne; (03) 9646 8249; www.echidnawalkabout.com.au

Indigenous tours

To grasp what Melbourne was like before the skyscrapers arrived you can take a two-hour Koori Heritage Trust walking tour. You will gain an insight into Indigenous history and the natural and cultural landscape of the area. A one-and-a-half-hour guided Aboriginal Heritage Walk also goes through the Royal Botanic Gardens, and includes a traditional smoking ceremony and information about traditional uses of plants. Bookings are essential for the tour and walk.

Koori Heritage Trust: (03) 8622 2600; www.kooriheritagetrust.com
Gardens visitor centre: Observatory Precinct, Birdwood Ave (opposite Shrine of Remembrance), Melbourne; (03) 9252 2429; www.rbg.vic.gov.au
Aboriginal Heritage Walk bookings: (03) 9252 2429

Learning about Koori culture in the Royal Botanic Gardens

Kayaking and canoeing

With everything from short, gentle kayak tours of the Docklands area and the Yarra to multi-day adventures further afield, including Wilsons Promontory, Seakayak Australia is bound to have something to catch your interest. The company will also hire out all gear if you want to head out on your own.

Adventure Canoeing runs popular canoeing and kayaking tours and hires gear on the upper Yarra River at Warrandyte, on Melbourne's north-eastern outskirts. If you go for a two-hour paddle or an overnight excursion you are likely to spot koalas, kangaroos and plenty of birds as you travel through Warrandyte State Park. The company also offers whitewater canoeing and whitewater rafting. You can do a one-day trip on the King River, a two-day trip on the Mitta Mitta or join a group expedition to the Mitchell or Snowy rivers in the east of the state.

Seakayak Australia: 12 Turner St, Abbotsford; (03) 8415 0997, 0410 329 090; www.seakayakaustralia.com

Adventure Canoeing: PO Box 255, Warrandyte; (03) 9844 3323 or 0423 636 936; www.adventurecanoeing.com.au

Melbourne Zoo

Melbourne has a choice of two excellent zoos: Melbourne Zoo, with more than 320 species on display; and the 225-hectare open range zoo at Werribee, about 30 minutes drive from the city centre (access from the Princes Highway). Werribee offers a Slumber Safari, staying overnight in an eco-friendly camp, with up-close animal encounters. Both zoos are involved in breeding programs for endangered species such as the eastern barred bandicoot.

Melbourne Zoo: Elliott Ave, Parkville; (03) 9285 9300; www.zoo.org.au

Werribee Open Range Zoo: K Rd, Werribee; (03) 9731 9600; www.zoo.org.au

Discovering a vast range of plants on a tour of the botanic gardens

Mountain-biking

With 20 kilometres of tracks developed by the Mountain Bike Association of Australia, Lysterfield Lake Park has something for all standard of mountain-biker, including family-friendly loops and exciting single-track descents. The park is also a good spot for a picnic and a swim and has a bird hide. All About Mountain Bike Tours can set you up for a day's mountain-biking here – either as a guided tour or on your own.

PV: 13 1963; www.parkweb.vic.gov.au

All About Mountain Bike Tours: (03) 5277 0817; www.allaboutmtbtours.com.au

Picnicking

With some 10 000 recorded plant species on 38 hectares of beautiful parklands along the Yarra, the Royal Botanic Gardens in Melbourne is a special spot in a bustling city for a stroll and a picnic. If you want to head slightly out of town, Warrandyte State Park has some excellent picnic and barbecue facilities, and swimming and bushwalking.

Gardens visitor centre: Observatory Precinct, Birdwood Ave (opposite Shrine of Remembrance), Melbourne; (03) 9252 2429; www.rbg.vic.gov.au

PV: 13 1963; www.parkweb.vic.gov.au

Coastal Victoria

Perhaps the most widely known of Victoria's landscapes, the glorious coast stretching from Croajingolong National Park in the east to Discovery Bay in the west has such iconic features as the Twelve Apostles and the Great Ocean Road, Wilsons Promontory and Phillip Island. But apart from these icons there is much more for the ecotourist, including 13 marine national parks and 11 marine sanctuaries. Within these magical places are towering kelp forests and sponge gardens, remote wind-swept beaches, seals, whales, dolphins and extraordinary birdlife. Ecotourists can choose from pursuits that include sailing, snorkelling, surfing, hiking, and whale-watching from specially built lookouts. In the hinterland there are lush rainforests, cycling tracks and bushwalks aplenty.

GREEN TRAVEL TIP Share the fun. With rising petrol costs and concerns about your carbon footprint when driving, why not go on holidays with friends? You can split the petrol costs and the driving, reduce your individual carbon output and you will have extra people with whom to enjoy the experience.

Windsurfing on Victoria's south coast

Mallacoota to Wilsons Promontory

WHERE TO STAY

Adobe Mudbrick Holiday Flats, Mallacoota

These 12 rustic mudbrick flats were ecologically designed to avoid the need for air-conditioning, and have solar hot water and rainwater tanks. The 32-hectare surrounds are managed as a Land for Wildlife property, providing habitat for lyrebirds, koalas, wombats, sugar gliders and yellow-bellied gliders. There is a rainforest gully that was in the process of being covenanted at the time of writing.

(03) 5158 0329 or 0409 580 329;
www.adobeholidayflats.com.au

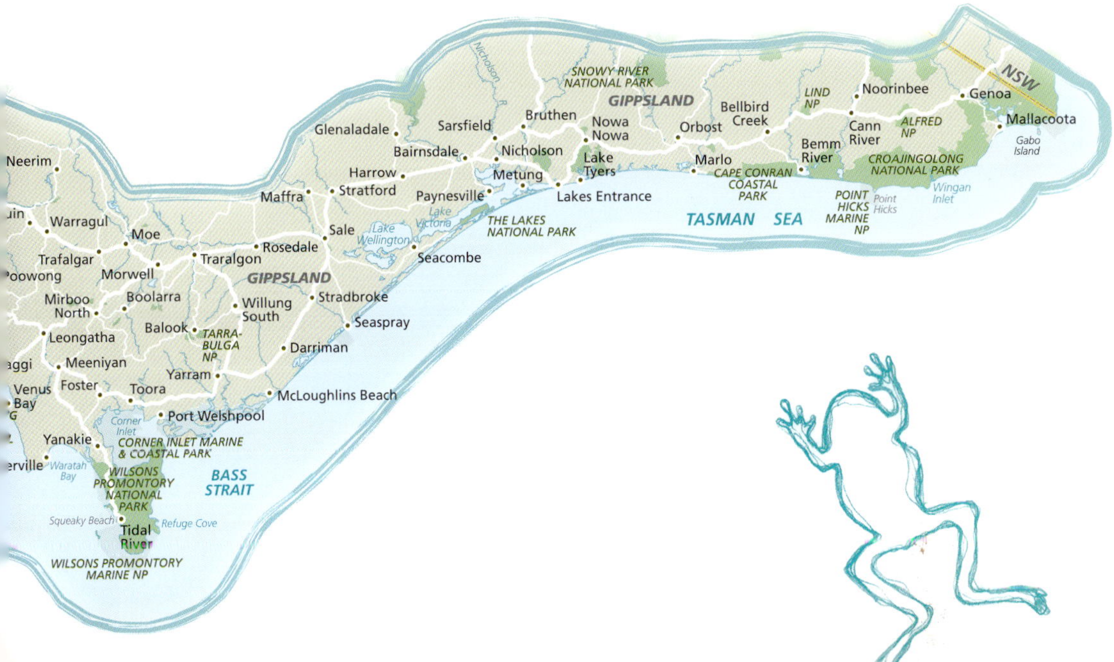

*Kayaking amid Australian fur-seals (*Arctocephalus pusillus*) in the waters off Croajingolong National Park*

Stringybark Cottages, near Bruthren

Situated inland from Bairnsdale, these four homely cottages have been designed to minimise power use, and rely nearly totally on wind and solar power.

(03) 5157 5245; www.stringybarkcottages.com

Waterholes Guest House, near Bairnsdale

This beautiful solar-powered guesthouse has large, luxurious rooms and is on a 17-hectare property on the Nicholson River, with its own wetland and powerful owl habitat, and has been covenanted as a Trust for Nature. It is about 30 kilometres north-east of Bairnsdale.

(03) 5157 9330; www.waterholesguesthouse.com.au

ACTIVITIES

Birdwatching

This stretch of Victorian coast offers some of the best birdwatching in the country. Two locations, both Ramsar-listed, are worth a visit. Protected by the northern arm of Wilsons Promontory, the wetlands of Corner Inlet, near Toora (22 kilometres east of Foster), have a bird hide from where you can observe some of the migratory species that nest in the area. The Sale Common Wetlands have a boardwalk and are also a top birdwatching spot. More than 130 bird species have been recorded here. Watch for glossy ibis, white-faced herons and cormorants in the swampy reed beds.

Central Gippsland visitor centre (Sale): (03) 5144 1108;
www.gippslandinfo.com.au
www.salecommunity.com/wetlands.php

Canoeing and kayaking

The peaceful bays and secluded creeks of the Gippsland Lakes are ideal for canoeing and kayaking. Lake Tyers Charters, or Director Boat Charters at Metung, west of Lakes Entrance, should have all the gear you need.

Lake Tyers Charters: 0428 565 003;
www.laketyerscharters.com
The Director Boat Charters: (03) 5156 2628;
www.thedirector.com.au

Cape Conran Coastal Park

A very popular camping spot in summer, this 11 700-hectare park has undeveloped swimming beaches and a range of accommodation options, including timber cabins for up to eight people, and safari-tent-style wilderness retreats for couples, just a stone's throw from the beach. Among the recommended short walks is the East Cape Boardwalk, which passes an Aboriginal midden site.

(03) 5154 8438; www.conran.net.au

Croajingolong National Park

One-third of Australia's bird species have been spotted in this 87 500-hectare park that stretches for 100 kilometres along the coast. The threatened ground parrot forages in the heath and lorikeets feed in the woodlands. The keen of eye may see yellow-tailed black-cockatoos, eastern yellow robins and superb fairy-wrens. The wetlands attract 40 species of migratory seabirds and waders, while the coastal heathlands and woodlands are the hunting grounds of hawks, eagles and falcons. A UNESCO World Biosphere Reserve, the park has beaches to explore and a range of walks – the 100-kilometre Wilderness Coast Walk explores some of the best, unspoiled scenery. There are several spots to camp, including Wingan Inlet. Campsite bookings are required during peak times and a ballot system operates for Wingan Inlet, Shipwreck Creek and Peach Tree Creek over the Easter holiday period (bookings online). Accommodation is also available at the Point Hicks Lighthouse keeper's cottages.

PV: 13 1963; www.parkweb.vic.gov.au

PV Mallacoota: campsite bookings for Wingan Inlet, Tamboon Inlet, Shipwreck Creek and Peach Tree Creek (03) 5161 9500

Point Hicks Lightstation: campsite bookings for Thurra and Mueller, and lighthouse keeper's cottage accommodation (03) 5158 4268

Cruises

More than just a cruise, a one- or two-hour Sea-Safari out of Lakes Entrance is an opportunity to add to research about the area. You will help document seabirds, marine life – including seahorses with an underwater camera – zooplankton and salinity levels. Any unusual findings are sent to the relevant government departments. The vessel takes a maximum of ten passengers.

Lazy Days Cruises operates a quiet electric motor in a quaint, century-old timber launch. In fact, the *Rubeena* claims to be Victoria's first completely electric-powered vessel. The cruises on pristine Lake Tyers last from one and a half hours to eight hours, with a focus on birdlife, ecology, history and natural beauty.

Sea-Safari: (03) 5155 5027 or 0458 511 438; www.lakes-explorer.com.au

Lazy Days Cruises: (03) 5156 5492 or 0418 994 235; www.rubeenacruises.com.au

Cycling

The 13-kilometre Grand Ridge Trail from Mirboo North to Boolarra is one of the many great rail trails in Victoria. It winds through

Passing Point Hicks Lighthouse on the Wilderness Coast Walk

*Eastern grey kangaroos (*Macropus giganteus*) near Tidal River in Wilsons Promontory National Park*

peaceful, scenic forests in the Strzelecki Ranges (you need to hire or bring a bike with you). Further south, the 39-kilometre Great Southern Rail Trail goes from Foster to Leongatha, passing through leafy forests and farmland and delivering coastal views along the way. Glenn's Sports and Gifts hires bikes in Foster.

Grand Ridge Trail: www.railtrails.org.au

Great Southern Rail Trail: www.promcountry.com.au/railtrail/index.htm

Glenn's Sports and Gifts: (03) 5682 2752

Fruit picking

At Trafalgar South, east of Warragul, you can pick organically certified berries, chestnuts and heritage apples at Sunny Creek farm.

Sunny Creek: (03) 5634 7526

Gabo Island

Just 500 metres off the sandy shores of Croajingolong National Park is Gabo Island, believed to be the site of the world's largest breeding colony of little penguins. Although there are no regular tours of the island, you can rent the relatively inexpensive assistant lightkeeper's cottage, with room for up to eight people, and have your own 154 hectares of paradise, with white-bellied sea-eagles overhead, little penguins, seals, shearwaters and other birds onshore, and whales and dolphins occasionally cruising past. Wilderness Coast Charters will take you out to the island for your stay, or for a day trip.

Gabo Island bookings: (03) 5161 9500

PV: 13 1963; www.parkweb.vic.gov.au

Wilderness Coast Charters: 0417 398 068 or 0418 553 809

Sailing

The 400 square kilometres of inland waterways known as the Gippsland Lakes is a top spot to learn to sail or simply enjoy being on the water, moving at the speed of wind. Plenty of companies have yachts to charter and many offer sailing lessons as well. Try Riviera Nautic at Metung, or anything from a two-hour to a four-day sail with Sail Safari at Paynesville.

Riviera Nautic: (03) 5156 2243; www.rivieranautic.com.au

Sail Safari: 0418 343 622; www.sailsafari.com.au

Tarra–Bulga National Park

Although only 2015 hectares in size, this lush, dense green park is breathtaking. Sixty-metre-tall mountain ash trees soar overhead, and

Corrigan's Suspension Bridge in Tarra Bulga National Park

Children cycling along the sand at Tidal River

The sandy beach at Norman Bay in Wilsons Promontory National Park

there are 39 species of fern, ancient myrtle beech, and waterfalls. There is no camping, but some beautiful picnic spots (although it is usually damp underfoot), and a few good short walks with the chance to glimpse superb lyrebirds. Some 200 kilometres east of Melbourne, access is via Traralgon or Yarram.

PV: 13 1963; www.parkweb.vic.gov.au

PV Traralgon: (03) 5172 2111

Wilsons Promontory National Park

Justifiably one of the most popular national parks in Victoria, Wilsons Promontory is brimming with natural treasures – from the mobs of eastern grey kangaroos and abundant common wombats that inhabit the surrounds of Tidal River to the wild coastline with its underwater forests of waving kelp, home to masses of fish and colourful corals. The landscape is characterised by eucalypt forests, fern-lined gullies and temperate rainforest, with wetlands and heathlands closer to the coast. The indented shoreline sweeps in and out of a multitude of sheltered coves and sandy beaches, ideal spots for beachcombing, birdwatching and picnicking. But many of the park's visitors come to hike the many walking trails. The two-to-five-day circular walk to Refuge Cove is an absolute gem if you do not mind carrying a pack. In more than 130 kilometres of tracks there are plenty of shorter walks too, among bright orange lichen-stained granite boulders, heathlands, forests and fern gullies. Take the short stroll to Squeaky Beach or set out on the 6-kilometre Lilly Pilly Gully Circuit.

The Prom is surrounded by marine parks, which provide excellent snorkelling in bays and around headlands, and plenty of places to swim and surf. Corner Inlet Marine and Coastal Park (*see* Birdwatching above) offers great opportunities to observe pied oystercatchers, grey plovers and red-necked stints. More than 180 bird species frequent the mudflats, beaches, heathlands and woodlands.

Most people stay at Tidal River, which has a vast campground and accommodation in huts and safari-style wilderness retreats. The retreats have been built to minimise their impact on the environment, are raised off the ground and require no concrete footings. Accommodation is also available in several cottages at the lighthouse (bookings essential). Long weekends and holiday periods are extremely busy but you need to book well in advance for stays at any time of year; for the summer-holiday period bookings are allocated via a ballot system (applications are accepted 1–30 June and drawn on 1 July).

PV Tidal River (campsite/accommodation bookings): (03) 5680 9555 or 1800 350 552 or 13 1963; www.parkweb.vic.gov.au

Lighthouse cottage bookings: (03) 5680 9500

Walkerville to Mornington

WHERE TO STAY

Phillip Island Eco Retreat and Day Spa

Designed and fitted out to be environmentally friendly, the two single-bedroom spa units here have solar hot water, green power and rainwater tanks, and all the wastewater is treated on site and recycled onto the garden. The units were built with sustainable timbers and use recycled PET bottles for insulation.

(03) 5952 6466; www.phillipislanddayspa.com.au

ACTIVITIES

Cycling

Bicycle-hire operator Ride on Bikes at Cowes recommends a 14-kilometre loop, suitable for families, to Rhyll and back along cycle paths and through a nature reserve. The company will also suggest a good range of off-road tracks for more experienced riders.

The 16-kilometre Bass Coast Rail Trail runs from the railway station at Anderson (located on the Bass Highway at the turn-off point to Phillip Island) to Wonthaggi, and is the only coastal rail trail in Victoria. It passes through coastal bushland, farmland and old mining areas, and crosses a historic trestle bridge over Bourne Creek at Kilcunda – offering sweeping coastal views. The first 5 kilometres is suitable for cycling and walking but the roughly surfaced remainder is currently suitable for mountain-biking and walking only.

Ride on Bikes: (03) 5952 2533;
www.rideonbikes.com.au
Bass Coast Rail Trail: (03) 9306 4846;
www.railtrails.org.au

Diving and snorkelling

There are some superb shore dives off the Mornington Peninsula, particularly around the piers at Rye, Portsea and Mornington, where you will see seahorses, stingrays, octopus, weedy sea dragons, corals and sponges. Aquatic Adventures at Rye are part of the flotilla of dive shops that will hire gear, offer advice and organise boat dives. Also in the area is Bayplay Adventure Tours, at Blairgowrie, who place an emphasis on educating clients about the marine environment during snorkelling and dive excursions in which you will see weedy sea dragons, sea stars, octopus, crabs and other creatures. South of Wonthaggi, Bunurong Marine Park also offers plenty of underwater fun, including snorkelling at The Caves and scuba diving at Shack Bay.

Aquatic Adventures: (03) 5985 8722;
www.aquaticadventures.com.au
Bayplay Adventure Tours: (03) 5984 0888;
www.bayplay.com.au
PV: 13 1963; www.parkweb.vic.gov.au
Bunurong Environment Centre (Inverloch):
(03) 5674 3738

French Island

Twice as big as Phillip Island, this place is a wildlife paradise in the heart of Western Port, south-east of Melbourne. It has the healthiest and most prolific colony of koalas in Australia, more than 250 bird species and the rare long-nosed potoroo. Seventy per cent of the island is national park, with environments ranging from mangrove salt marshes to heathlands and open woodlands, supporting 600 plant species, and 100 native orchids, including at least one that is only found here.

There is no bridge to the island, so you will need to either catch the passenger ferry from Stony Point or a small barge from Corinella in which you can bring your car if you must, but

One of the bedrooms at McLeod EcoFarm on French Island

you are better to bring a mountain bike or hire one from the general store.

French Island is perfect for a day tour, either on your own or with the highly recommended eco-accredited French Island Eco Tours in which you will almost certainly see active koalas up close. You can camp on the island, with free camping by the beach at Fairhaven, although it is 5 kilometres from where the ferry comes in. Alternatively, stay at McLeod EcoFarm, a certified biodynamic 220-hectare farm that grows garlic and vegetables, and has beef, lamb, pork and eggs. You can eat gourmet organic meals prepared by chefs from ingredients grown on the farm. About 50 per cent of the power comes from sun and wind, and there is a nine-hole organic golf course. There is accommodation for more than 100 people here, ranging from bunk rooms for two to a guesthouse with double rooms, and there are campsites as well.

Ferry information: (03) 9585 5730;
www.interislandferries.com.au
Corinella barge: 0428 880 729
French Island Eco Tours: 0429 177 532 or 1300 307 054;
www.frenchislandecotours.com.au
McLeod EcoFarm: (03) 5980 1224;
www.mcleodecofarm.com

Kayaking

For a great way to start the day, join a kayaking breakfast tour at Phillip Island Holiday Hire, which starts with a 45-minute paddle from Cowes and includes a civilised breakfast at a cafe. There is also a Devonshire tea option or a full-day paddle for the really keen. Bayplay Adventure Tours runs education-focused, sea-kayaking tours from Blairgowrie, on which you are likely to encounter dolphins, penguins and seals.

Phillip Island Holiday Hire: (03) 5952 5402 or
0419 556 224; www.phillipislandhire.com.au
Bayplay Adventure Tours: (03) 5984 0888;
www.bayplay.com.au

Swim with dolphins

In the warmer six months of the year, the eco-accredited Moonraker Charters will help you get in the water, swimming alongside Australian fur-seals and bottlenose dolphins. Of course, swimming is not compulsory on the three-hour tour that leaves from Sorrento, and from the vessel you will see seals, dolphins and Australasian gannets.

The guides at Polperro Dolphin Swims are activists who have supported dolphin research and campaigned for marine national parks,

The rocky shores of Cape Woolamai

regulatory reform and marine education. Displaying great environmental sensitivity, the company runs bay tours out of Sorrento from October to April, teaching people about the bay and its species. Seal swims are often part of the trips too.

Moonraker Charters: (03) 5984 4211 or 0419 205 060; www.moonrakercharters.com.au

Polperro Dolphin Swims: (03) 5988 8437 or 0428 174 160; www.polperro.com.au

Walking

Phillip Island has plenty of short walks, including one from the Woolamai Beach Surf Life Saving Club to the highest point on the island, on Cape Woolamai. The walking trail passes a shearwater rookery that is in use from October to April.

Visitor centre: 805 Phillip Island Rd, Newhaven; (03) 5956 7447 or 1300 366 422

Wildlife viewing

Phillip Island is best known for the little penguins that come ashore every night (bookings essential). But spend time exploring the area and you will find Seal Rocks, with Australia's largest colony of fur-seals, a busy silver gull nesting area at the Nobbies, and the superb Koala Conservation Centre. The eco-accredited Phillip Island Nature Park is the best place to start your wildlife viewing, with a range of tours including one in which you will be taken to a secluded beach and use night-vision technology to watch penguins come ashore.

There are some top birdwatching spots too, such as the hide beside Swan Lake – the only permanent freshwater lake on Phillip Island – and the mangroves of the Rhyll wetlands. There is usually pelican feeding at midday at the San Remo pier. Near Venus Bay, the Bald Hills Wetland Reserve also has a bird hide among the paperbarks and sand ridges, where you are likely to see spoonbills and shelducks.

Phillip Island Nature Park: penguin-viewing bookings (03) 5951 2800; www.penguins.org.au

Visitor centre: 805 Phillip Island Rd, Newhaven; (03) 5956 7447 or 1300 366 422

*A group of Phillip Island's little penguins (*Eudyptula minor*) returning to their burrows at dusk*

*Australian fur-seals (*Arctocephalus pusillus*) cavorting in the waves at Seal Rocks*

Melbourne to Port Campbell

WHERE TO STAY

Apollo Bay Youth Hostel

This relatively new hostel was built with an eco-friendly design, including thermal storage banks and other passive solar heating and cooling. It also has solar hot water, rainwater tanks, a worm farm, drought-tolerant native landscaping and an organic herb garden for guests.

(03) 5237 7899; www.yha.com.au

Cape Otway Centre for Conservation Ecology

There are not many better-thought-out ecotourism ventures than this superb multi-award-winning facility on Cape Otway. It has its own 66-hectare wildlife refuge and doubles as a shelter for injured and orphaned wildlife, including gliders, koalas and kangaroos. The hosts are dedicated to protecting, researching and conserving wildlife and offer intimate wildlife tours every day. There are only five bedrooms at the deluxe ecolodge, which includes a nature studies room and library.

(03) 5237 9297; www.capeotwaycentre.com.au

ACTIVITIES

Birdwatching

The permanent water and high-nutrient levels of sewage farms make them brilliant bird habitats and, for many years, the 11 000-hectare treatment plant at Werribee has been recognised as being in the top ten birdwatching spots in the country. It is a haven for tens of thousands of birds from more than 270 species, including the critically endangered orange-bellied parrot. There are currently no birdwatching tours on the site, but you can apply in advance for a permit to visit through Melbourne Water. Most long-term permits are for local birdwatchers who visit regularly, but interstate visitors can get a day pass.

The 227-hectare Serendip Sanctuary at Lara has excellent bird hides to spot some of the 150-plus bird species found in the wetlands and open grass woodlands there, including brolgas, bustards and blue-billed ducks. Some easy short walks link the habitats, and the picnic area has free electric barbecues. The sanctuary is managed by Parks Victoria.

Werribee sewage farm: (03) 9235 2828 or 13 1722;
www.melboca.org.au/birdingsites
www.birdobservers.org.au/BirdingMaps.asp
PV: 13 1963; www.parkweb.vic.gov.au

Canoeing

For a fantastic dawn or dusk paddle in which you have a 95 per cent chance of seeing a platypus, join Otway Eco Tours on Lake Elizabeth. Half-day trips to this remote lake in the ranges depart from the small hamlet of Forrest, north of Apollo Bay. Some of your tour fee will contribute to research into platypus diseases.

Otway Eco Tours: (03) 5236 6345;
www.otwayecotours.com

Great Ocean Walk

Why just drive the Great Ocean Road when you can walk it? In one of Victoria's best long-distance tracks, you can hike 91 kilometres from Apollo Bay to the Twelve Apostles, through spectacular gorges, past limestone cliffs and blowholes, and along white sandy beaches. There are plenty of accommodation options along the way, or you can camp in the seven campsites (you will need to book). Because of its relatively easy access, the track has a great range of short, medium and day

Hiking the Great Ocean Walk on a guided tour with Auswalk

walks. There are guided tours along the trek with everything arranged from transfers to four-star accommodation, gourmet meals and walking gear. Among the operators are the eco-certified Bothfeet, which has three-, four- and six-day options, Auswalk, and Ecotrek, which offers a five-day option with accommodation along the way.

www.greatoceanwalk.com.au
Bothfeet: 1300 767 416; www.bothfeet.com
Auswalk: (03) 5356 4971; www.auswalk.com.au
Ecotrek: (08) 8346 4155; www.ecotrek.com.au

Great Otway National Park

This vast 1030-square-kilometre national park extends from Anglesea to Princetown. You can walk through tall wet forests of mountain ash, myrtle beech, blackwood and tree fern to striking waterfalls such as Erskine, Stevensons, Triplet and Little Aire. Inland from Apollo Bay, Maits Rest Walk is an easy 1-kilometre stroll through rainforest with the chance to see king parrots and crimson rosellas. At Melba Gully, south-west of Lavers Hill, the short Madsens Track Nature Walk leads through fern gullies dotted with brightly coloured fungi and overshadowed by a closed canopy of ancient myrtle beech. Elsewhere in the park there are several mountain-biking loops through beautiful rainforest and plentiful picnic and camping areas with basic facilities, including Johanna Beach, renowned as one of the best coastal camping spots in the state. Accommodation is also available at the Otway lighthouse keeper's quarters (bookings essential).

PV: 13 1963; www.parkweb.vic.gov.au
Cape Otway Lightstation: (03) 5237 9240

Marine Discovery Centre, Queenscliff

Primarily set up to educate school children about the marine environment, this government-run facility also has an interesting holiday program and an interactive aquarium and touch tanks. Holiday activities include snorkelling tours both in-shore and by boat, canoe trips and the popular rockpool ramble, great for younger kids.

(03) 5258 3344; www.dpi.vic.gov.au/mdc

Mountain-biking

You Yangs Regional Park, north-east of Geelong, has more than 50 kilometres of mountain-biking tracks for all level of rider, with easier and flatter tracks through eucalypts in the Kurrajong Plantation, and other steeper and more testing single tracks in the Stockyards. There are obstacles such as log rides and boardwalks, and skills practice areas. All About Mountain Bike Tours can set you up for a day's mountain-biking here and almost anywhere else you want to go. Otway Eco Tours also has guided tours, particularly in Otway National Park, and hires mountain bikes with a drop-off service from the town of Forrest.

PV: 13 1963; www.parkweb.vic.gov.au

All About Mountain Bike Tours: (03) 5277 0817; www.allaboutmtbtours.com.au

Otway Eco Tours: (03) 5236 6345; www.otwayecotours.com

Sea-kayaking

In an exciting two-hour guided paddle, head out from Apollo Bay to Marengo Marine Sanctuary to get a close-up view of an Australian fur-seal colony. The seals often come out to swim around the kayaks.

0405 495 909; www.apollobaysurfkayak.com.au

Riding high over a jump in You Yangs Regional Park

Surfing

Perhaps the most famous break in Australia, the legendary Bells Beach is on this stretch of coast near Torquay, and there are plenty of waves to catch elsewhere as the Southern Ocean slams into the continent. There are also more sheltered spots to learn to surf. Go Ride a Wave at Torquay, Anglesea and Lorne has specialist, two-hour adult lessons and kids lessons so you do not have to embarrass yourself in front of the young surfies.

1300 132 441; www.gorideawave.com.au

Wild orchids on the Anglesea heath: yellow rabbit ears (Thelymitra antennifera) and a vibrant red species

Surfing action at Jan Juc near Torquay

Some of the remaining Twelve Apostles, which are gradually being eroded away

Port Campbell to South Australia

ACTIVITIES

Diving and snorkelling

Best known in diving circles for its multitude of shipwrecks, most of which are reached by boat dives, this area also has some great snorkelling and shore dives. Recommended spots include the Port Campbell jetty, Wild Dog Cove at Peterborough, and the breakwater wall at Warrnambool – particularly the outside wall. An area called The Gardens off Middle Island has superb kelp forests and swim-throughs. Stingray Bay, in the Merri Marine Sanctuary, is particularly good for snorkelling and is known for abundant fish and other creatures including crayfish, anemones and starfish. As well as the shipwrecks, deeper adventures can include the dramatic natural formations, because the awesome scenery of the Twelve Apostles Marine National Park does not stop at the waterline – under water there are dramatic arches, canyons and other formations. The Dive Inn at Warrnambool will fix you up with gear and give you the 'okay' signal.

(03) 5561 6108; www.diveinn.com.au

Great South West Walk

This 280-kilometre walk is a loop that starts and finishes at Portland, winding around Discovery Bay to the South Australian border then returning through Lower Glenelg National Park. Natural wonders along the way include a petrified forest, blowholes, an Australasian gannet colony, massive swells, seals, creeks, limestone gorges and forests. The walking is generally easier than many other long-distance walks, so most people can complete it in 12–14 days. Simple campsites, with pit toilets and fresh water, are located every 10–20 kilometres

The Petrified Forest at Cape Bridgewater

along the track, and there are a few places to have a comfy bed and a meal. South West Adventures runs guided tours of sections of the track, with overnight stops at B&Bs, talks by local historians and experts, and feasts of fresh crayfish barely out of the pots.

www.greatsouthwestwalk.com

South West Adventures: (03) 5523 3175 or 0428 358 139; www.southwestadventures.com.au

Mount Eccles National Park

At Mount Eccles you can walk for 2 kilometres around the rim of a volcanic crater then descend for a swim in the lake at its heart. It is a great spot for a picnic, with koalas and kangaroos, and the camping facilities include hot showers.

PV: 13 1963; www.parkweb.vic.gov.au

Picnicking

Lake Pertobe Reserve on Warrnambool's foreshore is known as one of the best adventure playgrounds around, with plenty for kids of all ages. There are paddleboats and canoes, a maze and flying fox, free barbecues and short walks with bird hides near the lake.

Seal watching

At Cape Bridgewater, 20 kilometres west of Portland, you will have the chance to see up to 1000 Australian fur-seals. On small craft holding 11 passengers, Seals by Sea Tours takes you out to rock platforms and a sea cave where the seals live. You can also walk to a seal-viewing platform from either Bridgewater Beach kiosk or the Blowholes carpark.

Seals by Sea Tours: (03) 5526 7247 or 0427 267 247

Tower Hill State Game Reserve

On a one-hour environmental or Aboriginal tour of this reserve near Warrnambool with the Worn Gundidj Aboriginal Cooperative, you will discover the area's fascinating volcanic

Whale watching at Logans Beach near Warrnambool

and cultural history. You can also do one of five self-guided walks, and there is abundant wildlife to see, including koalas, kangaroos and emus. A boardwalk leads across wetlands with the chance to see blue-billed ducks, herons, Australian ibis and other waterbirds.

(03) 5561 5315; www.worngundidj.org.au

Whale-watching

Warrnambool is well known as one of the best spots in Australia to spot southern right whales from the shore during their winter calving (June to September). At Logans Beach, the special whale-watching platforms even have binoculars to help you get a good look.

For a chance at seeing the largest animals on the planet – the awe-inspiring blue whales – head to Portland during December to May, when these 30-metre-long creatures can sometimes be spotted off Cape Nelson. They can occasionally be seen from the shore, but to get a good look you will need to join a boat, helicopter or light plane tour. Call the Portland visitor centre for details.

Warrnambool visitor centre: (03) 5559 4620

Portland visitor centre: (03) 5523 2671 or 1800 035 567

Eastern Victoria

Stretching north and east from Melbourne, this area encompasses some of Australia's most notable wine regions, along with Victoria's alpine country and some picturesque river environments along the Murray and in East Gippsland. At all times of year, the Victorian High Country and its surrounds offer great experiences for the ecotourist, and there is hopefully more to come, as resorts and accommodation providers realise the necessity of solid environmental practices. Outside the High Country are a scattering of national parks and reserves, the habitat of myriad wildlife, and opportunities for bushwalking, birdwatching, canoeing, cycling and caving. To appreciate the region, lace up those hiking or ski boots, hop on a bike or prepare for some serious picnicking.

Picnickers enjoying a Yarra Valley food and wine festival at De Bortoli

Around Healesville

WHERE TO STAY

Amarant Retreat

Ideal for bush lovers, this eco-certified retreat has five suites set in lush mountain ash forest, 400 metres above sea level, next to Yarra Ranges National Park.

(03) 5967 3416; www.amarantretreat.com.au

ACTIVITIES

Bicentennial National Trail

Acclaimed as the longest-marked, non-motorised, multi-use trekking route in the world, this track traverses an incredible 5330 kilometres from Healesville to Cooktown in north Queensland, passing through 18 national parks. Because of the distances involved, it is more suited to travelling on horseback or mountain bike but can be walked.

1300 138 724; www.nationaltrail.com.au

← *Amarant Retreat*

*Platypus (*Ornithorhynchus anatinus*) at Healesville Sanctuary* →

Cycling

The popular 40-kilometre Lilydale–Warburton Rail Trail winds through tea-tree bushland, over old railway bridges and through towns, with plenty of places to stop and take a break along the way. The Cog Bike Cafe in Mount Evelyn will not only hire bikes and organise transfers, but will also help you recover with a fair trade coffee afterwards.

www.railtrails.org.au

Cog Bike Cafe: (03) 9736 4999; www.cogbikecafe.com.au

Healesville Sanctuary

One of the most respected zoos in the country for its conservation work, Healesville has more than 200 species of Australian wildlife in 30 hectares of bush. Conservation efforts are targeted at endangered Australian species such as mountain pygmy-possums, orange-bellied parrots and spotted tree frogs. The sanctuary is near Healesville in Badger Creek Road.

(03) 5957 2800; www.zoo.org.au

Lake Eildon National Park

With eastern grey kangaroos and abundant birdlife on the lake, this is a popular spot to camp and swim in summer. Walking and mountain-bike tracks will get you around large parts of the rugged 27 750-hectare park, where you may encounter koalas, wombats, echidnas and other wildlife.

PV: 13 1963; www.parkweb.vic.gov.au

Organic market

Every Saturday morning, the Healesville Organic Market has all manner of chemical-free produce available at the Railway Station, from large certified producers to small backyard growers.

(03) 5962 5070; www.permaculturemelbourne.org.au

Yarra Ranges National Park

Home to the world's tallest hardwood forests, this tree-filled national park is a delight, with everything from ferny gullies and rainforest to semi-alpine woodland. Mount Donna Buang is one of the closest mountains to Melbourne on which it regularly snows. It is great in winter for tobogganing and snow play, and offers superb views year-round. There are walks through the tall mountain ash forests, including the Mount Donna Buang Skywalk at Cement Creek, which gets up to 17 metres above the forest floor. Lake Mountain, at more than 1400 metres, is a couple of hundred metres higher, and offers superb cross-country skiing in winter on 37 kilometres of groomed trails and excellent alpine hiking in the summer. You can hire ski gear there.

PV: 13 1963; www.parkweb.vic.gov.au

Lake Mountain: www.lakemountainresort.com.au

Wildlife tours

Most of Australia's marsupials and many other animals are most active at dusk or after dark. Guided, night-walking tours are therefore one of the best ways to see many wild animals,

← *A barking owl (Ninox connivens) at Healesville Sanctuary*

Cycling the Lilydale–Warburton Rail Trail →

Moss-covered boulders beside a mountain stream in Yarra Ranges National Park

and the eco-accredited Eco-Adventure Tours, based in Healesville, specialises in night tours, although the company offers day trips as well. On a night stroll you are likely to see bats, yellow-bellied and greater gliders, owls, wombats, wallabies and possums.

(03) 5962 5115 or 0418 999 936;
www.ecoadventuretours.com.au

Wine tasting

In the Yarra Valley, the renowned De Bortoli Wines has an environmental policy as extensive as its range of wines, and a cellar door that has won multiple tourism awards. The vineyard's eco-friendly practices include water management, biological farming, and packaging and waste management. De Bortoli is also a founding member of the Food for Trees program, which includes an aim to plant one million trees in the next decade.

De Bortoli; (03) 5965 2271; www.debortoli.com.au

East Gippsland hinterland

WHERE TO STAY

Buchan Caves

At this location there is a great campsite (bookings essential in peak periods), with abundant wildlife in the vicinity, including eastern grey kangaroos, lyrebirds and bellbirds. If you prefer not to camp, there is a good range of accommodation, from cabins to the relatively new safari-tent-style Wilderness Retreats, each with its own private deck (bookings essential year-round). There are guided walks through the two main limestone caves, both rich in elaborate features, and some nature walks above ground.

PV Buchan Caves Reserve: (03) 5162 1900
PV: 13 1963; www.parkweb.vic.gov.au

Stalactites at Buchan Caves

Jacarri Eco-Cottage, Goongerah

This rustic little cottage in East Gippsland sleeps four, and has solar power and a dry composting toilet. It has been built with sustainable timbers and uses a water wheel to fill the water tank. Organic fruit, vegetables, milk and eggs are available in season. It is situated in manna gum forest on the Brodribb River, at the western edge of Errinundra National Park. To reach the cottage, travel some 68 kilometres north along the Bonang Highway from Orbost then turn onto the Ellery Creek Track (bookings by email).

eegippsland@primus.com.au; www.eastgippsland.net.au/jacarri

ACTIVITIES

Caving

Wild Caving, based at Buchan, runs two-hour introductions to caving in Wilsons Cave, in which everything except footwear is supplied. The company describes the squeezing, twisting experience as 'a hard core yoga session'. There is no abseiling on that trip, but they offer another caving adventure for those looking for something even more extreme.

Wild Caving: (03) 5155 9305 or 0428 559 305

Mitchell River National Park

Although only 11 900 hectares in size, this rugged national park contains some of the best forest country in Gippsland. Great for experienced rafters, kayakers and canoeists, it also has some superb bushwalks. With a two-car shuffle, you can do the 18-kilometre Mitchell River Walking Track in a day, or camp overnight and spread it over two, encountering warm temperate rainforest, giant kanooka trees, the legendary Den of Nargun (in Aboriginal legend, the home of a fierce beast) and plunging cliffs in the gorge. The other main walk in the park is the 5-kilometre Den of Nargun loop, which takes in the awe-inspiring Bluff Lookout. You can camp in the park, and there are pit toilets at Angusvale. Billy Goat Bend and Angusvale have fireplaces, but campers must bring in all supplies.

PV: 13 1963; www.parkweb.vic.gov.au

Mountain-biking

Snowy River Expeditions hires mountain bikes and other gear from Karoonda Park in Gelantipy. The staff will set you up with maps and compass, and will provide a drop-off service if you require.

Snowy River Expeditions: (03) 5155 0220; www.karoondapark.com

Rafting

Rumours of the demise of rafting in the area because of the lack of water are untrue. Snowy River Expeditions (*see* details above) based in Gelantipy runs trips year-round, but varies the location depending on the conditions, and may raft the Snowy, Mitchell or Mitta Mitta rivers. A full-day experience with the company usually involves about three hours on the water, but there are also two- and four-day camping options for those keen to immerse themselves in this environment.

*The Gippsland water-dragon (*Physignathus lesueurii howitti*)*

High Country

Wildlife research

For a rare opportunity to observe native animals up close, in the wild, you can join a research trip with Gippsland High Country Tours, led by experienced naturalists eco-certified and recognised around the country for the work they do. You participate in monitoring frog populations, and trapping (and releasing) small creatures, such as tiny insectivorous forest bats, scientifically recording data on the ecology and distribution of species. The company, based in Bruthen, also has great walking tours in the High Country and East Gippsland, with an emphasis on native flora and fauna. Departure points vary but include Bairnsdale and Melbourne.

Gippsland High Country Tours: (03) 5157 5556; www.gippslandhighcountrytours.com.au

WHERE TO STAY

Arthur's Cottage, Cudgewa

This historic mudbrick, two-bedroom cottage was built around 1897, but now has solar-powered lights and a gas kitchen. It sits quietly on the Cudgewa Creek, with platypus drifting past. You will need to bring your own linen.

(02) 6077 4324 or 0427 774 324; www.visitvictoria.com

The Buckland, Bright

With the same architect as The Odd Frog (below), The Buckland's four luxury studio retreats have similar eco-design principles, and thousands of trees have been planted on the site. They are also powered by green energy.

(03) 5756 2383; www.thebuckland.com.au

The Odd Frog, Bright

This place comprises five funky new luxury studios on a 4-hectare Land for Wildlife property. The studios have been architecturally designed to have minimal impact on the environment, with thought even given to their eventual disassembly and recycling. There is solar hot water, LED lighting, a greywater recycling system that waters an orchard, and 4000 native trees have been planted on the site.

0418 362 791; www.theoddfrog.com

Funky studio deck amid the bushland at The Odd Frog

Luxury studio accommodation at The Buckland

The snow-capped peak of Mount Stirling

ACTIVITIES

Alpine National Park

Covering a vast 6460 square kilometres, this is Victoria's largest national park and cradles the state's highest mountains and dramatic alpine scenery, as well as the major downhill skiing resorts. The park has over 1100 species of plant – some found nowhere else – and some of the best bushwalking in the country. Bold, experienced walkers climb the 11 kilometres to the top of the 1922-metre Mount Feathertop in a strenuous day walk or overnight hike. The track starts just below Mount Hotham and has exposed walking on a narrow, rocky track, but spectacular 360-degree views from the summit.

Another taxing climb is to the top of Mount Bogong, which at 1986 metres is Victoria's highest peak. Hikers set out on the Staircase Spur from Mountain Creek picnic area to ascend through peppermint gums and snow gums and onto the exposed treeless plateau. The 16-kilometre walk will take a full day. As with all hiking in the High Country, be prepared for all conditions at all times of the year.

Hiking in Alpine National Park in summer

The Australian Alps Walking Track (*see* New South Wales/Australian Capital Territory/ Hiking and bushwalking) passes through the park. Sections can be walked as overnight or day trips. However, there are countless other walks of all lengths, with pretty wildflowers and melting snows in spring and summer.

If you want to walk large sections of this park with a guide, while staying in luxury accommodation, try the eco-accredited Hedonistic Hiking, which has multi-day walks focusing on history and gourmet food.

There are multiple camping areas scattered throughout the park – the Wellington River Valley is particularly popular.

PV: 13 1963; www.parkweb.vic.gov.au

PV Mansfield: (03) 5733 1200

Hedonistic Hiking: (03) 5755 2307; www.hedonistichiking.com.au

Baw Baw National Park

This 13 300-hectare national park cradles the low-key ski resort at Mount Baw Baw, the closest downhill ski resort to Melbourne. Near the resort are 10 kilometres of groomed cross-country trails (and you can hire gear at the resort), some longer ungroomed trails, and lovely alpine walks among the snow gums in summer. The most popular is probably the 5-kilometre-return walk to the summit.

1300 651 136; www.mountbawbaw.com.au

Burrowa–Pine Mountain National Park

Located near the New South Wales border, 430 kilometres north-east of Melbourne, and one of Victoria's lesser-known national parks, this has some remarkable features. The granitic Pine Mountain is one of the largest monoliths in Australia, one and a half times the size of Uluṟu. It is home to a number of rare and threatened plant species, including the Pine Mountain grevillea, fan grevillea and phantom wattle. The 1300-metre Mount Burrowa has more rainfall and is clothed by a range of forest types, from candlebarks and peppermints, to blue gums, alpine ash and snow gums on the highest parts. There are walks from short strolls to see waterfalls (do not miss the 4-kilometre Bluff Creek Nature Trail) through to multi-day hikes, and plenty of tracks for four-wheel drivers to explore. Camping is limited.

PV Tallangatta: (02) 6071 5301

PV: 13 1963; www.parkweb.vic.gov.au

Canoeing

You can paddle down the Murray for an hour or a day, or embark on overnight camping trips in canoes from Upper Murray Caravan and Tourist Park at Tintaldra. A pick-up and drop-off service is available if necessary. Snowy Mountains Holidays at Towong offers gentle, guided one-day canoeing trips on the upper Murray, or will help you with self-guided trips, including a drop-off and pick-up service.

Upper Murray Caravan and Tourist Park: (02) 6077 9207

Snowy Mountains Holidays: (02) 6076 8252; www.albury.net.au

Cross-country skiing

The home of our national cross-country team, Falls Creek is probably the best place to cross-country ski. It has 65 kilometres of groomed tracks, catering to beginners and intermediate skiers, as well as marked trails on the Bogong High Plains and plenty of scope for backcountry touring. The bulk of the tracks start at the Windy Corner carpark, where you can rent all the gear you need. Remember cross-country skiing is considerably cheaper – and a lot more peaceful – than downhill skiing. Falls Creek Sports also offers a guided two-hour introduction to snowshoeing.

The Mount Hotham and Dinner Plain region is another of the state's top cross-country areas, with more than 35 kilometres of tracks and circuits of 2–15 kilometres. Some trails start from Hotham village, but there is a free shuttle bus to Wire Plain where the bulk of the tracks start. Cross-country skis and other equipment can be hired from Hotham Equipe.

Mount Stirling, near Mansfield, has some 60 kilometres of cross-country ski trails leading to the summit, and plenty of areas for advanced

Cross-country skiing at Falls Creek

Scaling the granite cliffs of Mount Buffalo National Park

skiers. Hire gear at the cross-country trailhead near the carpark.

Mount Beauty visitor centre: (03) 5754 1962
Falls Creek: 1800 204 424; www.fallscreek.com.au
Mount Hotham: (03) 5759 3672; www.hotham.com.au
Dinner Plain visitor information: 1800 670 019
Mount Stirling: (03) 5777 6441; www.stirling.au.com

Kayaking

The operator 5 Star Adventure Tours offers a huge range of eco-accredited tours and activities in the High Country, particularly targeting those who like a few little luxuries on the way. One of the most popular trips is a one-day kayaking experience, leaving from Bright at the respectable time of 9am, and hitting whichever local river is likely to give the most satisfactory paddle at the time. The trips generally run from November to May, and have a focus on caring for first-time paddlers, and on providing information about the environments experienced along the way.

(03) 5759 2555; www.5staradventure.com.au

Mount Buffalo National Park

One of the must-see national parks in Victoria, this dramatic mountain rises spectacularly in granite cliffs loved by rock climbers, abseilers and hang-gliders. There are tumbling waterfalls, snow-gum woodlands, snow-grass plains, masses of wildflowers and plunging gorges. In winter the area is perfect for snowshoeing and cross-country skiing (particularly the road up to the Horn picnic area) and the rest of the year it offers superb bushwalking on more than 100 kilometres of tracks, with everything from short strolls to strenuous hikes through a landscape that includes plants found nowhere else in the world. Recommended short walks with great views are the Monolith Track, The Gorge, the Cathedral-Hump Track and the climb to the summit of the Horn from the picnic area. In winter, free snowshoeing tours, with

Hang-gliding in Mount Buffalo National Park

Lake Catani offers a tranquil environment in which to camp or paddle a canoe

Rafting the rapids of the Mitta Mitta River

equipment supplied, are regularly given by the park's rangers, in which you will learn a lot more about the park and its wildlife than you would otherwise do on your own. These tours provide a great introduction to the park and are a fun way to get around in the snow for a couple of hours. Bookings are essential.

There are simple facilities for camping at Lake Catani, but you will need to ski there during winter.

(03) 5756 2328 or 13 1963; www.parkweb.vic.gov.au

Paragliding

Ecotourism is not generally about thrills for their own sake, but soaring in the thermals in the Victorian Alps really has to be a glorious way to see this part of the country, flying in silence, and using wind and air currents alone. There are several operators that offer tandem paragliding for those who want a taste without having to learn the ropes. Alpine Paragliding at Bright emphasises that they take people with disabilities and Active Flight will also get you up in the air.

Alpine Paragliding at Bright: 0428 352 048; www.alpineparagliding.com

Active Flight: 0428 854 455; www.activeflight.com.au

Rafting

Adventure Rafting Victoria only takes a few months off, from April to June, and runs exciting day trips down the foaming Murray Gates, and two-night paddles down the Mitta Mitta, staying overnight in the legendary Blue Duck Inn at Anglers Rest. The company has excellent environmental practices, including helping with removal of invasive willow trees.

Adventure Rafting Victoria: (02) 6077 1164 or 1800 997 238; www.raftingaustralia.com

The North East

WHERE TO STAY

Camping

The straggling reserves along the Murray River offer some quiet waterside camping spots (except during the peak of Easter and Christmas holidays), among river red gums and birds. Try Stantons Bend (near Wahgunyah, north-west of Rutherglen), Taylors Bend (near Yarrawonga) and around Sharps Bend (just west of Yarrawonga). There are some 50 sandy beaches between Yarrawonga and Barmah, which provide excellent swimming, canoeing and kayaking.

PV: 13 1963; www.parkweb.vic.gov.au

Lake Waranga Caravan Park, Rushworth

Situated on the shores of the Waranga Basin, the owners of this caravan park are to be commended for completely redesigning their new guest amenities to be more environmentally conscious, with the use of many water- and power-saving technologies. The complex is mainly suitable for those set up for camping, but it does have some cabins.

(03) 5856 1243; www.lakewaranga.com

River red gums in the Barmah wetlands

ACTIVITIES

Barmah wetlands

In Barmah State Park bushwalkers can stroll among some of the elder statesmen of the bush, the 500-year-old river red gums, more than 30 metres tall, along the Murray. The park rims the river in separate sections, from Barmah to Strathmerton. A few medium-length walking tracks of 4–7 kilometres are signposted near the Dharnya Centre (on the southern edge of the park just north of Barmah). There are some great camping options along the Murray, including in established campgrounds or bush camping. For a deeper appreciation of the Barmah forest and its internationally recognised wetlands, visitors can take an eco-accredited, one- or two-hour cruise in the MV *Kingfisher*, a small vessel that carries only 30 passengers. Alternatively, explore the area on your own by hiring canoes and kayaks from Gondwana Canoe Hire in Barmah.

PV: 13 1963; www.parkweb.vic.gov.au

Kingfisher cruises: (03) 5480 1839, (03) 5855 2855 or after hours 0428 552 854; www.kingfishercruises.com.au

Gondwana Canoe Hire: (03) 5869 3347; www.geocities.com/gondwanahire

Berry-picking

You can pick your own blackberries and occasionally other berries from Newtons Organic Prickleberry Farm, an organic berry, hops and herb farm at Whitfield (and they swear not all the branches are prickly). Frozen berries are available year-round (by appointment), and fresh berries from December to March.

(03) 5729 8272 or 0427 298 278; www.visitwangaratta.com.au

Chiltern–Mount Pilot National Park

A favourite among birdwatchers, this park is one of the only places to see the endangered and rather pretty regent honeyeater, as well as turquoise parrots, painted button-quail and 220 other bird species. The park is dominated by some of the last box-ironbark forest in Victoria. There are a couple of walks and the forest tracks are great for some gentle mountain-biking.

PV: 13 1963; www.parkweb.vic.gov.au

Cycling

With 100 kilometres of safe, sealed bitumen surface to pedal on, the Murray to the Mountains Rail Trail is the most developed rail trail in the state, and therefore very popular, with more than 40 000 people estimated to

Pedalling up the solid climb to Beechworth on the Murray to the Mountains Rail Trail

ride it each year. It links Wangaratta, Bright and Beechworth, and travels through the picturesque Ovens and King valleys, passing farmland, bushland and beautiful alpine scenery. There is a 15-kilometre solid climb into Beechworth, and a fun descent the other way. An average rider will take about six hours to ride from Wangaratta to Bright. Add about two hours for the Beechworth detour. V-line has a scheduled coach service between the towns, and will take bikes. Dean Woods Cycles in Wangaratta has comfy hybrid bikes for hire, including panniers.

The pretty 35-kilometre High Country Rail Trail follows the southern shore of Lake Hume, near Wodonga, with plenty of picnic spots along the way. Unfortunately it has one section in the middle on the Murray Valley Highway that is unsuitable for inexperienced riders, but the stretches either side are long enough on their own to provide a very pleasant family cycle. You will have to bring your own bikes or walk a section (no bike hire in town at the time of publication).

www.railtrail.com.au
V-line: 13 6196; www.vline.com.au
Dean Woods Cycles: 1800 353 123;
www.deanwoods.com.au
www.highcountryrailtrail.org.au

Indigenous tour

A free, short, bush-tucker tour is available from the Bangerang Cultural Centre in Shepparton. You will need to book, but you can visit the centre on weekdays to see the wide range of artefacts from the area, and from Indigenous groups in other regions.

(03) 5831 1020; www.bangerang.org.au

Wine-tasting

The Rutherglen region in the far north of the state is renowned particularly for its fortified

Tasting a Rutherglen muscat

ports and muscats, perfect for a winter's night. There are no organically certified wineries in the area, although several wineries are adopting organic principles, including Valhalla Wines and Scion Vineyard (which has a cellar door partially built with recycled timbers). Lilliput Wines is a chemical-free wine-maker and a registered Land for Wildlife property. All three establishments have tastings on site. You can travel between the wineries on a mountain bike rented from the visitor centre in Rutherglen (bookings required on weekends). And later, you can work off those calories from the wine with a self-guided stroll through historic Rutherglen. The walk takes about an hour and includes everything from historic pubs and buildings from the mid-1800s, through to gardens, convents, churches and schools.

Valhalla Wines: (02) 6033 1438;
http://valhallawines.com.au
Scion: (02) 6032 8844; www.scionvineyard.com
Lilliput: (03) 5726 5055;
www.lilliputwinesofrutherglen.com.au
Mountain-bike hire: (02) 6032 9166 or 1800 622 871
Rutherglen visitor centre: (02) 6033 6300

Western Victoria

Western Victoria is primarily agricultural, but contains a wealth of natural features and national parks that blossom with spring wildflowers and harbour wildlife year-round. Green experiences out here include everything from testing your nerves on a rock face at Mount Arapiles to the more sedentary sampling of organic wines. The premier park in the region is the Grampians, but there are plenty of other places for bushwalking, picnicking and mountain-biking.

Hiking in the Grampians on an Inn-to-Inn tour with Auswalk

*The koala (*Phascolarctos cinereus*) is common in Brisbane Ranges National Park*

The Goldfields

WHERE TO STAY

MillDuck, Harcourt North

This strawbale house won a Most Energy Efficient Home award (North West Region) when it was built. More than 1000 trees have been planted on the property since it was purchased, and it is now an alpaca stud. The B&B, with passive solar-design features, takes two couples in separate units.

(03) 5439 6451; www.millduck.com.au

ACTIVITIES

Brisbane Ranges National Park

With a vibrant koala population, this relatively small national park only 80 kilometres west

of Melbourne has picnic areas, walking tracks through rocky gorges and a basic camping area.
PV: 13 1963; www.parkweb.vic.gov.au

Food and wine sampling

Wineries Avonmore Estate near Elmore, just north of Bendigo, is certified biodynamic and has cellar-door sales Wednesday to Sunday or at other times on request, but as wines are produced in small volume, they sometimes sell out completely. Paul Osicka Wines near Graytown uses no insecticides or herbicides near the vines, some of which have been around for 50 years. The vineyard has cellar-door sales if the shiraz, cabernet sauvignon and merlot have not sold out. Langanook Winery, near Faraday, uses solar power and organic principles for its award-winning range. Jasper Hill vineyard at Heathcote has been producing wines using organic/biodynamic principles since they started in 1975. Their small range is noted for its excellent quality. Bress, near Harcourt, is a winery and cidery that focuses on sustainable practices. It is closed June–October.

Fruits You can pick your own fruits straight off the tree at the certified organic Mount Alexander Fruit Gardens in Harcourt. In the November–December cherry-picking season, the orchard is open Friday to Sunday, and open on Sundays during the January–Easter season for peaches, nectarines, plums, pears and apples. You can also pick your own certified organic cherries and apricots at Maldon Cherry Farm, mid-November to January, or just turn up and buy them once the hard work is done.

Avonmore Estate: (03) 5432 6291; www.avonmoreestatewine.com
Paul Osicka Wines: (03) 5794 9235; www.heathcotewinegrowers.com.au
Langanook Winery: (03) 5474 8250; www.langanookwines.com.au
Jasper Hill: (03) 5433 2528; www.jasperhill.com
Bress: (03) 5474 2262; www.bress.com.au
Mount Alexander Fruit Gardens: (03) 5474 2808 or 0409 706 784; www.mafg.com.au
Maldon Cherry Farm: (03) 5475 2178

Golden Nugget Discovery Tours

This carbon-neutral business in Ballarat runs small, personalised tours of no more than six people in the Goldfields region, with three themes – wild nature, gold history and heritage, and food and wine.
(03) 5332 9199 or 0407 542 796; www.golden.nuggettours.com.au

Picnicking

There are some lovely picnic spots and parks to explore in this region. The volcanic Mount Buninyong Scenic Reserve, 745 metres above sea level and overlooking Ballarat, is a year-round favourite.
(03) 5320 5500; www.ballarat.vic.gov.au

Orchards in the Goldfields region produce luscious fruits in season

Far west

Aquila Eco Lodges are surrounded by natural bushland

WHERE TO STAY

Aquila Eco Lodges

Emus, echidnas and myriad other wildlife visit the 40 hectares of bushland on this property, which has been covenanted with Trust for Nature, preserving it as a wildlife reserve. Aquila collects all its own water, generates its own power through solar panels and a generator that partly runs on biodiesel, made on site with waste cooking oils, and deals via a worm farm with waste and sewage on site. Two of the four lodges have won design awards and feature passive heating and cooling.

(03) 5577 2582 or 0425 745 933; www.ecolodges.com.au

Grampians YHA Eco-Hostel

At this eco-hostel you sleep under roof tiles that are actually solar panels. Any extra power generated is fed back to the electricity grid. The passive solar building, featuring rammed earth walls, also has solar hot-water heaters, greywater treatment and recycling, an organic herb garden and chickens with tasty eggs free to the first guests up in the morning. Although bathroom facilities are shared, there are double rooms and twin rooms, as well as dormitories.

(03) 5356 4544; www.yha.com.au/hostels

Little Desert Nature Lodge, Nhill

Set on 117 hectares of bushland beside Little Desert National Park, the lodge has 24 rooms with ensuite bathrooms, or 16 bunkrooms with shared facilities. By staying here, you are helping support projects such as the mallee fowl sanctuary, an 80-hectare, covenant-protected reserve with active breeding pairs. There is a captive breeding program where chicks raised are released back into the wild, and revegetation of areas to provide suitable breeding and feeding habitat for the mallee fowl. Guests can also go on tours of the sanctuary and view the captive breeding program in operation.

(03) 5391 5232; www.littledesertlodge.com.au

Pomponderoo Bush Retreat, Dimboola

With solar power, rainwater tanks and tree planting to offset carbon emissions, these three self-contained timber cabins are a great accommodation option near the north-eastern edge of Little Desert National Park.

(03) 5389 1957 or 0419 824 618

ACTIVITIES

Canoeing

Wild Side Outdoors, based at Red Cliffs on the outskirts of Mildura, lead ecotours of the Murray River and outback. You can canoe across Kings Billabong, near Mildura, at sunset, sharing the water with multitudes of swans, pelicans, cormorants, grebes and ducks.

(03) 5024 3721; www.wildsideoutdoors.com.au

The architect-designed Brambuk Cultural Centre

Grampians National Park

There are many, many reasons to go to this remarkable 1680-square-kilometre national park: its spectacular spring wildflowers, its dramatic cliffs and sandstone features, its bushwalking, the stunning views from its lookouts, and its Aboriginal cultural centre.

There are numerous guided activities including walking, abseiling and mountain-bike riding. The area is well known internationally for its superb rock climbing, and the best way to start that potentially dangerous activity is with a guide. The eco-accredited Grampians Personalised Tours and Adventures is one of many happy to help you.

Picnic spots abound, such as the kangaroo-friendly Zumstein, but for the able-bodied the best choice is to strap on a day pack and head out on any of the walks that lead up the mountains and enjoy the stunning views.

One of the most convenient ways to enjoy a walking holiday in the Grampians is using the services of the eco-accredited Auswalk Walking Holidays. On one of their Inn-to-Inn walks, they will book your accommodation and look after your baggage each day as you spend three days walking between B&Bs, carrying nothing but your day pack. You cover 14–22 kilometres each day, which is not too far, but enough to deserve an extra drink or two in the evening.

PV: 13 1963; www.parkweb.vic.gov.au

Park visitor centre: (03) 5361 4000

Grampians Personalised Tours and Adventures: (03) 5356 4654 or 0429 954 686; www.grampianstours.com

Auswalk: (03) 5356 4971; www.auswalk.com.au

Hattah–Kulkyne National Park

This 48 000-hectare national park with its network of creeks and lakes linked to the Murray is a refuge for many bird species, including some of the more spectacular Australian parrots, such as Major Mitchell cockatoos, and regent, bluebonnet, mulga and mallee ringneck parrots. You might also spy mallee fowl, emus, and red and western grey kangaroos. Camping facilities are basic, and access to some areas can be difficult, but the main Lake Hattah campsite is accessible by 2WD. The 6.5-kilometre walk, cycle or driving loop, Hattah Lakes Nature Discovery, is a great introduction to the area, or you can do a six-hour driving and walking tour with Wild Side Outdoors, an operator based in Red Cliffs.

(03) 5024 3721; www.wildsideoutdoors.com.au

PV: 13 1963; www.parkweb.vic.gov.au

Indigenous tours

Brambuk, the Grampians National Park and Cultural Centre, houses an Aboriginal cultural centre explaining much of the history and stories associated with the area. There is also a bushfoods cafe, where you can try emu, kangaroo and native vegetarian dishes. During the holidays there are activities such as boomerang throwing and painting, bushfood walks and didgeridoo performances, but all year, Monday to Friday, there are guided tours to Aboriginal rock-art sites.

(03) 5361 4000; www.brambuk.com.au

Aerial view over the Pink Lakes in Murray–Sunset National Park

Little Desert National Park

This park contains one-fifth of all flowering plant species in Victoria. The elusive mallee fowl and rare scrub robin live amid the 600 kilometres of tracks that go out to remote sections of the park near the South Australia border. There are three basic camping sites, but access can be difficult in a 2WD. Birdwatching, bushwalking and 4WD tours are all available.

PV: 13 1963; www.parkweb.vic.gov.au

Mount Arapiles–Tooan State Park

The mecca of Australian rock climbing, this lump of sandstone that towers over the surrounding Wimmera Plain has more than 2500 recorded climbs, from beginner-level meanders to some of the hardest routes in the world. There is some bushwalking as well, including a track to the summit, and basic campsites (usually full of climbers), but the main way to come to grips with this park is attached to a rope a long way off the ground. Arapiles Climbing Guides and others listed on the Parks Victoria website will help you get started.

Arapiles Climbing Guides: (03) 5384 0376; http://users.netconnect.com.au/~climbacg

PV: 13 1963; www.parkweb.vic.gov.au

Murray–Sunset National Park

A relatively untouched semi-arid wilderness of mallee scrub, this is one of the few areas in Victoria where red kangaroos are found. Birdwatchers come to search for the elusive mallee fowl and the rare black-eared miner. The majority of the terrain is accessible by 4WD only. One of the special highlights is the unusual Pink Lakes, in the south-east of the park. Most colourful on late-summer early mornings or late afternoons, they are coloured by carotene, secreted by alga on the lake. The camping site on the southern shore of Lake Crosbie, the largest of the four lakes, has toilets, gas barbecues, picnic tables and fireplaces, but you will need to be self-sufficient with drinking water. You can also stay at a hostel-style Shearer's Hut in the west of the park, with cooking facilities, bunks and a hot shower.

PV: 13 1963 (includes Shearer's Hut bookings); www.parkweb.vic.gov.au

Wine-tasting

Robinvale Wines, near Robinvale, produces a wide variety of wines, certified organic and biodynamic, with no chemicals used.

(03) 5026 3955; www.organicwines.com.au

South Australia

South Australia is a state full of surprises. It is proving to be quite progressive and diverse when it comes to ecotourism, with everything from free bikes offered to tourists in some cities and towns, through to swimming with dolphins and sea-lions. Kangaroo Island is an ecotourism hotspot, attracting vast numbers of national and international visitors each year to view its abundant wildlife.

Many South Australian producers, such as vineyard owners, are setting benchmarks for sustainable practices throughout the country and overseas. Inland, 4WD tours and tracks are rapidly increasing in number, and there are countless bushwalking trails that traverse the dramatic, ancient landscape.

WESTERN SOUTH AUSTRALIA is a vast region with amazing natural landscapes such as Lake Eyre, the Nullarbor and Great Australian Bight. Ecotourism here is varied and widespread.

EASTERN SOUTH AUSTRALIA includes the wider Adelaide Hills, the Barossa and McLaren Vale, the Fleurieu Peninsula, Kangaroo Island, the Coorong, far south-east and the area around the Murray, the Flinders Ranges and beyond to Innamincka in the north-east corner of the state.

South Australian Visitor & Travel Centre: 18 King William St, Adelaide; (08) 8303 2220 or 1300 655 276; www.southaustralia.com

Department of Environment and Heritage (DEH): (08) 8204 1910; www.environment.sa.gov.au

TOP TEN

1 Dive or snorkel with thousands of breeding cuttlefish off Whyalla

2 Camp near Cullyamurra Waterhole in the remote Innamincka Regional Reserve

3 Munch on an organic, carbon-neutral pizza beside the Torrens River

4 See rare species of the arid zone at Arid Recovery Reserve, near Roxby Downs

5 Cycle some of the 900 kilometres of the Mawson Trail, which runs from the eastern outskirts of Adelaide to Blinman in the northern reaches of the Flinders Ranges.

6 Soak away your troubles in Dalhousie Mound Springs in Witjira National Park

7 Stay in completely self-sustainable accommodation on wildlife-rich Kangaroo Island

8 Join an Aboriginal tour of the Coorong to appreciate the environmental dilemmas of this endangered habitat for birds

9 Hike the Yurrebilla Trail, sampling wines and staying in B&Bs

10 Visit Banrock Station or one of the other wineries showcasing sustainable practices

GREEN TRAVEL TIP If the green operator you contact cannot fit you in at the time you wish to travel, ask them if they can recommend any other green operators in the vicinity – they are likely to know of new operators or others in the area with similar environmental credentials.

Adelaide

Sitting picturesquely on the Torrens River, Adelaide has been building up a solid range of ecotourism activities and innovative ideas. It is one of Australia's solar cities, so the place has an encouraging focus on sustainable living, although more accommodation operators need to pick up on this theme. Whether it is picnicking up in the hills, cycling on the free bikes or hiking the Yurrebilla Trail, ecotourism activities here are fun and varied.

View of Adelaide and the River Torrens

WHERE TO STAY

Clarion Hotel Soho

Completed at the end of 2008, this five-star boutique hotel was designed with many hidden environmental features, such as water-recycling systems, sustainable building materials and airflow and passive cooling to reduce reliance on air-conditioning.

264 Flinders St, Adelaide; (08) 8412 5600; www.clarionhotelsoho.com.au

WHERE TO EAT

Goodlife

This innovative restaurant and takeaway not only makes carbon-neutral pizzas, but also places an emphasis on sourcing produce that is organic and local. Takeaway pizzas here even come tied up with string.

Goodlife: 44 Jetty Rd, Glenelg (08) 8223 2618 or (08) 8376 5900; North Adelaide (08) 8267 3431; 170 Hutt St, Adelaide (08) 8223 2618; www.goodlifepizza.com

ACTIVITIES

Aboriginal gallery

The Australian Aboriginal Cultures Gallery at the South Australian Museum holds the largest collection of Aboriginal artefacts in the world. Some 3000 are on display at any one time.

North Tce, Adelaide; (08) 8207 7500; www.samuseum.sa.gov.au

Adelaide Zoo

With its catchphrase 'We exist to save animals from extinction', this is another of Australia's excellent zoos. The sea-lion display and walk-through rainforest aviary are particularly recommended. Behind the scenes this establishment does a lot of conservation work.

Frome Rd, Adelaide; (08) 8267 3255; www.adelaidezoo.com.au

Belair National Park

South Australia's oldest national park has rich birdlife, a lake, walking and cycling tracks, free barbecues and an adventure playground. The best walk is the 6.5-kilometre Waterfall Hike.

DEH Belair: Upper Sturt Rd, Belair; (08) 8278 5477; www.environment.sa.gov.au

Cycling

A superb scheme allows you free use of bikes anywhere within Adelaide's city limits as long as you return them within the day. All you need is a driver's licence or passport. It is first come first served and you can pick up bikes from the Rundle Street Market on Sundays, Bicycle South Australia in Franklin Street or Adelaide Travellers Inn in Hutt Street. One of the best routes is the 33 kilometres of sealed track along the River Torrens, finishing at the coast. At Port Adelaide Visitor Centre you can also get free bikes, and cycle along the beautiful coastal path from Semaphore to North Haven.

Free bikes: (08) 8168 9999; www.southaustralia.com

Diving and snorkelling

Most of the best diving around Adelaide is boat-based. However, there is excellent snorkelling and some shore dives around Port Noarlunga, including the very popular Port Noarlunga Reef, and Onkaparinga Estuary Aquatic Reserve, which has an underwater trail on which you will see sponges and myriad fish species. Adventure Blue at Port Noarlunga will set you up and get you in the water. Divers Service in Welland is the longest-running dive shop in Australia and provides a friendly service. Another alternative is to combine a day out diving with sailing on a 16-metre, two-masted ketch with Blue Ice Charters.

Adventure Blue: 9 Saltfleet St, Port Noarlunga; (08) 8186 0066; www.adventureblue.com.au

Divers Service: 80 Grange Rd, Welland; (08) 8346 3422 or 0409 326 698; www.diversservice.com.au

Blue Ice Charters: 0412 631 586 or 0401 337 894; www.blueicecharters.com.au

*Adelaide Zoo: yellow-footed rock-wallaby (*Petrogale xanthopus*) and southern hairy-nosed wombat (*Lasiorhinus latifrons*)*

Lunch at Bridgewater Mill in the Adelaide Hills

Hiking

Experience the best of the Adelaide Hills on the 54-kilometre Yurrebilla Trail, which starts at Belair National Park and goes to Black Hill Conservation Park, taking in Cleland and Morialta conservation parks, great views, wineries and historic townships. You can walk it in three days, staying in B&Bs, or make a series of day walks. Ecotrek runs guided and supported two-night walking tours on the Yurrebilla, staying in quality accommodation and with a focus on local food and wine.

Another recommended hike is the Bridgewater Mill to Mount Lofty Summit section of the Heysen Trail. It is 10 kilometres each way, so makes for a solid day walk. A shorter option is the 3.5-kilometre-return walk to the summit from Waterfall Gully.

Around 40 kilometres north-east of Adelaide, the steep 2.2-kilometre-return Devils Nose walk in Para Wirra Recreation Park has great views.

Yurrebilla Trail: (08) 8204 1910; www.environment.sa.gov.au
Ecotrek: 1300 948 911; www.ecotrek.com.au
Heysen Trail: (08) 8204 1910; www.environment.sa.gov.au
DEH Para Wirra Office: (08) 8280 7048; www.environment.sa.gov.au

Kayaking

Kayak around a ship's graveyard, mangroves and prime dolphin habitat in the Adelaide Dolphin Sanctuary, leaving from the Garden Island boat ramp at Gillman. Adventure Kayaking runs fully guided and self-guided tours, with a 99 per cent chance of seeing the dolphins. To see dolphins from land, there are vantage points along the Port River Dolphin Trail.

Adventure Kayaking: (08) 8295 8812 or 0429 019 141; www.adventurekayak.com.au
Port River Dolphin Trail: www.portenf.sa.gov.au

Morialta Conservation Park

One of the most stunning parks in the region and located only 10 kilometres north-east of Adelaide, this has waterfalls and deep gorges, woodlands, koalas, echidnas and southern brown bandicoots. The pick of the walks is the 7-kilometre Three Falls Grand Hike, but there are shorter walks, free barbecues and a playground.

DEH Morialta: (08) 8336 0901; www.environment.sa.gov.au

Mountain-biking

Eagle Mountain, 12 kilometres south-east of the CBD, is well set up for mountain-bikers, with around 21 kilometres of cross-country tracks, a skills development park and a jumps area. You can hire mountain bikes for the day from Bicycle South Australia in Adelaide. For more fun off the bitumen, hop onto a section of the 900-kilometre Mawson Trail, Australia's premier off-road cycling trail. It takes in the Barossa and Clare valleys, the Adelaide Hills and the southern Flinders. You need about two weeks to do the whole thing, with accommodation options including country pubs and campsites, or just ride a section in a day, such as the trail through the picturesque Torrens Gorge and Chain of Ponds near Athelstone in Adelaide's north.

Bicycle SA: 111 Franklin St, Adelaide; (08) 8168 9999; www.bikesa.asn.au

Picnicking

Pretty Adelaide and its surrounds offer no shortage of great picnic spots. For a seaside outing, try the copious grass or sand along the Semaphore shoreline. There is also a 7.5-kilometre bike and pedestrian path. In the Adelaide Hills, the 97-hectare Mount Lofty Botanic Garden has several great walking trails, quiet spots and views. About 30 per cent of the garden is still native bushland.

Adventurous kids will love the award-winning adventure playground at St Kilda, 20 kilometres north of the CBD, with giant slides, flying foxes, climbing structures, a pirate ship and a maze of tunnels. There are coin-operated barbecues.

Mt Lofty Botanic Garden: Summit Rd or Piccadilly Rd, Crafers; (08) 8370 8370; www.environment.sa.gov.au

Platypus tour

Join a maximum of ten people on a sunset tour to a 10-hectare feral-proof private bush sanctuary that was once a market garden and introduced pine grove. Platypus Eco Tours at Cumbungi Sanctuary takes you around an underwater observatory and guarantees sightings of platypus, but you are also likely to see other local endangered animals, such as southern brown bandicoots, woylies, potoroos, quolls and koalas.

Lot 14 Williams Rd, Mylor (Adelaide Hills); (08) 8370 8628 or 0439 366 606; www.platypusecotours.com.au

St Kilda Mangrove Trail

Just 20 kilometres north of the CBD, a raised 2-kilometre boardwalk winds through the mangrove forest of the Barker Inlet Aquatic Reserve, where 200 species of bird have been recorded. The trail complex includes a lookout tower and interpretive centre.

Off Fooks Tce (adjacent St Kilda marina); (08) 8280 8172 or 0413 975 064; www.salisbury.sa.gov.au

Solar-powered bus

Hop aboard Tindo, the free green bus that claims to be the world's first community, solar-powered electric bus. It has no noisy engine, is recharged using solar panels, and travels a useful route around North Adelaide and the city centre.

Timetable and map: Council Customer Service Centre, 25 Pirie St, Adelaide (08) 8203 7203;
Rundle Mall Information Centre, Rundle Mall, Adelaide (08) 8203 7611; www.cityofadelaide.com.au
Tindo Solar Bus: www.adelaidecitycouncil.com

Swimming with dolphins

Since 2002, the eco-accredited Temptation Sailing has offered a 'swim with the dolphins sail' on a 17-metre catamaran out of Glenelg, in which the bottlenose and common dolphins reputedly come to the vessel – it does not have to go looking for them. The three-and-a-half-hour tour includes snorkels, masks, wetsuits and a 'shark shield' in the water that emits an electronic signal to keep great whites at bay, or you can pay less and stay dry on board.

Holdfast Shores Marina, Glenelg; 0412 811 838; www.dolphinboat.com.au

Cycling the Mawson Trail north of Adelaide

Looking for dolphins near Glenelg

Eastern South Australia

From the ancient wonders of Naracoorte Caves to the latest in environmentally friendly wine-making, this region is a delight for today's ecotourist. Kangaroo Island is popular for its abundant wildlife among international and Australian travellers alike, and many operators are committed to sustainable practices. Reach the summit of a rugged peak in the Flinders Ranges and the view opens up, over diverse landscapes of ancient volcanoes, flood plains and red ranges. Further out, in the far north-east of the state, there is a wealth of Indigenous and European heritage to discover. From the correct vantage point you can also spy ecotourism in this entire region opening up, with growing numbers of educational 4WD tours, Aboriginal involvement and marine experiences, adding to a solid base of bushwalking, birdwatching and boating activities.

Ancient hills of the Black Ridge in the northern Flinders Ranges

Adelaide Hills and Fleurieu Peninsula

WHERE TO STAY

Ridgetop Retreats

Three funky, architecturally designed cabins sit in quiet seclusion in Deep Creek Conservation Park at the tip of the Fleurieu Peninsula. They have solar hot water, composting toilets, two bedrooms, floor-to-ceiling windows, rainwater, and have been built from sustainable timbers.

(08) 8598 4169; www.southernoceanretreats.com.au

Saunders Gorge Sanctuary

This hilly, 1364-hectare, eco-accredited property some 55 kilometres east of Adelaide combines conservation and sheep grazing with habitat preservation, particularly of some rare grasslands. Some 8000 to 9000 trees are planted every year. Located near Mount Pleasant, there are great views over the riverlands on a few of the walks and 4WD routes. A restaurant and six self-contained B&Bs are on the property, including four semi-circular eco-cabins (with solar power, wind power and a fascinating natural air-conditioning system using a well). There are also some campsites.

(08) 8569 3032; www.saundersgorge.com.au

WHERE TO EAT

The Locavore

The Locavore ('local eater') at Stirling in the Adelaide Hills sticks to the '100-mile' philosophy of sourcing food, which in its case includes the Barossa, Adelaide Hills, McLaren Vale and the Clare Valley. The lusciously tempting menu includes salt and pepper squid, rabbit pie, and a chocolate, fig and apricot pudding.

(08) 8339 4416; www.thelocavore.com.au

The Organic Market and Cafe

This bustling cafe and organic produce outlet in Stirling was the national winner of the best organic retailer award. Something of an institution in the area, it has delicious antipasto platters and great coffee. About 90 per cent of ingredients used in the cafe are organically certified.

(08) 8339 7131; www.organicmarket.com.au

ACTIVITIES

Birdwatching

Abutting the Coorong, and with wetlands, beaches and a wide variety of terrain, the Fleurieu Peninsula is a top spot for birdwatching. There is a hide off Barrage Road at Goolwa, and the Goolwa Effluent Ponds can have blue-billed ducks, white-fronted chats and birds of prey. Nearby, Hindmarsh Island is known as a good spot for waders, and bush birds are abundant at Nangawooka Flora Reserve at Victor Harbor. Nearby Hindmarsh Falls – spectacular after heavy rain – is known for scrubwrens and bassian thrush.

Cycling

South of Adelaide, the sealed 34-kilometre Coast to Vines rail trail goes from Hallett Cove railway station to Willunga, taking in the magnificent cliffs of Hallett Cove, the natural beauty of the Onkaparinga River and the McLaren Vale wine district. Oxygen Cycles at McLaren Vale hires entry-level mountain bikes and is based close to the rail trail. Onya Bike Tours and Hire at The Carriage Cafe in McLaren Vale has bikes, tandems and rickshaws suitable for families.

The 30-kilometre Encounter Bikeway, going from Victor Harbor to Goolwa along some pretty stretches of coastline, is suitable for rollerbladers, cyclists and walkers. It links Port Elliot and Middleton. You can hire bikes from Victor Harbor Cycle. Cycling Tours Australia caters for three-to-five-day, self-guided cycling tours on the Fleurieu Peninsula, staying in four-star hotels and B&Bs. The company provides roadside assistance and luggage transfers each day.

Coast to Vines rail trail: (03) 9306 4846; www.railtrails.org.au

Oxygen Cycles at McLaren Vale: (08) 8323 7345; www.oxygencycles.com

Onya Bike Tours and Hire: (08) 8323 7689

Victor Harbor Cycle: (08) 8552 1417

Cycling Tours Australia: 0411 256 908; www.cyclingtoursaustralia.com.au

Deep Creek Conservation Park

This 4500-hectare park at the southern end of the Fleurieu Peninsula is renowned as one of the most attractive wild spots in the area, with spectacular views, waterfalls, secluded bush camping and abundant wildlife, particularly

Cabins at Ridgetop Retreats

Semi-circular eco-cabin at Saunders Gorge Sanctuary

Hiking in Deep Creek Conservation Park

around Tent Hill. Take the 3.5-kilometre-return Waterfall Track, the Deep Creek Cove Hike, the 5-kilometre Spring Wildflower Walk or one of the others on the extensive track network. Stringybark Campground has hot showers, flush toilets and rainwater tanks, and Trig, Tapanappa and Cobbler Hill campgrounds have toilets and rainwater tanks.

Deep Creek CP: (08) 8598 0263;
www.environment.sa.gov.au

Diving and snorkelling

Some of the state's best diving – particularly in-shore and around jetties – is on the Fleurieu Peninsula, with leafy sea dragons, shipwrecks, dolphins and myriad fish species. Second Valley is great for snorkelling and diving, with schools of fish off the rocks; Rosetta Harbor in Encounter Bay near Victor Harbor has great snorkelling, including weedy sea dragons, and the Bluff jetty is also recommended. Rapid Bay jetty is very popular with divers and is one of the best locations for leafy sea dragons. The Bluffs at Victor Harbor is good for novice divers and reaches depths of up to 12 metres. You can hire gear from the Courthouse Cafe and Dive in Normanville (bookings are recommended).

Courthouse Cafe and Dive: (08) 8558 3532

Granite Island Nature Park

This great natural treasure near Victor Harbor is best known for its 700 little penguins. Every night there is a tour of the colony just after dusk. A pleasant 45-minute, 3-kilometre-loop walk leads around the island, with several lookouts and spectacular views. To reach the island you need to walk 1 kilometre along a causeway, or take a horse-drawn tram.

Nature park: (08) 8552 7555;
www.graniteisland.com.au

Walking across the causeway to Granite Island

Kayaking

For those after an adventurous day out, join Adventure Kayaking on a tour from Rapid Bay on the lower Fleurieu Peninsula. You will paddle on open water, past towering cliffs, into sea caves and onto remote beaches, with the opportunity to observe a colony of sea-lions. Another company, Surf and Sun, offers a three-hour kayak tour from Victor Harbor to uninhabited Wright Island, where you can swim and snorkel in rockpools. The paddle finishes with a circumnavigation of the island and paddling under the Victor Harbor Bluff cliffs. The company also offers surfing lessons at Middleton and Robe.

Adventure Kayaking: (08) 8295 8812 or 0429 019 141;
www.adventurekayak.com.au
Surf and Sun: 1800 786 386 or 0400 881 565;
www.surfandsun.com.au

Mount Barker Summit Reserve

With a couple of short walks, panoramic views, birdlife and plants such as the Mount Lofty grass tree and the rock correa, this is a top spot for a picnic or short visit if you are in the area.

Onkaparinga River National Park

The main feature of this national park is the magnificent gorge, with cliffs up to 50 metres high, but it also has remnant woodlands of pink gum, grey box, she-oak and native pine, and a beautiful wildflower display in spring. There is a range of short-to-medium-length walks, such as the 4-kilometre Sundews Ridge Loop, with an option to hike down into the gorge if you are feeling up to it. The 4.5-kilometre Wetlands Walk is known for its birdlife.

DEH Belair: (08) 8278 5477;
www.environment.sa.gov.au

Organic produce

Taste the sensational fresh, organically grown berries and nuts at Nirvana Organic Farm in Heathfield (south of Stirling in the Adelaide Hills), or go on a two-hour tour of the farm, learning about the sustainable methods used here. At B.-d Farm Paris Creek at Meadows (around 45 kilometres south-east of Adelaide), a new cafe is the best place to try out the farm's biodynamic yoghurts and quark.

Nirvana Organic Farm: (08) 8339 2519;
www.nirvanaorganicfarm.blogspot.com
B.-d Farm Paris Creek: (08) 8388 3339;
www.bdfarmpariscreek.com.au

Picnicking

There is no shortage of coastal picnic areas, but for something a bit different, head to

Discovering whaling history at Victor Harbor

Ingalalla Falls near Parawa in the centre of the lower Fleurieu (due west from Victor Harbor, with access via Range Road), particularly after rain or in the wetter winter months. In summer the falls can become little more than a trickle.

Swimming

There are plenty of great swimming beaches along the peninsula. Victor Harbor has a plethora to choose from – including Kent Reserve and Dump Beach – but there is also Horseshoe Bay at Port Elliot, and the pristine white sand and calm waters of Normanville Beach, which is patrolled at weekends in summer. Carrickalinga and Lady Bay, near Normanville, are recommended if you want more secluded options. Maslin Beach is a nudist beach.

Warrawong Wildlife Sanctuary

With a superb reputation for its conservation efforts and restoration of degraded farmland, this sanctuary near Stirling is sure to delight nature lovers, particularly the 90-minute guided nocturnal tour or the one-hour feeding tour for families at dusk.

(08) 8370 9197; www.warrawong.com

Whale-watching

Between May and October, southern right whales often cruise right next to the shore of the Fleurieu Peninsula. Popular viewing spots include Port Elliot, Goolwa, Middleton and Victor Harbor, but your best starting point is the South Australia Whale Centre in Victor Harbor. The centre advises on where the latest and best whale sightings have been, and has two floors of exhibits on whales and sharks, including a complete skull of a southern right whale.

(08) 8551 0750; www.sawhalecentre.com

Boardwalk across the wetlands at Warrawong Wildlife Sanctuary

Wildlife art

The Wildlife Gallery in Porter Street at Goolwa has an emphasis on wildlife art, including sculptures and the bird paintings of artist-in-residence Brenda Holden.

(08) 8555 1911; www.brendaholdenart.com.au

Wine-tasting

Sinclair's Gully is a small eco-accredited vineyard and cellar door near Morialta Conservation Park. The winery not only follows biodynamic principles, but also protects 8 hectares of endangered candlebark forest and has won Landcare awards for its conservation work. After trying the sparkling pinot noir or the wooded chardonnay, you can join a guided

Hahndorf Hill vineyard

wildflower walk, or engage in some wine-tasting around a campfire, with wallabies and bettongs jumping around.

Hahndorf Hill is a 5.4-hectare biodynamic winery, and offsets its carbon use by tree planting. Grapes are hand-picked and irrigated as little as possible. There is a lovely tasting area and cafe that is open on weekends.

On the main road from McLaren Vale to Willunga, stop at the Salopian Inn to try wines from Gemtree Estate, which has been farmed biodynamically since 2007. Part of the proceeds from every bottle in the Tadpole range goes to Greening Australia to enable the ongoing development of the Gemtree Wetlands in the vineyards. More than 20 000 native trees and shrubs have been planted so far.

Sinclair's Gully: (08) 8390 1995;
www.sinclairsgully.com
Hahndorf Hill: (08) 8388 7512;
www.hahndorfhillwinery.com.au
Salopian Inn: (08) 8323 8769; www.salopianinn.com.au
Gemtree Estate: (08) 8323 7428;
www.gemtreevineyards.com.au

Gawler to Innamincka

WHERE TO STAY

Arkaroola Wilderness Sanctuary

Located in the northern reaches of the Flinders Ranges, Arkaroola is a 610-square-kilometre private sanctuary that is one of the longest-running ecotourism ventures in the state. Accommodation varies from lodges and motel-style rooms to a caravan park, and organised trips range from astronomy and wildlife tours to the signature, four-hour, eco-certified Ridgetop tour in which you will discover 1.6 billion years of geological history.

(08) 8648 4848 or 1800 676 042;
www.arkaroola.com.au

Bendleby Ranges, near Orroroo

In the process of being organically certified at the end of 2008, this 15 000-hectare sheep farm north-west of Peterborough has a focus on sustainable farming and offers accommodation from shearer's quarters and a self-contained cottage, through to camping sites. There is plenty of scope for mountain-bike riding and bushwalking with two sets of ranges and beautiful gorges.

(08) 8658 9064; www.bendlebyranges.com

Horseshoe Rim, near Carrieton

This remote wilderness cabin, situated midway between Peterborough and Hawker, has solar power, a gas refrigerator, log fire, cooking equipment, rainwater and room for up to ten people. In August–September, guests are invited to watch shearing on the property.

(08) 8648 6438; www.thehorseshoe.com.au

*A flock of galahs (*Cacatua roseicapilla*), a common sight on outback stations*

Iga Warta, near Nepabunna

This entirely Aboriginal-owned cultural centre in the northern Flinders region has permanent safari tents, ten cabins and a campground, and offers half-day, full-day and overnight tours with the Adnyamathanha people. There are visits to art sites, ochre pits and women's sites, and the opportunity to learn about local bushfoods and culture.

(08) 8648 3737; www.igawarta.com

Quorn Caravan Park

Although it has a fair way to go, this caravan park seems serious about becoming more sustainable, and is a good place to keep an eye on and support. There is a range of cabins as well as camping sites.

(08) 8648 6206; www.quorncaravanpark.com.au

Artist Amy Fatt demonstrates dot painting at Iga Warta

Rawnsley Park Station

Eight modern strawbale eco-villas with grand views perch on this sheep station, on the southern slopes of Wilpena Pound. Tourism is now the main industry on the property, and the one- and two-bedroom eco-villas are the prime places to stay, although there are other options. One of the first tourism operators in the state to gain ecotourism accreditation, Rawnsley Park also recently put a covenant over 1000 hectares to protect Rawnsley Bluff. One of the villas' 'star' features is a large skylight over the bed, so you can lie in bed and look at the night sky.

(08) 8648 0030; www.rawnsleypark.com.au

Warraweena Conservation Park

An ex-sheep station in the northern Flinders Ranges, Warraweena's 355 square kilometres were bought by the non-profit Wetlands and Wildlife company in 1996. Accommodation includes huts, shearer's quarters and campsites.

(08) 8675 2770; www.warraweena.com

Willow Springs Station, near Wilpena Pound

Another working sheep station, Willow Springs on the edge of the national park is home to the legendary six-hour 4WD route Skytrek, passing through Bunkers Conservation Reserve and

The vast natural amphitheatre of Wilpena Pound

culminating at the 921-metre-high summit of Mount Carnarvon, the highest point of vehicle access in the Flinders Ranges. Self-contained accommodation includes an old School of the Air building, a 1950s homestead and a remote, solar-powered hut. There is also limited camping.

(08) 8648 0016; www.skytrekwillowsprings.com.au

ACTIVITIES

Bushwalking

The Flinders Ranges and surrounds are renowned as one of the best bushwalking destinations in the country. Whatever your previous bushwalking experience, there will be something appealing for you here. The steep 6.4-kilometre-return walk up Mount Ohlssen Bagge provides great views over Wilpena Pound, and the short Wilpena Solar Power Station walk will give you a look over one of Australia's largest solar-power stations. Bunyeroo Gorge is a peaceful 7.5-kilometre walk. In Mount Remarkable National Park, the 2-kilometre-loop walk through Alligator Gorge to The Narrows is spectacular, and experienced walkers love the 12-kilometre-return hike up Mount Remarkable, with views all the way to Spencer Gulf.

Wilpena Visitor Centre: (08) 8648 0048; www.environment.sa.gov.au

Mount Remarkable NP: (08) 8634 7068; www.environment.sa.gov.au

Cycling

In the Barossa, you can hire bikes from the visitor centre in Tanunda and take the paved 7-kilometre cycle path to Nuriootpa. For a guided, multi-day supported bike tour, sampling the best of the region's cuisine along the way, try Barossa Classic Cycling Tours. The company also offers longer off-road cycling tours through the Flinders Ranges, and an on-road tour following the course of the professional Tour Down Under.

Tanunda visitor centre: (08) 8563 0600

Barossa Classic Cycling Tours: 0427 000 957; www.bccycletours.com.au

Four-wheel-drive tours

The area around the Flinders Ranges has become something of a 4WD hotspot, with quite a number of properties opening up routes on their land to tourists. Local visitor centres can point you in the direction of some of the best self-drive 4WD routes.

Alternatively, there are plenty of 4WD tours to join: Derek's 4WD Tours Australia is eco-accredited and provides half- and full-day tours of the Flinders Ranges and surrounds, with a focus on the plants, animals and geology of the region; and Wallaby Tracks Adventure Tours offers one-, two- and three-day tours of the Flinders and Wilpena Pound.

4WD information: www.quornadventures.com
Derek's 4WD Tours Australia: 0417 475 770 or home (08) 8648 4057; www.dereks4wdtours.com
Wallaby Tracks Adventure Tours: (08) 8648 6655; www.wallabytracks.com

Heysen Trail

Some 1200 kilometres long, this renowned walking track stretches from Cape Jervis on the Fleurieu Peninsula all the way to Parachilna Gorge in the northern Flinders. It covers a vast range of scenery from coastal cliffs and sandy beaches to grazing pastures, pine forests, vineyards, bushland and the rugged peaks of the Flinders Ranges. The whole, superb track takes about six to eight weeks to walk. There are campsites, shelters and huts along the way, and the track passes near several towns if you want to stock up on supplies or rest in a comfy bed. There are also plenty of places to get on or off the track for shorter walks or day walks. The track is usually closed from 1 November to 30 April because of fire risk.

Several organisations run guided walks along parts of the track. Ecotrek runs catered five-night excursions along the northern sections, through the Flinders Ranges, and World Expeditions do a seven-day highlights package. The Friends of the Heysen Trail conduct twilight walks and treks along the whole trail, and have a wealth of information about current conditions. They may even be able to help find you a walking partner if you are on your own.

Ecotrek: 1300 948 911; www.ecotrek.com.au
World Expeditions: 1300 720 000; www.worldexpeditions.com
Friends of the Heysen Trail: (08) 8212 6299; www.heysentrail.asn.au
www.heysentrail.sa.gov.au

Indigenous tours

The Aboriginal-owned-and-operated Bookabee Tours runs two-to-seven-day outback 4WD tours in the northern Flinders and outback South Australia, visiting significant Aboriginal sites and offering an interpretation of the landscape through Aboriginal eyes, with plenty of creation stories. There are also short tours in and around Adelaide.

Bookabee Tours: (08) 8235 9954 or 0408 209 593 or 0434 161 421; www.bookabee.com.au

Setting out for a walk at Rawnsley Park Station

Haydyn Bromley of Bookabee Tours holds a western blue-tongued lizard (Tiliqua occipitalis)

Nildottie Gorge near Blinman, south of Vulkathunha–Gammon Ranges National Park

Innamincka and Coongie Lakes

With internationally significant wetlands, abundant wildlife, and a rich Indigenous and European heritage, this regional reserve and national park is one of the best outback areas to explore in the country, with a wide range of terrain nearby – big red sand dunes, gibber plains, spinifex and coolibah trees.

Do not miss beautiful Cullyamurra Waterhole in the reserve. Aboriginal stone engravings, middens, tool-making sites and stone arrangements are common along the Cooper and around Coongie Lakes. Cooper Creek is also indelibly etched into the national psyche as the final resting place of the ill-fated explorers Burke and Wills. There are plenty of top camping spots, but many areas are only accessible by 4WD.

DEH Innamincka: (08) 8675 9909;
www.environment.sa.gov.au

Organic produce

If you are nearby, stop at Taralee Orchards near Wirrabara (north-east of Port Pirie), for certified biodynamic dried fruit and fresh fruit in season. There are a couple of cottages here too if you want to stay the night.

(08) 8668 4343; www.taralee.com.au

Vulkathunha–Gammon Ranges

This rugged and spectacular national park wilderness next to Arkaroola Wilderness Sanctuary has deep gorges, freshwater springs and animals such as yellow-footed rock-wallabies and painted dragons. You can stay in old shearer's quarters or solar-powered huts, or camp out at designated sites.

DEH Balcanoona: (08) 8648 4829;
www.environment.sa.gov.au

Wine-tasting

Elderton Wines near Nuriootpa is a carbon-neutral winery. Its cellar door is partially solar-powered and the vineyard is using biodynamic methods of production. Yalumba in Angaston has three organic wines and an increasing environmental consciousness.

Elderton Wines: (08) 8568 7878;
www.eldertonwines.com.au
Yalumba: (08) 8561 3200; www.yalumba.com

The south-east

WHERE TO STAY

Coorong Wilderness Lodge

Opened early in 2009, the five beautiful cabins here on a limestone cliff on Aboriginal lands have 180-degree views over the Coorong, with pelicans, ducks and other birds flying past at window height. The cabins have solar hot water and recycled greywater, and a wind generator provides some of the power. The Ngarrindjeri custodians run informative tours by 4WD or canoe, covering bush tucker, history, traditional crafts and environmental issues. There is also an excellent restaurant, with hearty meals and wattleseed cappuccinos, a campground with powered sites and a bunkhouse.

(08) 8575 6001; www.coorongwildernesslodge.com

WHERE TO EAT

Mallyons on the Murray, near Morgan

Eighty per cent of the produce served in this solar-powered cafe, in a restored 1850s stone barn between Morgan and Taylorville, is organic, much of it from the owner's orchards on the Murray River. You can wander through the orchards and pick up fresh produce in season (open Thursday to Monday, 10am–4pm).

(08) 8543 2263

Banrock Station Wine and Wetland Centre

ACTIVITIES

Banrock Station, Kingston-On-Murray

A world leader in sustainable wine-making and tourism, Banrock Station Wine and Wetland Centre should be high on any ecotourist's South Australian wish list. Sample the inexpensive wines at the centre, which is 40 per cent solar-powered, built with renewable materials on a former sheep farm, and was designed to have a minimal environmental footprint. Head out on one of the walking trails (up to 8 kilometres long) through the wetlands, where there are four bird hides, information huts and myriad birds, including regent parrots. Banrock Station's extensive green credentials include donating over $5 million to environmental projects in Australia and overseas.

(08) 8583 0299; www.banrockstation.com

The black-winged stilt (Himantopus himantopus) inhabits the saltmarshes of the Coorong

Returning from a canoe trip at Coorong Wilderness Lodge

Birdwatching

See brolgas and other wetland birds south of Naracoorte at Bool Lagoon Game Reserve and the adjoining Hacks Lagoon Conservation Park, a Ramsar-listed site that is one of the largest freshwater lagoons in southern Australia. There are boardwalks over the wetlands, and basic camping, but no drinking water provided. The 1.4-kilometre Pat-Om Walk skirts the deepest water, and has some of the most prolific birdlife, and the Gunawar Walk heads across the water to Hacks Island.

In the far south-east of the state, spy reed-warblers and beautiful southern emu-wrens at Lake Frome Conservation Park. Walk 1.8 kilometres through tea-trees out to a bird hide on the water's edge. Not to be confused with Lake Frome Recreation Reserve in the Strzelecki Desert, way to the north, the conservation park is near Southend. Nearby Lake McIntyre at Millicent has bird hides, walking tracks and barbecues.

Up on the Murray, the 4-kilometre Border Cliffs Customs House Wetland Walk in Chowilla Game Reserve, 30 kilometres north-east of Renmark, goes through riparian and wetland zones to a lagoon with large numbers of waterbirds, including white-faced herons. Cadell, east of Morgan, also has a trail through the wetlands and bird hides by the Murray.

DEH Naracoorte: (08) 8762 3412 (Bool and Hacks lagoons); www.environment.sa.gov.au

DEH Berri: (08) 8595 2111; www.environment.sa.gov.au

Bushwalking

Take the 3.6-kilometre-circuit walk of Blue Lake at Mount Gambier, which offers commanding views of the surrounding area along the ridge left by a volcano. As it changes temperature, the lake changes colour from turquoise (November–March) to steel grey in winter. Short walking tours down into the lake bowl leave from the reception centre every hour, in which you will learn about Aboriginal legends of the area, the volcanic history and the local environment. There is no need to book.

Mount Gambier visitor centre: (08) 8724 9750 or 1800 087 187

Canoeing

Getting out on the Coorong's waters, or on the Murray River itself, is one of the best ways to understand and appreciate the ongoing water issues and environmental dilemmas in this watery wonderland. Ecotrek runs two-night, canoe–camping tours on the Coorong and the Murray, and Coorong Wilderness Lodge runs canoe tours on the Coorong when there is enough water. Canoe South Australia has a complete list of canoe-hire places, canoe guides and recommended paddles around the state.

Ecotrek: 1300 948 911; www.ecotrek.com.au

Coorong Wilderness Lodge: (08) 8575 6001; www.coorongwildernesslodge.com

Canoe South Australia: (08) 8240 3294; www.canoesa.asn.au

Camping at Godfreys Landing near the Murray mouth in Coorong National Park

Naracoorte Caves National Park

Caving

Naracoorte Caves National Park has been declared a World Heritage area for its impressive fossil record that includes such spectacular creatures as diprotodon, the so-called giant wombat, and marsupial lions. The park is now home to creatures such as the threatened southern bent-winged bat, and in spring you can watch – via infra-red camera – these small bats raise their young in one of the 26 caves. Daily tours include a 30-minute wander through Alexandra Cave, and the Victoria Fossil Cave. There are also adventure caving options, and a three-hour, behind-the-scenes World Heritage Tour for those with a particular interest in the fossils.

For more underground wonders, check out the beautiful features in Tantanoola Caves Conservation Park. Wheelchair and pram accessible, the pretty cave is seen on a self-guided tour, after a short introductory talk.

In Mount Gambier, you can take a short cave tour under the city streets to a small pool that is the launching point for cave divers who explore the underground aquifer. You may even spy some cave divers suiting up.

Naracoorte Caves: (08) 8762 2340

Tantanoola Caves: (08) 8734 4153

www.environment.sa.gov.au

Mount Gambier cave tour: 1800 087 187

Coorong National Park

With 240 bird species and 145 kilometres of lagoons, Coorong National Park remains one of the best birdwatching sites in the country, despite its degradation in recent years. Some of the recommended spots are at Pelican Point, Parnka Point, Salt Creek, the Murray mouth and the Goolwa barrage. A large pair of binoculars has been installed on the 1.2-kilometre Jack Point Pelican Observatory Walk, overlooking bird-breeding colonies.

There are plenty of camping areas, including Parnka Point, 42 Mile Crossing, and the pink gum forest near Salt Creek. Most stops have some short walks, or you can tackle the Nukan Kungun hike, 27 kilometres each way from Salt Creek to the beach at 42 Mile Crossing.

However, to really see this park, you will need to get out on the water. Spirit of the Coorong Cruises runs a four-and-a-half-hour and a six-hour cruise from its base at Goolwa, in a low-emission boat that was designed to produce only a small wake. The cruise stops for a guided walk and a visit to an Aboriginal site.

(08) 8575 1200; www.environment.sa.gov.au

Spirit of the Coorong Cruises: (08) 8555 2203 or 1800 442 203; www.coorongcruises.com.au

*Red-necked avocets (*Recurvirostra novaehollandiae*) breed in the wetlands of the south-east*

*Monarto Zoo provides habitat for mallee fowl (*Leipoa ocellata*)*

Gluepot Reserve

Birds Australia's publicly funded reserve preserves 51 300 hectares of the largest block of intact mallee left in Australia. It is home to nationally endangered birds such as black-eared miners, red-lored whistlers, regent and scarlet-chested parrots, as well as stunning other species such as orange chats. There are bird hides, bushwalks and a visitor centre. As it is a bit of a hike to get here (one and a half hours along a good dirt road north of Waikerie), you will probably want to stay a night or two, but you will need to be completely self-sufficient, bringing all your own water, camping gear, food and gas cooker. Jolly Goodfellows Birding runs guided tours.

(08) 8332 1204; www.riverland.net.au/gluepot
Jolly Goodfellows Birding: (08) 8583 5530 or 0407 609 160; www.birding.com.au

McCormick Centre for the Environment

This solar-powered and energy-efficient building in Renmark holds environmental displays, including a model of the Murray–Darling Basin showing land use, irrigation methods, and more. It is open Monday to Friday, 10am–4pm.

(08) 8586 4777; www.austlandscapetrust.org.au

Monarto Zoo

Located near Murray Bridge, this open-range zoo has mallee fowl and bilbies among the meerkats, bison and other animals.

(08) 8534 4100; www.zoossa.com.au/monarto-zoo

Murray River National Park

This 13 000-hectare park comprises three separate wetland areas. There is great camping along the river in the Katarapko section, and the easy 5-kilometre Ngak Indau Wetland Walk is recommended. It winds through giant river red gums and along a creek.

DEH Berri: (08) 8595 2111; www.environment.sa.gov.au

Picnicking

Mount Gambier has some extraordinary picnic spots around collapsed caves that are now beautiful sinkhole gardens. Try Cave Gardens or the stunning Umpherston Sinkhole, which has free barbecues and good facilities. Compare these sites with sinkholes just outside Mount Gambier that have been left in their natural state, such as Hells Hole and Caroline Sinkhole.

Snorkelling and diving

Renowned as one of the most unusual snorkelling and dive spots in Australia, Piccaninnie Ponds Conservation Park has crystal clear freshwater (visibility up to 40 metres) with amazing limestone features covered in green algae. There is a deep chasm and an underwater cave. You need a permit to snorkel or dive here and timeslots are allocated. The park is situated on Discovery Bay, 32 kilometres south of Mount Gambier. The nearby Ewens Ponds Conservation Park is more suited to snorkelling than diving, with spring-fed channels, pygmy perch and crayfish.

DEH Mount Gambier: (08) 8735 1177; www.environment.sa.gov.au

Kangaroo Island

WHERE TO STAY

Antechamber Bay Ecocabins

This low-key, out-of-the-way spot in the east of the island is next to a beautiful and isolated beach. There are two fairly basic self-contained and solar-powered cabins with room for up to eight people each, half a dozen camping spots, and a funky solar-powered amenities block complete with composting Natureloo toilets and semi-outdoor showers.

(08) 8553 1557; Kiecocabins.com.au

Camping

There is a host of great camping locations on Kangaroo Island, but one of the best out-of-the-way spots is Western River Cove in the island's north-west. It has minimal facilities but is cheap as chips, and the slippery red dirt of the access road makes it feel like a major adventure.

Cape Cassini Wilderness Retreat

This is one of the absolute-best examples of sustainable ecotourism in the country. Situated on the edge of 80-metre-high mudstone cliffs, the homely B&B is fully solar- and wind-powered, with a daily update of how much power has been generated, and how much is available, so that all guests are aware of the power they are using. There are superb fairy-wrens, beautiful firetails, western grey kangaroos, 4WD tours, nocturnal tours, and excellent meals with an emphasis on local produce. All wastewater is treated on site, going to the organic orchard, and the property preserves 360 hectares of prime coastal habitat.

(08) 8559 2215; www.capecassini.com.au

Eleanor River Homestead

This beautiful two-bedroom log cabin in the middle of the island is solar-powered, has rainwater and a sewage worm farm.

(08) 8559 5234; www.eleanorriverhomestead.com.au

Sea-lions, fur-seals, penguins, koalas, wallabies, echidnas, goannas, emus, kangaroos and myriad birdlife – it is not hard to see all of these in the wild in just one day on Kangaroo Island. Almost a large free-range zoo, the island is a hotspot for ecotourism, with plenty of great places to stay whatever your budget or tastes. The island is larger than many people think (4500 square kilometres!) so allow extra days to explore it properly. There is an airstrip, or you can take a 45-minute car ferry from Cape Jervis, near the southern tip of the Fleurieu Peninsula.

Car ferry: 13 1301; www.sealink.com.au

*Common wildlife species on Kangaroo Island are Rosenberg's goanna (*Varanus gouldii rosenbergi*) and the short-beaked echidna (*Tachyglossus aculeatus*)*

Southern Ocean Lodge perches on a clifftop on a remote stretch of coast

Flour Cask Bay Sanctuary

Stay in luxury eco-campervan tents or camp in secluded camping spots on 200 hectares of yacca (grasstrees), forest, grasslands, samphire and hyper-saline lakes. The land is managed by a private conservation trust that plants some 9000 trees a year. The tents have solar-powered lights and ensuites with a chemical toilet. There are 20 kilometres of walking and cycling tracks, and bikes and canoes for hire.

(08) 8553 7278; www.eco-sanctuaries.com

Lighthouse cottages

Stay in eco-accredited lighthouse keeper's cottages on wind-swept hills at opposite ends of the island: Cape Borda, Cape Willoughby and Cape du Couedic. There are also daily tours of the lightstations.

(08) 8559 7235; www.environment.sa.gov.au

Nautilus Lodge

This solar-powered, four-bedroom house is surrounded by Cape Gantheaume Conservation Park and is situated right on the beach. It can sleep up to 12 people.

(08) 8553 1140; juliehelyar@internode.on.net

Southern Ocean Lodge

Jaw-droppingly beautiful, this very high-end lodge and spa attracted considerable criticism during its construction for being environmentally unsuitable, but local opinion changed as the lodge took shape. With floor-to-ceiling windows providing spectacular views along the entire ocean side, the building has clever architectural features that make it more sustainable: recycled timbers, ethanol fires, super-efficient heat-pump technology for hot water, sewage worm farms, cross-flow louvre windows, and rainwater. In addition to that, the food and wine (which is all included) is South Australian and the property protects more than 100 hectares of quiet bushland that is about as far away on the island from the ferry arrival point at Penneshaw as you can get.

(08) 8559 7347; www.southernoceanlodge.com.au

ACTIVITIES

Caving

Kelly Hill Conservation Park holds one of the rarest types of limestone caves in the world – formed by collapse, rather than water. Take a 45-minute guided cave tour or put on some old clothes and go on the two-hour adventure tour.

(08) 8559 7231; www.environment.sa.gov.au

Cape Gantheaume Conservation Park

Go for a two-day, one-way trek from D'Estrees Bay to Bales Bay along an isolated stretch of coast with limestone cliffs, New Zealand fur-seals and wild coastal scenery. The conservation park also encircles Murray Lagoon, the island's largest lagoon and a major bird-breeding area. There are walking trails around the lagoon and some basic camping.

(08) 8553 8233; www.environment.sa.gov.au

Diving and snorkelling

The sheltered north coast of Kangaroo Island is favoured for water activities, and is home to some 270 temperate fish species – such as blue devils, boarfish and blue groper – along with seals, dolphins and gorgonian corals.

KI Diving Services at Cooinda Fishing Charters has scuba and snorkelling gear for hire, runs Discover Scuba experiences and recommends snorkelling along the outer breakwater wall at Penneshaw or in-shore-diving at Western River Cove. KI Diving Safaris guarantees that you will see a leafy sea dragon in two days of diving, and a high chance of seeing seals and dolphins in the water.

KI Diving Services: (08) 8553 1072; www.kidiving.com
KI Diving Safaris: 0427 102 387;
www.kidivingsafaris.com

Emu Ridge Eucalyptus

See a working eucalyptus distillery that produces about 3 per cent of Australia's supply, run by ex-sheep farmers. It looks a bit rough, but much of the place is made from recycled materials – for example, the old shearing shed is the plant nursery – and runs on solar and wind-generated power. The property has a 28-hectare plantation of Kangaroo Island narrow-leafed mallee, and the by-products from the oil-production process are recycled back into the plantation. There is a cafe and you might even see one of the orphaned or injured animals that the owners are looking after.

(08) 8553 8228; www.emuridge.com.au

Flinders Chase National Park

There is so much to do in this park, and so many people give it too little time. The most popular sights are the lichen-stained artist's treasure, Remarkable Rocks, and a playful colony of New Zealand fur-seals near Admirals Arch. But there is also great camping, plenty of other wildlife, an excellent information-filled visitor centre, and walks such as the 3-kilometre Snake Gully hike. For the really adventurous, there is the four-day trek from Cape du Couedic to Cape Borda lightstation.

(08) 8559 7235; www.environment.sa.gov.au

Kangaroo Island Marine Tours

This well-respected, eco-accredited outfit runs a variety of wildlife-focused tours out of Kingscote in a low-emission, rigid, inflatable vessel that takes up to 12 people. Swim with dolphins, see a New Zealand fur-seal colony, look at albatross and land on remote beaches accessible only by boat.

0418 816 515 or 0427 315 286; www.kimarinetours.com

Organic produce

Kangaroo Island produces some excellent food and wine, so make sure you indulge your tastebuds while there. Particularly recommended are the certified organic Ligurian

The boardwalk at Seal Bay Conservation Park

bee honey at the Island Beehive at Kingscote, which has a great range of honeys to try, and the chemical-free Island Pure sheep dairy at Cygnet River.

Island Beehive: (08) 8553 0080; www.island-beehive.com.au

Island Pure: (08) 8553 9110; http://goodfoodkangarooisland.com

Rustic Blue

This great little art gallery and cafe, 8 kilometres west of Vivonne Bay, has a strong nature focus in both the artwork on display, and its surrounds. The owners care for orphaned and injured wildlife and have dedicated the 160-hectare property to wildlife. Rainwater is collected and they serve organic and fair-trade coffee.

(08) 8559 7371 or (08) 8559 7370 or 0408 685 901

Seal Bay Conservation Park

One of the star attractions of Kangaroo Island, Seal Bay is known as one of the best places in the country to get up close to Australian sea-lions. Guided visits are very carefully controlled, with an emphasis on 'observation, not interaction', but you will get to stand on the beach within a few metres of some of the lumbering mammals, watching the male pups playfully fighting and the bull seals engaged in more serious confrontations. There is also an 800-metre boardwalk to an observation point over the beach.

(08) 8559 4207; www.environment.sa.gov.au

Stokes Bay Bush Garden

It will take you about an hour to wander through the 3 hectares of densely packed gardens here, with a very comprehensive, written guide that names nearly every plant, particularly identifying those native to South Australia and the island. If you have even the slightest interest in botany, it is well worth the small price of admission.

(08) 8559 2244; jcstan98@bigpond.net.au

Swimming

Kangaroo Island's many beaches and white sands are inviting but not all are safe so take extreme care when swimming. Those to the north of the island are usually the spots with the calmest waters. Do not miss Stokes Bay's hidden beach, reached by squeezing through a secret 'smuggler's tunnel'. Vivonne Bay is sublime (and has camping) and Browns Beach is sheltered and suitable for children. Island and Hog Bay beaches are also recommended.

*Australian sea-lions (*Neophoca cinerea*) at Seal Bay*

Wildlife tours

Kangaroo Island's wildlife is so abundant you really just have to walk, drive or cycle to see it, but for a better interpretation and understanding of the unique ecosystem, use one of the local guides. David Welford at Cape Cassini is eco-accredited and runs 4WD tours for couples and small groups. Australian Wildlife Walkabouts is run by an ecologist and committed environmentalist, and supports wildlife conservation and research. The company operates a variety of small-group day tours with a focus on wildlife and the environment. The eco-accredited Exceptional Kangaroo Island day tour takes in key wildlife experiences on the island, but also dips into some of the island's other treasures, such as the eucalypt distillery and food producers. The company has a reasonable environmental policy and has been rehabilitating a former sheep farm. It can also organise a whole holiday package on the island. Kangaroo Island Wilderness Tours runs small, one-to-four-day 4WD tours.

Hanson Bay Wildlife Sanctuary runs brilliant 90-minute nocturnal tours, in which you are likely to see koalas, possums, kangaroos and wallabies. You can also take self-guided tours here during the day, and choose from a variety of different accommodation options. Alkirna Tours runs two-and-a-half-to-three-hour nocturnal wildlife tours out of American River. You will see little penguins, tammar wallabies, possums, echidnas and maybe a few other animals, as well as doing a bit of star-gazing.

For 45-minute tours to see the little penguin colony at Penneshaw, go to the Penneshaw Penguin Centre at Lloyd Collins Reserve. Small groups and families can purchase tickets on the night, but groups of ten or more will need to book. The Kangaroo Island Marine Centre at Kingscote runs nightly tours of the penguin colony there. The tours include a guided aquarium tour and some astronomy if the night is clear.

Stokes Bay Bush Garden

David Welford: (08) 8559 2215; www.capecassini.com.au
Australian Wildlife Walkabouts: (08) 8553 5350 or 0400 035 300; www.australianwildlifewalkabouts.com.au
Exceptional Kangaroo Island: (08) 8553 9119; www.exceptionalkangarooisland.com
Kangaroo Island Wilderness Tours: (08) 8559 5033; www.wildernesstours.com.au
Hanson Bay Wildlife Sanctuary: (08) 8559 7344; http://hansonbay.com.au
Alkirna Tours: (08) 8553 7464; www.alkirna.com.au
Penneshaw Penguin Centre: (08) 8553 1103; ppenguincentre@bigpond.com.au
Kangaroo Island Marine Centre: (08) 8553 3112; www.kimarinecentre.com.au

Western South Australia

Threaded through the wide open spaces of South Australia are ancient dreaming tracks, far-flung national parks and wild ecotourism experiences unique to the state. The Eyre Peninsula, in particular, has an array of ecotourism options stretching out towards the seemingly endless plains of the Nullarbor, where mobs of red kangaroos can be seen, and southern right whales congregate at the base of the dramatic Bunda Cliffs. In the arid lands of the far north is a spring-fed oasis (complete with date palms, a testament to early attempts at settlement).

Murphy's Haystacks near Streaky Bay on the Eyre Peninsula

Yorke and Eyre peninsulas

WHERE TO STAY

Baird Bay Ocean Eco Apartments

Located on the Eyre Peninsula's north-west coast, the two rammed-earth units here were architecturally designed and are suitable for families and large groups. They are right by the sea. All water is recycled.

(08) 8626 5017; www.bairdbay.com

Shboo Shelly Beach Lodge

Completely wind- and solar-powered, with rainwater and greywater recycling, this beautiful and relatively new three-bedroom apartment at Mount Dutton Bay near Coffin Bay National Park (on the south-east coast of the Eyre Peninsula) has stunning waterfront views. It is fully self-catering or meals can be provided.

(08) 8685 4192; www.shboo.com.au

Tanonga Eco Lodges, Charlton Gully

On the southern reaches of the Eyre Peninsula, midway between Louth Bay and Wanilla, lies Charlton Gully. Set on 200 hectares of native bush, with walking tracks to explore, the two architecturally designed eco lodges here are solar-powered, and have limestone interiors providing natural insulation. The owners have regenerated part of the property, planting more than 25 000 native trees, grasses and sedges.

(08) 8684 5066 or 0427 812 013; www.tanonga.com.au

Wide-sweeping views from an eco lodge at Tanonga

ACTIVITIES

Australian Arid Lands Botanic Garden

Located at Port Augusta West (at the head of Spencer Gulf) and spread over 200 hectares, this centre showcases the Australian arid landscapes and their vegetation. There are 12 kilometres of walking tracks, guided tours every morning, a cafe, and displays explaining the natural and economic value of the arid lands. There is also what is believed to be the largest collection of *Eremophila* species (commonly known as emubush) in the world.

(08) 8641 1049;
www.australian-aridlands-botanic-garden.org

Coffin Bay National Park

A park of contrasts, this Eyre Peninsula highlight has pounding surf, windswept cliffs and towering dunes on the southerly, ocean side, and protected quiet bays on the northern side. Great camping spots include Black Springs and Yangie Bay. A sealed road will take 2WDs as far as Yangie Bay.

(08) 8688 3111; www.environment.sa.gov.au

Diving

Port Lincoln Diving Services recommends a few in-shore dives around the south-east of the Eyre Peninsula, including Coles Point, with a reasonable chance of seeing crayfish and abalone, and the Tumby Bay jetty, with its population of leafy sea dragons.

Port Lincoln Diving Services: (08) 8682 1656

Diving with cuttlefish

Every year between May and September, thousands of Australian giant cuttlefish converge on the rocky coastline between Fitzgerald Bay and False Bay at Whyalla (on the Eyre Peninsula's north-east coast) to breed and lay their eggs. The cuttlefish can rapidly change colour and shape, and can weigh up to 5 kilograms and grow up to 60 centimetres long. In September the eggs hatch. The spectacle is

Visitor centre at Australian Arid Lands Botanic Garden

great for divers, but also ideal for snorkellers, as the cuttlefish gather in just 2 to 3 metres of water right on the coast. Whyalla Diving Services and Whyalla Diving Adventures are the two operators in town who will set you up with gear and provide advice about where to go.

www.whyallacuttlefish.com

Whyalla Diving Services: (08) 8645 8050

Whyalla Diving Adventures: (08) 8645 5693

Diving with sharks

Although controversial in some parts of the world, cage-diving with great white sharks in the Neptune Islands – home of Australia's largest seal colony – has a longstanding, very good reputation. Rodney Fox has set up a foundation to study and promote the conservation of these huge predators. Cage-diving trips leave from Port Lincoln, usually last several days and, surprisingly, you do not have to be a certified diver to get in the cage.

(08) 8363 1788; www.rodneyfox.com.au

Four-wheel-drive tours

Explore everywhere from the outback to the sea with Gawler Ranges Wilderness Safaris based near Wudinna in the north of the Eyre Peninsula. Each night you will return to luxury safari tents in a solar-powered camp, mainly built from recycled materials, on the edge of Gawler Ranges National Park.

Based in Port Lincoln, the eco-accredited Great Australian Bight Safaris offers tag-along and fully guided 4WD tours of the Eyre Peninsula, the Great Australian Bight, the Gawler Ranges and other areas. There are short half-day tours, sunset wildlife tours and multi-day adventures.

Gawler Ranges Wilderness Safaris: (08) 8680 2045 or 1800 243 343; www.gawlerrangessafaris.com

Great Australian Bight Safaris: (08) 8682 2750 or 1800 352 750; www.greatsafaris.com.au

*A giant cuttlefish (*Sepia apama*) in the waters off Whyalla*

Ecology cruise

Departing from Port Augusta, Augusta Westside Cruises operates a small vessel up past Redbank to the Salt Works Conservation Zone, with informative commentary on the ecology of the region, and you have about a 90 per cent chance of seeing bottlenose dolphins. The boat has solar power. This eco-accredited company also runs 4WD tours into the Flinders Ranges.

0438 857 001; www.augustawestside.com.au

Gawler Ranges National Park

This underrated 1200-square-kilometre park in the Eyre Peninsula's northern section has dramatic gorges and cliffs, volcanic hills, abundant wildlife and wildflowers. It is one of the best spots to see southern hairy-nosed wombats, yellow-footed rock-wallabies and beautiful Major Mitchell cockatoos and scarlet-breasted parrots. Most tracks are unsuitable for 2WD vehicles. Recommended bush camping sites (minimum facilities) include Yandinga, Kolay Hut and Mattera, but you will need to take your own water.

(08) 8688 3111; www.environment.sa.gov.au

*Emus (*Dromaius novaehollandiae*) on the beach at Innes National Park*

Inland aquaculture

Stuart High School Murray Cod Enterprises offers tours of an aquaculture farm in which you will see growth stages of the Murray cod. You will learn how the farm minimises dependence on mains water and how wastewater is recycled to grow native plants and vegetables. Contact the Whyalla Visitor Centre for bookings.

Whyalla Visitor Centre: (08) 8645 7900

Innes National Park

On the tip of the Yorke Peninsula, Innes National Park is known for its abundant wildlife, including emus, western grey kangaroos and western whipbirds. It receives the full impact of the wind-whipped Southern Ocean, so offers some wild walking along rocky headlands, cliffs, coastal dunes and beaches. The 2-kilometre Stenhouse Bay Lookout Walk will enable you to capture this experience. For a full day's look at the park through the eyes and dreaming stories of the Adjahdura people, join an award-winning Aboriginal Cultural Tour. There are plenty of camping sites in the park.

(08) 8854 3200; www.environment.sa.gov.au

Aboriginal Cultural Tour: 0429 367 121; www.adjahdura.com.au

Lincoln National Park

One of the best-kept secrets out this way is the stunning Memory Cove, a beautiful secluded cove surrounded by mallee. You need a 4WD and a permit and key from the Port Lincoln Visitor Centre. The rest of the 31 531-hectare park, on the south-eastern end of the Eyre Peninsula, is more accessible and has limestone cliffs, sand dunes and spectacular wildflowers.

Looking at shell fragments from an Aboriginal midden in Innes National Park

There are quite a number of camping sites available, or up to six people can stay in an old lighthouse keeper's cottage, with stunning views over Spalding Cove. Do not miss the short hike to Stamford Hill lookout, with views over Boston Bay and Port Lincoln.

Port Lincoln Visitor Centre: (08) 8683 3544 or 1300 788 378; www.visitportlincoln.net
DEH Port Lincoln: (08) 8688 3111; www.environment.sa.gov.au

Mangrove walk

The most southerly mangroves in Australia can be explored at Berryman Crescent in Tumby Bay on the east coast of the Eyre Peninsula, with an excellent boardwalk with interpretive signs.

(08) 8688 2584; www.tumbybay.com

Picnicking

The development of 10 hectares of wetlands at Whyalla has opened up a pleasant picnic and barbecue area, with short walks around the lakes and birdlife such as reed warblers and herons. Ten kilometres north of town, Whyalla Conservation Park has a much drier terrain, with red and grey kangaroos and occasionally euros around the saltbush and western myall. A 30-minute walking trail traverses the park.

Five kilometres out of Port Lincoln visit Winters Hill Lookout, which has barbecues, a playground and bushwalks in the vicinity. In town, anywhere along the foreshore is also good, with free electric barbecues near the yacht club.

For something a bit different, have a picnic near the beautiful pink granite outcrops known as Murphys Haystacks, near Streaky Bay (on the north-west coast of the Eyre Peninsula). There are picnic facilities, but the area is fairly unprotected and can be bitterly cold on a winter's day.

Murphys Haystacks: www.murphys-haystacks.com

Wadlata Outback Centre

Sea-lion viewing

On the Eyre Peninsula, across Baird Bay from the township of the same name, on the Calca Peninsula, is Point Labatt Conservation Park, with a mainland breeding colony of Australian sea-lions. There is a viewing platform, interpretive signs and once every 17 months or so you will see new pups.

Swimming with seals

Baird Bay Ocean Eco Experience takes small groups out on a 6.5-metre boat to swim with Australian sea-lions and dolphins from September to May. Masks, snorkels and wetsuits are supplied. The animals are not fed, and may or may not choose to interact with swimmers. Sunscreen cannot be worn prior to swimming with the animals, so wear a T-shirt or long-sleeved shirt and a hat.

(08) 8626 5017; www.bairdbay.com

Wadlata Outback Centre

Much more than a regional information centre, this brilliant centre at Port Augusta includes a 1300-square-metre interactive outback museum, in which you can see 22 films and 30 exhibits showcasing the area's geological, Aboriginal, European and environmental history. It will take a couple of hours to digest the information.

(08) 8642 4511; www.wadlata.sa.gov.au

Whyalla Eco Renovation Info Centre

Although not on the main tourist list, this centre could be great for those interested in sustainable living. It shows typical two- and three-bedroom homes and gardens that have been renovated using ecological principles. There are some interactive displays and occasionally seasonal fresh produce is available for sale from the garden. The centre is open Monday to Thursday, 10am–1pm.

(08) 8645 5999; www.advancingwhyalla.org.au

Nullarbor and outback deserts

ACTIVITIES

Arid Recovery Reserve

Initially a public relations exercise for BHP Billiton's massive Olympic Dam mine, the Arid Recovery Reserve at Roxby Downs is now an excellent example of how industry, government and the community can work together to have a positive impact on the natural environment.

The 86 square kilometres here are now nearly completely free of feral pests, leading to the dramatic return of wildlife – both by natural 'rebounding', and by successful adaptation of re-introduced species. On a three-hour sunset tour, run by volunteers, you have a good chance of seeing burrowing

The wetlands at Purnie Bore

bettongs, bilbies, western barred bandicoots and some of the other rarely seen species of the arid lands. Bookings are essential through Roxby Downs visitor centre.

(08) 8671 2001; www.aridrecovery.org.au

Cross the Nullarbor

Many tour companies will transport you across the Nullarbor – either speedily or by taking a more leisurely approach. The eco-certified Nullarbor Traveller offers a ten-day, Adelaide-to-Perth tour, focusing on wildlife and Indigenous experiences, including a nocturnal spotlight tour, swimming with sea-lions and visiting national parks.

(08) 8687 0455 or 0428 870 455 or 1800 816 858; www.thetraveller.net.au

Nullarbor National Park

The legendary Nullarbor is only for well-prepared travellers, but offers expansive and remote wilderness. As well as horizons of bluebush and saltbush, there are southern hairy-nosed wombats, big red kangaroos, countless reptiles, and Aboriginal sites. Do not miss the six lookouts on the Bunda Cliffs, the magnificent 90-metre-high, 200-kilometre-long precipice that drops straight into the Southern Ocean. Fifteen minutes north of Nullarbor Roadhouse you can explore Murrawijinie Caves, the only easily accessible caves on the Nullarbor. They are called 'twilight' caves as they are not completely enclosed, and you can see ancient Aboriginal handprints.

(08) 8625 3144; www.environment.sa.gov.au

Witjira National Park

Although extremely remote (straddling the Northern Territory border and adjacent to the Simpson Desert), Witjira is a popular desert park. It is most famous for Dalhousie Mound Springs, where artesian waters have formed thermal pools and a lush environment.

In the east of the park is Purnie Bore, an exploratory well drilled in 1963 then used as a water source, which has created an artificial wetland. In 1987 the flow of water from the bore was reduced to help maintain the output at Dalhousie Springs. Purnie Bore wetland, still impressive in size, attracts more than 60 species of birds. A bird hide is on the western edge.

There are excellent camping facilities at the springs and elsewhere in the park. In good conditions, the park can be reached by 2WD. Access from Adelaide is via Oodnadatta.

DEH Port Augusta: (08) 8648 5300; www.environment.sa.gov.au

Whale-watching from the Head of Bight cliffs

Cooling off at Dalhousie Springs

Whale-watching

One of the best spots in Australia to see southern right whales is Yalata, at Head of Bight, the most northerly point of the Great Australian Bight. Here the Bunda Cliffs of the Nullarbor end, and there are boardwalks offering great views of the whales during the May–October season. There is a charge. Camping is available on the Yalata lands.

(08) 8625 6201; www.yalata.org

Tasmania

Tasmania is probably the state best set up for ecotourism. Almost anywhere you go seems inherently beautiful, with outstanding natural values, and more than a third of the state is protected by World Heritage areas and reserves. The wildlife often comes to you, whether it is possums and quolls moving around outside while you sit by a log fire in a cabin, or pademelons and Tassie devils scurrying out of the lights as you drive along the roads at dusk.

Combine the fresh, clean air and ancient mountain ranges with some 3000 kilometres of managed walking tracks and nearly 900 separate walks, and you have the makings for some innovative and exciting ecotourism opportunities. As the state is relatively small, it is tempting to zoom around everywhere, but travel times on winding roads here can blow out unexpectedly and, as always, you may be better to slow down and fully experience one region.

NORTHERN TASMANIA has a beautiful blend of highlands, lakes and coastline, with plenty of forested areas in between, and ecotourism ranging from penguin and platypus watching to solar-powered retreats.

BASS STRAIT ISLANDS might be slightly harder to access, but provide exceptional green holiday options in dramatic settings.

THE WILD SOUTH has vast, untouched areas that can only be accessed by multi-day hikers, kayakers and rafters. But there are also some more accessible ecotourism spots, particularly in the south-east.

Tasmanian Travel and Information Centre: 20 Davey St, Hobart; (03) 6230 8233; www.discovertasmania.com

Parks and Wildlife Service (PWS): 134 Macquarie St, Hobart; 1300 135 513; www.parks.tas.gov.au

TOP TEN

1 Raft the mighty Franklin River, an internationally renowned whitewater-rafting destination south-east of Queenstown

2 Encounter Bruny Island's wildlife – seals, quolls, penguins, forty-spotted pardalotes, myriad birds, and white Bennetts wallabies (*see* image above)

3 See a platypus in the wild at Latrobe on the north coast near Devonport

4 Soak in an outdoor bath at Huon Bush Retreats, and watch the wildlife watch you

5 Nibble on gourmet, organic sheep's cheese at Birchs Bay, south of Hobart

6 Dive amid the towering kelp forests of Fortescue Bay on the east coast of the Tasman Peninsula

7 Hike the Port Davey or South Coast tracks, some of the wildest walking routes in the country

8 Paddle a kayak across Great Oyster Bay to Freycinet National Park on Tasmania's sublime east coast

9 Climb to the summit of majestic Cradle Mountain and marvel at the magnificent glaciated landscape of this World Heritage wilderness area

10 Watch wild devils up close with Kings Run Wildlife Tours at Marrawah

GREEN TRAVEL TIP To reduce the amount of road kill, try to avoid driving on rural roads at dawn and dusk when the majority of animals are likely to be moving around. If you do see an animal on the road, do not swerve, but brake firmly in a straight line, sounding your horn.

Hobart

Most residents of Hobart are so relaxed and gentle in their approach to life that the island capital often does not feel like a city at all. In recent years, its waterfront on the River Derwent has become recognised as suitable for kayaking ecotours, and the looming presence of Mount Wellington is a constant reminder of the natural beauty on the doorstep of most Tasmanians. There are some great food and tour options around the city, but for environmentally sensitive accommodation, it may be best to stay out of town.

Hobart cityscape and the River Derwent

ACTIVITIES

Island Cycle Tours

This innovative company offers guided and self-guided cycling tours, ranging from three-hour jaunts in and around Hobart, to three-week expeditions on the west coast. There are trips to combine cycling and hiking, and private family-friendly cycling holidays with special activities for children along the way. The same company runs Under Down Under Tours (*see* below).

204 New Town Rd, New Town; (03) 6228 4255 or 1300 880 334; www.islandcycletours.com

Kayaking

Two operators will take you on a two-hour kayak tour from Hobart – mornings, afternoons or sunset – around the historic waterfront. No experience is necessary. Freycinet Adventures is based in Coles Bay on the east coast but bookings for their 'Hobart paddle' can be made online or by phone.

Blackaby's Sea Kayaks: 0418 124 072

Freycinet Adventures: PO Box 226, Coles Bay; (03) 6257 0500; www.freycinetadventures.com.au

Mount Wellington Walks

You can quite easily pick up a map and explore Hobart's wilderness playground on your own but, for initiates, the maze of tracks may be best travelled with a guide who will show you bushfoods and wildlife, teach you about the geology and history of the area, and provide great food along the way. Mount Wellington Walks runs a Greenfleet bus and offers a few different walks, including a gentle or a more adventurous half-day option. Do not miss the view from the 1270-metre summit, which sometimes has a covering of snow.

0439 551 197; www.mtwellingtonwalks.com.au

Salamanca Market

With so much excellent fresh produce in Tasmania, you should consider picking up some local organic fruits and vegetables and cooking up your own feast. Try the famous Salamanca Market (Saturday 8.30am–3pm) or City Organics in Criterion Street.

Historic waterfront at Sullivans Cove

Salamanca Market: Salamanca Place, Hobart; www.hobartcity.com.au

City Organics: 34 Criterion Street, Hobart; (03) 6231 1465; www.cityorganics.com.au

Under Down Under Tours

This eco-accredited Hobart-based tour company offers guided tours of one to nine days for low-budget travellers, with a focus on discovering Tasmania's fragile environment. You can choose from walking, cycling (the same company runs Island Cycle Tours, *see* above), kayaking or bus tours to all parts of Tasmania. Overnight accommodation is usually in hostels.

204 New Town Rd, New Town; (03) 6228 4255 or 1800 064 726; www.underdownunder.com.au

The Mount Wellington summit lookout

Walking to Cape Tourville lookout in Freycinet National Park with Island Cycle Tours

The wild south

Many Tasmanians have a saying, 'There's no such thing as bad weather, just bad clothing', and this is probably most applicable to nature-based tourism in the wild south, where conditions can change quickly and help is often a long way away. But do not let that daunt you! Although much of the wild region is best explored via multi-day trips on foot or in rafts, there are plenty of more relaxing ecotourism options for those less inclined to rough it for a week at a time – whether it is eating organic sheep's cheese while gazing out at Bruny Island, admiring the birdlife along the Huon River or staying in a secluded and romantic solar-powered cabin with its own outdoor bath.

Experiencing the rugged Tasman Peninsula coast with Tasman Island Cruises

NATURE WATCH An endangered plant in Tasmania's south-west, King's lomatia (*Lomatia tasmanica*) reproduces by cloning itself, hence all the 500 remaining plants have an identical genetic structure. One stand of this species has spread over 1.2 kilometres and is estimated to be at least 43 000 years old.

Forestier and Tasman peninsulas

ACTIVITIES

Diving

One of the most coveted Tasmanian diving experiences is through the towering kelp forests found along areas of the east coast. These plants can grow as much as a metre a day, reaching heights of nearly 50 metres in some conditions. The clear water of Fortescue Bay, on the east coast of the Tasman Peninsula, is one of the most accessible spots to dive the kelp forests, but there are other great dives around here too, including on shipwrecks and near seal colonies.

Eaglehawk Dive Centre: (03) 6250 3566;
www.eaglehawkdive.com.au

Tasman Island Cruises

In an extension of the widely loved ecotourism venture Bruny Island Charters, which has been operating for nearly a decade, the reputable company launched a similar three-hour cruise off the Tasman Peninsula, available all year-round. This trip takes in the highest sea cliffs in

*Weedy sea dragon (*Phyllopteryx taeniolatus*) swimming in kelp at Waterfall Bay, south of Eaglehawk Neck*

the Southern Hemisphere and guarantees seal sightings, and offers the chance to see dolphins, migrating whales, sea caves and abundant seabirds. The rigid inflatable boats zip around but the focus is on great information.

(03) 6250 2200; www.tasmancruises.com.au

Tasman National Park

While so many tourists visit Port Arthur, only a small number explore this dramatic national park, with its 200-metre sea cliffs and outstanding views. The three-to-five-day hike along the Tasman Coastal Trail comes highly recommended, but the main campground at Fortescue Bay can be booked out over the Christmas and Easter holidays.

PWS Seven Mile Beach: (03) 6214 8100; www.parks.tas.gov.au

Camp bookings: (03) 6250 2433

Tasmanian Devil Conservation Park

There are many 'wildlife parks' (read 'zoos') in Tasmania, most of which endeavour to help the wildlife in some way. Although it also has other exhibits, this park near Taranna on the west coast of the Tasman Peninsula has a particular focus on conserving Tasmanian devils and has been involved in the care then release into the wild of devils orphaned by the destructive facial tumour disease.

(03) 6250 3230; www.tasmaniandevilpark.com

South and south-west of Hobart

WHERE TO STAY

Huon Bush Retreats

When you make it up the steep dirt road to this well-thought-out eco retreat, co-owner–manager Paul Dimmick may well meet you with an orphaned pademelon or other animal in his arms. The owners are dedicated wildlife carers and conservationists (they bought the place to protect it from loggers) and have set up Huon Bush Retreats on a private 11-square-kilometre nature reserve among towering swamp gums, sassafras and dogwoods. There is a range of secluded solar-powered cabins with

Teepee accommodation at Huon Bush Retreats

Peppermint Ridge Retreat

Boardwalk at Hartz Mountains National Park

composting toilets, and two intimate, carpeted tepees, as well as a few campsites with some of the best amenities you will find anywhere. There are no TVs or hairdryers to destroy the peace, and each cabin (and the camping area) has its own, completely private outdoor bath, where you and your loved one can snuggle under the stars and watch the wildlife watch you. The retreats are in the Huon Valley, some 50 minutes drive south of Hobart.

(03) 6264 2233; www.huonbushretreats.com

Peppermint Ridge Retreat, Woodbridge

Even without the stunning views over the D'Entrecasteaux Channel from 6-metre-high windows, the pademelons that hop around, or the free-range eggs and organic vegetable garden that guests are allowed to raid in summer, the two-bedroom apartments here would be worthy of inclusion. Their funky design involves environmentally friendly straw-stubble walls, recycled corrugated iron, recycled and natural timbers and a non-smell composting toilet. Woodbridge is less than 40 kilometres south of Hobart.

(03) 6267 4192; www.peppermintridge.com.au

ACTIVITIES

Grandvewe cheese and wines

Grandvewe organic sheep's 'cheesery' and winery at Birchs Bay (just south of Woodbridge) uses no chemicals in the farming process. Treat your tastebuds to the range of beautiful cheeses, including curd, pecorino, blue and an exquisite lavender-infused cheese. Wines include a chardonnay and pinot noir. There is a stunning view from the cafe across lush green paddocks to the D'Entrecasteaux Channel and Bruny Island. During milking season you can also have the novelty of watching the sheep milked from 4.30pm each day.

(03) 62674099; www.grandvewe.com.au

Hartz Mountains National Park

If you want something less urbane than the Tahune AirWalk, then head up the potholed, winding gravel road to this national park that lies adjacent Southwest National Park (access via Geeveston). In Hartz Mountains the walking is on rough boardwalks, but this is surprisingly easy and the environment is wonderfully wild and alpine. Delightful Ladies Tarn, at

Stalactites and stalagmites at Hastings Caves

1000 metres above sea level, is just a half-hour power-walk away. Surrounded by gnarled King Billy pines, pandani and cushion plants, you walk through snow gums and swirling winds. Adventurous and experienced walkers can keep going on the steep and exposed track to Hartz Peak, although there is no guarantee of a view. Precipitous Waratah Lookout is just off the road further down the hill, and promises Tasmanian waratahs in early summer and other flowers at other times beside a waterfall that tumbles off the dolerite range.

PWS Huonville: (03) 6264 8460;
www.parks.tas.gov.au

Hastings Caves and Thermal Springs

Not only is Newdegate Cave the largest tourist cave in Australia, it is one of the few made of dolomite rather than limestone. Here, some 98 kilometres south of Hobart, you can take a 45-minute tour and a short bushwalk, and finish with a picnic and swim in the 1.2-metre-deep thermal pool (28°C year-round). There is also a paddling pool.

PWS Hastings Caves: (03) 6298 3209;
www.parks.tas.gov.au

Kayaking

On Bathurst Harbour on the wild south-west coast you can experience the soul of the Tasmanian Wilderness World Heritage Area with a seven- or three-day kayaking expedition with Roaring 40s Kayaking, which includes six to eight hours travel each day and a stay in a different campsite most evenings. 'Whilst you won't need to be an expert paddler to participate, this expedition will offer challenges even if you are', the company boasts. The company also offers shorter trips in the area and in other locations, and hires equipment from Kettering.

Roaring 40s Kayaking: (03) 6267 5000;
www.roaring40skayaking.com.au

Living History Museum of Aboriginal Cultural Heritage

Set in a former Methodist church that had strong ties with the Tasmanian Aboriginal community, this little museum near Cygnet showcases Indigenous history, artefacts, art and bush tucker. It is generally open on weekends in summer and spring.

(03) 6295 0004; info@setac.org.au

Snorkelling

Tinderbox Bay south of Kettering has a sheltered beach and Tasmania's only underwater snorkel trail, suitable for young and old, snorkelling novices and divers. The beach and foreshore are included within the Tinderbox Marine Reserve, which extends 1.4 kilometres north-east of Tinderbox Bay to Piersons Point. You are likely to see a vast range of different seaweeds and fish in the clear water and, if you are lucky, weedy sea dragons, seahorses, octopus and squid.

PWS: (03) 6233 6560; www.parks.tas.gov.au

Tahune AirWalk

Located 29 kilometres from Geeveston, this unashamed public relations exercise for Forestry Tasmania starts on the serpentine drive out to the AirWalk, where signs clearly state when an area was last logged. There are some delightful short walks and picnic spots along the way. At the site, the temptation is to head straight to the disabled-accessible, 1.6-kilometre AirWalk, rising to nearly 40 metres above the forest floor.

However, of the three walks on offer, the best is the short and flat Huon Pine Walk, where the grand old pines, clothed in a green lichen garb, are hundreds or thousands of years old. You will also be introduced to celery-top pines, native laurel, stringybark, dogwood, fish-bone ferns and tree ferns. The whole experience gives you a great appreciation of the trees that the foresters would love to chop down. In summer, this attraction is packed – it is the second biggest tourist attraction in Tasmania (after Port Arthur). You can camp for free at the site, where Tasmanian devils and other wildlife roam around at night, but there are no hot showers.

Tahune AirWalk towers above the forest floor, amid sassafras, celery-top pine and stringybarks

Forestry Tasmania: (03) 6297 0012; www.forestrytas.com.au

PWS Huonville: (03) 6264 8460; www.parks.tas.gov.au

Trekking in Southwest National Park

Tasmania's largest national park, this wild World Heritage area comprises more than 6000 square kilometres of wild rivers, jagged mountain ranges, buttongrass plains and thick

*Along the South Coast Track: Little Deadmans Bay (left) and pandani plants (*Richea pandanifolia*) in the Ironbound Range (right)*

forest. It is the home of two of the greatest long-distance treks in the country, the South Coast Track and the Port Davey Track. Both are incredibly isolated, will take about a week, and should only be undertaken by hardened bushwalkers. The two walks meet at Melaleuca, the main breeding ground of the extremely endangered orange-bellied parrot. Melaleuca is only accessible by plane or boat.

Several companies offer guided tours of these muddy tracks including Tasmanian Expeditions, but you need to carry all your gear. Other classic long-distance, strenuous treks in this national park include Federation Peak and the rugged Western Arthur Range.

Tasmanian Expeditions: (03) 6339 3999 or 1300 666 856; www.tas-ex.com

PWS: (03) 6288 1283 (entrance via Maydena); (03) 6264 8460 (entrance via Cockle Creek); www.parks.tas.gov.au

Tall eucalypt forest on Bruny Island

Bruny Island

Bruny is an amazing wildlife paradise. Even southern elephant seals and leopard seals occasionally haul out here, among the quolls, wallabies, birds and 1000 nesting little penguins. The island has a growing population of white Bennetts wallabies, and some of the possums are starting to turn white too. Do not miss the lush rainforest of the Mavista Nature Walk. There is also a hike up Mount Mangana, the highest mountain on the island, the long and remote Labillardiere Peninsula, and the mid-length Fluted Cape walk. But it is just as good to take an isolated stroll along any of the quiet beaches or bays.

WHERE TO STAY

Inala

Although a working cattle farm, this Land for Wildlife property is managed primarily for the copious wildlife on site, and 80 per cent of the 200 hectares has not been cleared. 'I haven't even been in a lot of it', says the owner, biologist Dr Tonia Cochran. 'I figure it's for whatever was here before I got here.' The property is tucked away on the Cloudy Bay

Cottage at Inala

Yellow banksia on Bruny Island

A Bruny Island Charters' boat negotiating a towering rock stack

Road, on south Bruny, and contains one of the largest remaining colonies of the endangered Tasmanian endemic species, the forty-spotted pardalote. There are two comfy cottages with all the mod cons, and Tonia is a brilliant tour guide with astounding natural history knowledge, who will take you on day, evening or multi-day, wildlife-watching experiences around Bruny or further afield. Vehicular ferries for the island depart from Kettering (pick-ups from Hobart are also available), and Inala is a 45-minute drive from the island's ferry terminal.

(03) 6293 1217 or 0418 124 934;
www.inalabruny.com.au

ACTIVITIES

Bruny Island Charters

This very popular eco-accredited tour company proudly uses 'the cleanest motors that money can buy' on its rigid inflatable boats. In a three-hour experience set against the towering cliffs and remote bays of South Bruny National Park, you are likely to see a haul-out for Australian fur-seals, a breeding colony of New Zealand fur-seals, sea-eagles, albatross, sea caves, towering sea stacks and penguins swimming past. While you cruise over kelp forests in crystal-clear water, the guides provide an interesting discourse on explorers, early settlers, whaling history and botany.

(03) 6293 1465; www.brunycharters.com.au

West of Hobart

WHERE TO STAY

Curringa Farm

Near Hamilton, about an hour's drive west of Hobart, this eco-accredited 300-hectare farm gives visitors a taste of sustainable farming practices on a mixed property with hundreds of sheep, opium poppies and other crops. Give a couple of day's notice and you can tour the farm, or have a one-hour tour seeing Landcare and tree-planting efforts, native plants and animals. The property has one of the longest-

Russell Falls in Mount Field National Park

running farmstay B&Bs in the state, located on the Lyell Highway.

(03) 6286 3333 or 0418 863 337;
www.curringafarm.com

ACTIVITIES

Mount Field National Park

This lush rainforest overflowing with tree ferns and waterfalls offers a variety of great short and medium-length walks. Although your gaze will constantly be drawn upwards to the towering forest canopy, keep an eye out for brilliantly coloured fungi, platypus and glow worms.

PWS Mount Field: (03) 6288 1149;
www.parks.tas.gov.au

Rafting

For many, rafting the Franklin is the ultimate eco-friendly adventure in Australia. This is the river that was saved from damming by a long and controversial conservation campaign, and the trip provides more than a week of independent travel through pristine areas that many have heard about, but few have seen. Guided trips are not as expensive as you might think, and the experience leaves many with a fresh commitment to conservation. Operators are very environmentally conscious in their approach, even carrying out solid human waste. There are five-, seven-, nine-, ten- and 11-day rafting options, ex-Hobart, the longer ones including an optional walk to Frenchmans Cap. Prospective rafters generally have to be over 16 years of age.

Water by Nature: 1800 111 142;
www.franklinrivertasmania.com
Rafting Tasmania: (03) 6239 1080;
www.raftingtasmania.com
Tasmanian Expeditions: (03) 6339 3999 or 1300 666 856; www.tas-ex.com

Something Wild

This is a huge 450-hectare wildlife sanctuary for orphaned and injured animals, about an hour's drive west of Hobart (2 kilometres east of Mount Field National Park). Visitors see a variety of animals, but the aim is to nurture the injured back to good health and release them into the sanctuary. On a three-hour night tour you can be shown platypus, wallabies, bandicoots, quolls, wombats and devils, and will help set up special remote cameras to take photographs of animals after you have gone. The images will then be emailed to you later.

(03) 6288 1013; www.somethingwild.com.au

Rafting the Franklin River

Near Strahan

ACTIVITIES

Beachcombing

Wander the wilds of Ocean Beach on the west coast, its shores battered by waves and winds, and strewn with kelp. This is western Tasmania at its finest.

Gordon River paddle

What a way to experience the mirror-like surface of the Gordon River – a kayak and cruise combination. Running only in the summer months, this trip starts on the morning cruise across Macquarie Harbour from Strahan, on the *Lady Jane Franklin II*. Then at Heritage Landing, the furthest point that cruise boats can reach, a small group of kayakers will get in the water for an incredible three-hour kayaking experience, plus a lunch at Eagle Creek. The kayakers are picked up on the evening cruise and returned to Strahan.

(03) 6471 4300 or 1800 084 620; www.puretasmania.com.au

Scenic view of the Gordon River and surrounds

West Coast Wilderness Railway

In a remarkable trip through 35 kilometres of wild Tasmanian forest, the West Coast Wilderness Railway offers a look into steep gorges and rivers between Strahan and Queenstown. A stop in dense rainforest at Dubbil Barril allows passengers to wander along forest paths and discover remote creeks running down to the King River. Travel is one way by rail then by coach back to your starting point.

1800 084 620; www.westcoastwildernessrailway.com.au

Cruising the Gordon River on the Lady Jane Franklin II

Northern Tasmania

Tasmania's north promises many intimate encounters with wildlife, from guaranteed sightings of wild platypus and penguins, through to white-bellied sea-eagles, tawny frogmouths, Tasmanian devils, Bennetts wallabies and forester kangaroos. The iconic terrain here ranges from peaceful Wineglass Bay in Freycinet National Park through to the jagged dolerite of Cradle Mountain. Not surprisingly, ecotourism is booming.

Paddling on Dove Lake in Cradle Mountain–Lake St Clair National Park

NATURE WATCH Two of the often-mentioned macropods (literally 'big feet') in Tasmania are subspecies that have different common names on the mainland. The forester kangaroo is a subspecies of the eastern grey kangaroo, and Bennetts wallaby is a subspecies of what is known as a red-necked wallaby on the mainland.

East coast

WHERE TO STAY

Mount Paul on Freycinet

This stunning 300-hectare Land for Wildlife property in the centre of the Freycinet Peninsula includes six endangered forest communities and the 282-metre summit of Mount Paul, and the owners have been told it has more density of wildlife than Freycinet National Park, with myriad creatures including wombats, quolls, Tasmanian devils, echidnas, Bennetts wallabies and tawny frogmouths. The beautifully designed, wheelchair-accessible and ecologically sound cabins have such great commanding views over Oyster Bay and the Hazards in the national park that it is hard to leave the celery-top pine deck. The steep but short walk up Mount Paul is worth the effort for its 270-degree views.

(03) 6257 0300 or 0408 504 414; www.mtpaul.com

Cabin at Mount Paul on Freycinet

Rainbow Retreat

The owners of this 30-hectare nature reserve at St Marys are wildlife carers who rehabilitate then release wildlife on the property, so there are plenty of their old friends wandering around, including wombats, pademelons and Bennetts wallabies. The cosy cabins are completely solar- and wind-powered, yet

Taking the four-day guided walk at the Bay of Fires

amazingly include low-voltage LCD TV. The owners also plant trees on the property to offset any carbon used, such as for fuel or gas. One of the owners is a pastry chef who will deliver meals to the cabin, including gourmet wood-baked pizzas, or you can use the kitchenette in the cabin. A great deck overlooks forest and the ocean at Falmouth and Scamander, and on a clear day there are views to Flinders Island in Bass Strait. Even though it is close to 600 metres above sea level, you can still hear the waves hitting the shore.

(03) 6372 2168; www.rainbowretreat.com.au

WHERE TO EAT

Purple Possum Wholefoods and Cafe

Purple Possum is in the great little town of St Marys, midway between St Helens and Bicheno. The cafe is wholly vegetarian, and you can take away a range of organic fruit and vegetables and locally grown supplies.

(03) 6372 2655; www.purplepossum.com.au

ACTIVITIES

Bay of Fires Walk

A deluxe four-day walk along the magnificent north-east coast at the edge of Mount William National Park, staying in solar-powered accommodation designed for sustainable living, is one of the newer ecotourism treats in Tasmania. You dine on fresh local produce, go snorkelling or swimming, and walk moderate distances, carrying a light load each day.

(03) 6391 9339; www.bayoffires.com.au

Diving and snorkelling

Although diving might not be your first thought when you head south to Tasmania, the temperate waters usually provide much greater visibility than tropical waters, and offer a surprisingly rich and diverse range of flora and fauna. For information on some of the best dive spots on offer, check out the internet (*see* below) or call in at one of the local dive shops. The pretty seaside town of Bicheno has several great snorkelling and in-shore dives, with huge sponge gardens, seahorses and weedy sea dragons. One of the best snorkelling sites is near the breakwater in Waubs Bay but try to keep an eye out for boats. The Bicheno Dive Centre will provide advice and hire gear. If you want to see the plentiful marine life without getting wet, take an inexpensive, 40-minute cruise in a glass-bottom boat. There is also some lovely

*An amphipod or beach hopper (*Talorchestia sp.*) in the waters off Bicheno*

Eco-friendly luxury for hikers doing the Bay of Fires Walk

swimming and surfing, at places such as Redbill and Waubs Bay beaches.

Dive trail information: www.tchange.com.au/recreation/divetrail.html

Bicheno Dive Centre: (03) 6375 1138; www.bichenodive.com.au

Boat tour: (03) 6375 1294 or 0407 812 217; www.bichenoaquarium.com.au

Douglas–Apsley National Park

The premier feature of this gorge-cut national park is a beautiful opal-coloured waterhole five minutes walk from the carpark. It is great for a dip on a hot day, but to preserve the water clarity you are asked to leave the sunscreen at home (it is suggested you swim with a shirt on instead). Take a three-hour walk up the gorge to see Oyster Bay pines and the largest remaining dry eucalypt forest in Tasmania. If you are desperate to stay here, there are some fairly ordinary campsites about five minutes walk from the car, within hearing of lowing cattle.

PWS Freycinet: (03) 6256 7000; www.parks.tas.gov.au

Freycinet Adventures

One of the best ways to experience the Freycinet environment is a morning paddle with Freycinet Adventures. You glide across Great Oyster Bay to a beautiful secluded beach, indulging in a scrumptious morning tea with real coffee while sea-eagles soar overhead and bait fish shimmer as they fly out of the water. The helpful guides will surprise you with information about whaling, granite quarrying and wildlife in the national park. The paddle is long enough to know you have done some exercise, but not too long – past clients have ranged in age from two to ninety-two. This award-winning company also conducts other activities in the national park such as multi-day trips that combine walking and kayaking, and

The famously beautiful Wineglass Bay

abseiling and rock climbing, and will hire out kayaks to experienced kayakers.

(03) 6257 0500; www.freycinetadventures.com.au

Freycinet National Park

By far the most popular walk in this spectacular coastal park is the uphill trudge past huge pink granite boulders to Wineglass Bay Lookout. It is a stunning view, but do not think you will get a chance to sit and contemplate how beautiful the scene is – a constant stream of visitors and chatter ensures there is no serenity. Few make the effort to walk down the other side to the beach, which beckons swimmers in summer, but the local tip is that even fewer walk up the steep and slightly scary Mount Amos, which delivers a much more dramatic – and peaceful – view down onto Wineglass Bay. Camping in this national park is very popular in summer and you have to book via a ballot system. The campsite at the far end of Wineglass Bay is recommended, but you will need to walk for a couple of hours to get there.

PWS Freycinet: (03) 6256 7000; www.parks.tas.gov.au

Freycinet Sea Cruises

This eco-accredited company runs luxury catamaran tours of a few hours duration into Freycinet National Park and around nearby Schouten Island, where you are likely to

The sculptured iron-stained Triassic sandstone of the Painted Cliffs on Maria Island

see Australian fur-seals, dolphins and other wildlife. On the Beach To Bush cruise and walk, you sail into beautiful Wineglass Bay before taking a guided walk in the national park.

(03) 6257 0355; www.freycinetseacruises.com

Maria Island National Park

This beautiful island, just a short ferry ride from near Triabunna, is a haven for wildlife both on land and offshore. Not-to-be-missed features include the beautifully patterned Painted Cliffs, and the sea creatures entombed in Fossil Cliffs. You can head out to the island for just a few hours, catching the afternoon ferry back, or stay at either the bunkhouse in the old penitentiary, or at one of the three campsites. There is great diving and snorkelling at the ferry pier and Painted Cliffs, mountain-biking, and of course walking. One of the most enjoyable ways to see the island is the four-day guided Maria Island Walk, where you carry just a few personal belongings and lunch, are treated to fine dining and wine, walk only moderate distances each day and stay in very comfortable fixed camps and a historic house. The guided walks are only held from October to April.

PWS Seven Mile Beach: (03) 6257 1420;
www.parks.tas.gov.au
Park ranger: (03) 6357 1420;
maria.island@parks.tas.gov.au
Guided walks: (03) 6234 2999;
www.mariaislandwalk.com.au

Mount William National Park

Mount William at the north-eastern tip of Tasmania is a park that entices visitors for a multitude of reasons. There are the dazzling white beaches, azure waters and granite headlands splashed with orange lichen; there is the abundant wildlife at dusk – countless forester kangaroos, wallabies and wombats; and then there is the surfing at Picnic Rocks, the walk to Mount William summit or the diving around Stumpys Bay. The campsites are basic.

PWS St Helens: (03) 6376 1550;
www.parks.tas.gov.au
Park ranger: (03) 6356 1173

Penguin tours

Every evening, inexpensive one-hour tours leave at dusk to go through the little penguin rookery near Bicheno.

(03) 6375 1333; www.bichenopenguintours.com.au

Near Launceston

ACTIVITIES

Forest Ecocentre, Scottsdale

The uniquely designed building is probably the key attraction here. Designed to use 20 per cent less energy than conventional structures, it has a building within a building, with a central funnel and large fan. Learn about

history, local animals and, being a Forestry Tasmania site, the local forestry industry.
(03) 6352 6466; www.forestrytas.com.au

Low Head Penguin Tours

Every night at dusk this comprehensive but inexpensive tour takes visitors to a little penguin-nesting site near the mouth of the Tamar River, where you can watch the penguins waddle ashore to return to their nests.
The tour includes commentary on penguin behaviour, maritime and colonial history of the area, and pickup can be arranged from your accommodation in Launceston.
0418 361 860; www.penguintours.lowhead.com

Mole Creek Karst National Park

There are 50 limestone caves in this national park, including some of the most visited caves in Tasmania. Two caves are open to the public, including one with an underground creek, and a dry cave with a relatively flat walk to some beautiful calcite formations.
PWS Launceston: (03) 6363 5182;
www.parks.tas.gov.au
Park office: (03) 6363 5182

Tamar Island

This important wetland habitat just 10 minutes from the heart of Launceston features a great bird-viewing hide, 3.2 kilometres of easy walking tracks and an interpretation centre.

Tasafari

Holding advanced eco-accreditation, this tour company combines some of the best day walks in Tasmania with camping in remote areas. A total of nine people is permitted on a tour.
1300 882 415; www.tasafari.com.au

Trowunna Wildlife Park, Mole Creek

One of the most respected and long-running wildlife parks in Tasmania, Trowunna is involved in conservation, education and rehabilitation. There is a wide range of wildlife on display, including devils, reptiles, quolls and birds, and educational guided tours daily.
(03) 6363 6162; www.trowunna.com.au

Near Devonport

ACTIVITIES

Giant crayfish research

Tasmania has the largest freshwater crayfish in the world, and they can grow up to a metre in length, with claws that could cut a person's hand off. You can go out on a research trip with the world's expert on these endangered creatures, Todd Walsh, helping him catch and tag the incredible invertebrates. Day trips generally leave from Ulverstone.
0439 693 377; giantlobsters@hotmail.com

*Eastern quoll (*Dasyurus viverrinus*) in Mount William National Park*

*Female Tasmanian devil (*Sacrophilus harrisii*) near her den at Trowunna Wildlife Park*

*Freshwater crayfish (*Parastacoides tasmanicus insignis*) at its burrow entrance*

Hiking

If you want to embark on a little-known, but highly varied Tasmanian bushwalk, try part or the entire 80-kilometre Penguin to Cradle walk. It starts at the coast, goes through a mix of rural areas, woodlands, canyons, mountain ranges and rainforest, and finishes at Cradle Mountain–Lake St Clair National Park. It can be done as a five-to-seven-day trek, or reduced to four, long, day walks. You can download maps from the website.

www.nwwc.org.au/penguin_cradle_maps.htm

Narawntapu National Park

Narawntapu National Park, just east of Devonport, was previously known as Asbestos Ranges National Park, but for understandable reasons that did not seem to attract people. A shame, because the wildlife is abundant – particularly wombats, forester kangaroos and birds – and the beaches are pretty. There is a bird hide, short walks and three camping areas, including a shower block at Springlawn.

PWS Narawntapu: (03) 6428 6277; www.parks.tas.gov.au

Platypus Encounters, Latrobe

Three brothers almost single-handedly turned an old quarry site into one of the most reliable places in the world to see wild platypus. In fact, the guided tours have never failed to encounter a platypus in Warrawee Reserve, beside the Mersey River. You can go to the reserve for free and enjoy the picnic and barbecue facilities under towering white gums, or book in at the Latrobe Visitor Centre for the guided tour on which you may see the local tawny frogmouths, wombats and possums, as well as the wary monotremes.

(03) 6426 1774; www.latrobetasmania.com.au

Central tablelands

WHERE TO STAY

Camping

There are sites with and without power at Cradle Mountain Tourist Park, 3 kilometres north of Cradle Mountain Visitor Centre, outside the national park. There is no camping within the Cradle Mountain day-walk area.

Camp bookings: (03) 6429 1395

Cradle Mountain Lodge

Live in the lap of luxury – old style – with a warm and welcoming central lodge, surrounded by individual cabins. Like nearly any large lodge, it does not have a perfect environmental record, but this eco-accredited accommodation is the ideal spot to recuperate after you have been doing some of the best bushwalking you can do in the country. It also offers a comprehensive program of guided walks and activities, including canoeing, nocturnal-spotlighting tours and mountain-biking.

(03) 6492 1303; www.cradlemountainlodge.com.au

Mountain Valley, Loongana

Mountain Valley is off the beaten tourist track, situated around 64 kilometres south-west of

Devonport (due south of Burnie). Visitors here stay in rustic cabins with open fireplaces on a private and remote 60-hectare nature reserve. Platypus are visible in the tannin-stained Leven River and wild quolls and devils come right to your door, attracted by chopped up roadkill occasionally left there by the owners, which helps keep the devils themselves off the road. There is abundant birdlife and beautiful walks through wet sclerophyll forest on a lush carpet of lime moss to glow-worm caves. Despite its isolation you can access the Penguin to Cradle walk (*see* Near Devonport/Hiking), or go for a challenging hike up Black Bluff.

(03) 6429 1394; www.mountainvalley.com.au

Waldheim Cabins

You can steal a march on everyone else in the morning by staying in historic cabins at a beautiful spot within Cradle Mountain–Lake St Clair National Park, operated by the Parks and Wildlife Service. The cabins are inexpensive and fairly basic, with shared amenities, but vary in size with space for four, six or eight people, and include a gas stove, refrigerator, cutlery and crockery. You need to book months ahead for summer.

(03) 6492 1110; cradle@parks.tas.gov.au

Cradle Mountain Lodge

Pencil Pine Falls near Cradle Mountain Lodge

ACTIVITIES

Cradle Mountain–Lake St Clair National Park

This is the most iconic park in Tasmania, and rightfully so, as it is a very special place indeed. A spectacular World Heritage area, it has ancient forests, alpine moorlands and amazing wildlife, and offers classic bushwalks of various lengths and for all abilities. The climb to Marions Lookout and the Cradle Mountain summit, then back via Twisted Lakes and Hansons Peak, is a highly recommended day walk – allow at least six hours – as the route quickly takes you above the hordes of sightseers strolling around Dove Lake. Take extreme care on the exciting rock scramble to the summit of Cradle Mountain as even without ice or snow the rocks are slippery and require a steady head. Go in late April or early May to see the hillsides ablaze with deciduous beech (*Nothofagus gunnii*), and stop in at the Ronny Creek carpark to have a look for wild wombats. There is a fairly flat 8.5-kilometre track from the visitor centre to Dove Lake, and you can combine walking sections with catching a shuttle bus.

Barn Bluff hut, one of several Cradle Huts on the Overland Track

Behind the Cradle Mountain Lodge, the one-and-a-half-hour Speeler Track Circuit is a great way to stretch the legs and to get acquainted with some of the beautiful plant communities, such as the buttongrass plains, sphagnum bogs and King Billy pine forest dripping with lichens.

PWS Cradle Mountain: (03) 6492 1110; www.parks.tas.gov.au

PWS Lake St Clair (Derwent Bridge): (03) 6289 1172

Devils@Cradle

A visit to this sanctuary on the northern edge of Cradle Mountain–Lake St Clair National Park is a great way to see and learn about Tasmanian devils, with daytime viewing and night tours. The centre is also involved in ongoing studies of the wild devil population.

(03) 6492 1491; www.devilsatcradle.com

Gunns Plains Cave

Located just south-west of Gunns Plains (some 23 kilometres south-west of Ulverstone), this is yet another great limestone cave. It has one of the largest shawl formations in the Southern Hemisphere, glow worms aplenty and an underground creek. There are 45-minute guided tours available.

(03) 6429 1388; www.parks.tas.gov.au

Leven Canyon

Tucked away in a small regional reserve, south of Gunns Plains (access via Nietta), a mere 500-metre stroll from the carpark leads to a stupendous lookout that hangs over the Leven River some 300 metres below. Further down the road, another slightly longer track will take you to the valley floor of this deep limestone gulch.

The Overland Track

Deservedly the most well-known, multi-day walking route in Australia, this 65- to 80-kilometre route through Cradle Mountain–Lake St Clair National Park is a classic (for national park information, *see* park entry above). Starting at Cradle Mountain, the track leads through the rainforests of Cradle Valley before heading south over alpine moors, through ancient rainforest, past giant pandani groves and finally down into forested valleys with cascading waterfalls to Lake St Clair, at the southern end of the park. Most groups take about five days to walk the trail, but there are quite a few recommended side trips, such as to Mount Oakleigh, so allow a few extra days for these, if the weather allows. Because of the 10 000 or so walkers who trek along here each

Bennetts wallaby (Macropus rufogriseus), found throughout the north of Tasmania

Hikers on the Overland Track

year, the management of the track in recent years has become more sustainable: composted human waste from the toilets is flown out, tracks are regularly maintained, boardwalks are being added, and walkers are required to book – and travel from north to south – during the busy November to April period. Independent walkers can use the huts along the way, but will need to bring a tent as well, in case the huts are full, or for emergencies.

Several guiding companies will take you out on the Overland, including Tasmanian Expeditions. However, the deluxe option is particularly popular. For those choosing this experience, five private helicopter-supplied huts are tucked off the main Overland Track route, and small groups of walkers get to stay in them in style, drinking wine, having tasty dinners and hot showers, and sleeping in a bed, carrying only their personal belongings during the day.

(03) 6492 1133; www.overlandtrack.com.au

PWS track bookings: (03) 6233 6047; www.parks.tas.gov.au

Tasmanian Expeditions: (03) 6339 3999 or 1300 666 856; www.tas-ex.com

Deluxe option: (03) 6392 2211; www.cradlehuts.com.au

The Wilderness Gallery

At this Cradle Mountain venue, adjacent to Pure Tasmania's Cradle Mountain Chateau, you can take a quiet break to absorb ten rooms of absolutely stunning wildlife and wilderness photographs taken in Tasmania and further afield. The gallery is open seven days, and the exhibitions change regularly and include some of Australia's best photographers. You will leave inspired to capture more images of your own.

(03) 6492 1404; www.wildernessgallery.com.au

Walls of Jerusalem National Park

Serious bushwalkers often say this special alpine wilderness is even prettier than the adjacent Cradle Mountain–Lake St Clair National Park. Its glacial terrain studded with alpine lakes and tarns has stands of pure pencil pine forest. It is inaccessible by road, and conditions can change quickly and dangerously. Most trekkers go for at least a couple of nights.

PWS: (03) 6363 5133 or 1300 135 515

Park ranger: (03) 6363 5182; www.parks.tas.gov.au

Colourful display of honey richea (Richea scoparia) *in Walls of Jerusalem National Park*

The north-west

This region of Tasmania encompasses the 447 000-hectare Tarkine wilderness, which is the area bounded by the Bass and Murchison highways, south to Rosebery and Zeehan. The Tarkine includes the largest tract of temperate rainforest in the Southern Hemisphere, a spectacular wild coastline, stands of the tallest hardwood trees in the world, dramatic mountain ranges and wild rivers, habitat for over 50 threatened wildlife species, and is rich in Indigenous cultural-heritage sites.

WHERE TO STAY

Corinna

Corinna is a lovely modern ecotourism story. An old mining and forestry ghost town on the Pieman River in the Tarkine Wilderness has been turned into an ecotourism venture with an emphasis on preserving the natural heritage, and powered almost entirely by solar power. You can stay in one of 20 new eco-cabins, the old butcher's shop or general store, the pub that has been converted to accommodate backpackers, or camp (14 campsites). There are canoe trips into the Tarkine and a 500-metre, wheelchair-accessible boardwalk amid ancient huon pines, as well as a multitude of longer walks. There is no mobile phone coverage, no TVs and no hairdryers – just the wilderness.

Corinna (and Pieman River Cruises): (03) 6446 1170; www.corinna.com.au

ACTIVITIES

Arthur River Cruises

Take a guided cruise and walk in cool temperate rainforest along the Arthur River, on the edge of the Tarkine Wilderness. You are likely to see sea-eagles, azure kingfishers and occasionally a platypus. Canoe hire is also available.

Arthur River Cruises: (03) 6457 1158; www.arthurrivercruises.com

Arthur River Canoe and Boat Hire: (03) 6457 1312

Creative Paper, Burnie

Make your own paper with recycled bits and pieces on a half-hour tour at this non-profit, community-based enterprise. They use all sorts of odds and ends to make their eco-friendly papers, including old jeans, fruit pulp and even dried kangaroo scats. Staffed by volunteers, the place is worth visiting, even if you do not do the tour, to see the unbelievable papier-mâché artworks and learn a little about Burnie's paper-making history. Bookings are advised for tours, and the place is open 9am–5pm weekdays, 9am–4pm weekends (but only open Sundays from September to April).

(03) 6430 7717; www.creativepapertas.com.au

Kings Run Wildlife Tours

A wildlife tour in which the host starts by attaching a road-killed wallaby to the back of his utility and dragging it for several kilometres through his property is unusual to say the least. But this extraordinary wildlife tour on land that used to be grazed, until the owner had his eyes opened to its natural values, is a treat. As well as learning about Aboriginal and natural history of the area, encountering wombats, wallabies and birds such as the yellow-throated honeyeater, you have a 90 per cent chance of seeing wild Tasmanian devils. They smell the carcass and come in to feed on it, within metres of a cabin where you look out while sharing snacks and a glass or two. The tour leaves from either Marrawah or Arthur River on the far north-west coast, and it is worth staying nearby, not only because this remote coastline

is so beautiful, but also because the evenings can finish quite late, particularly in summer.
(03) 6457 1191; www.kingsrun.com.au

Rocky Cape National Park

There is great snorkelling and in-shore diving among the sponge gardens and myriad marine life here, and a wreck, the *Southern Cross*, is lying in a few metres of water off the cape. The coastal heath has prolific birdlife and wildflowers including orchids. There are Aboriginal sites and shelters to discover and a variety of walks, ranging from less than 20 minutes to a full day. These take in Aboriginal rock shelters and caves, tranquil beaches, and rocky headlands abounding in rockpools.
PWS Smithton: (03) 6452 4997;
www.parks.tas.gov.au

Tarkine Forest Adventures at Dismal Swamp

This is a strange mix of natural history, art installations, public relations for Forestry Tasmania and a wild and riotous 110-metre slide. The experience is set in the only known sinkhole in the world with a thriving blackwood forest, and it is not hard to find locals who wish it had been left as it was. You can see the chimneys built by nocturnal burrowing crayfish and, if you visit in spring, look out for beautiful white Gunns Plains tree orchids. It is rather a hike to get there (some 32 kilometres south-west of Smithton, along the Bass Highway towards Marrawah), so make the most of the barbecue, picnic and cafe facilities.
(03) 6456 7199; www.dismalswamp.com.au

The slide through the treetops in the Tarkine Forest

Tarkine Trails

Delve deeply into the temperate rainforest of the Tarkine Wilderness on a multi-day bushwalk with Tarkine Trails. Unashamedly made up of conservation activists, the company is keen to show you why the Tarkine area should become World Heritage listed. It also offers guided multi-day walks along the Tarkine coast and a walking option with accommodation along the way.
(03) 6223 5320 or 0427 397 815;
www.tarkinetrails.com.au

Common wombat (Vombatus ursinus) in the Tarkine

Canoeing on the Pieman River near Corinna

Bass Strait islands

From tiny Swan Island, just off the north-east tip of Tasmania, you can gaze out at parts of the old land bridge that linked Tasmania to the mainland in the last ice age. The wind-lashed mountain range pokes out of the shallow Bass Strait, forming islands such as Clarke, Cape Barren and Flinders. The islands provide vital habitats for a range of wildlife, and stepping stones for hardy kayakers and boaters who travel from Tasmania to the mainland. Further away to the west is King Island, renowned for its wildlife and remote beauty.

These islands offer limited but unique ecotourism options, both on the water and on land. There are top diving spots, national parks to explore on foot and by boat, food and wine, and incredible birdlife. And if you thought the Tasmanian mainland was quiet, wait until you set foot on some of these remote landscapes.

View from Walkers Lookout in Strzelecki National Park on Flinders Island

Swan Island

WHERE TO STAY/ACTIVITIES

Relax in the shade of a lighthouse on a 240-hectare island, with no more than a handful of people on the whole place. Just 3 kilometres off the northern tip of the Tasmanian mainland, the privately owned Swan Island is a wild delight, brimming with little penguins, Cape Barren geese and plenty of other birds. There are eight sandy beaches, and dolphins, orcas and whales sometimes cruise offshore. The lighthouse keeper's cottage comfortably holds two to six people, and all power is generated by solar and wind. Spend your days exploring, beachcombing, snorkelling, skinny dipping or taking private art lessons in this quiet piece of paradise. The plane flight from Bridport takes no more than a few minutes. You will need to bring your own food, but linen is supplied. Children under 16 are not welcome.

(03) 6357 2211; www.swanislandholidays.com.au

Flinders Island

ACTIVITIES

Birdwatching

Logan Lagoon in the south-east is an internationally recognised wetland, vital for rare migratory species such as the red-necked stint, common greenshank, eastern curlew and bar-tailed godwit.

Bushwalking

The best-known walk here is the four-to-five-hour-return Strzelecki Track to the distinctive Strzelecki Peaks, in the 4216-hectare Strzelecki

*Cape Barren geese (*Cereopsis novaehollandiae*) in Strzelecki National Park*

Boulder-strewn beachscape in Strzelecki National Park

The largest of the Bass Strait Islands, Flinders is a mecca for bushwalkers, birdwatchers and increasing numbers of rock climbers. It also has some great diving and snorkelling off 120 beaches, and is a jump-off point to explore some of the other nearby islands. It is accessed by plane from either Launceston or Victoria.

National Park. Located in the south-west corner of the island, the national park has pristine white-sand beaches, granite mountain ridges and abundant wombats and Cape Barren geese. There are plenty of free camping areas, and the campgrounds at Trousers Point and Allports Beach have gas barbecues and toilets.

Strzelecki National Park: (03) 6359 2217; www.parks.tas.gov.au

Flinders Island Adventures

To experience the island fully, join a 4WD tour of two to eight days with a focus on bushwalking, birds and the natural environment.

(03) 6359 4507; www.flindersisland.com.au

Snorkelling and diving

Flinders Island Dive hires snorkelling gear and can take you on snorkelling tours in quiet bays, or you can swim just offshore at Fotheringate Bay in Strzelecki National Park. It is possible to dive off more than 50 islands of eastern Bass Strait, with rich fish life, rock shelves, sponge gardens, coral reefs and generally warmer water than off the coast of the Tasmanian mainland.

(03) 6359 8429; www.divetasmania.com

Kent Group

WHERE TO STAY/ACTIVITIES

The two islands that can be visited here are Deal and Erith islands, both part of the Kent Group National Park. There is camping (fuel stove only) on both these islands, a composting toilet on Erith and some walking tracks on Deal. Tasmanian Parks are hoping to turn the lighthouse keeper's cottage on Deal Island into solar-powered accommodation for rent. It is generally only people in boats who make it to

these beautiful islands, but charters can be secured from Flinders Island or Victoria.
(03) 6359 2217; www.parks.tas.gov.au

King Island

ACTIVITIES

Diving and snorkelling

King Island is a renowned diving destination and you can dive through kelp forests or near the local seal colony with King Island Dive Charters.
(03) 6461 1133 or 1800 030 330

Kelp harvesting

King Island has a vibrant bull kelp industry, in which storm-cast kelp is collected from the beaches and processed. This is one of the only places where you will see this happening, and there is information about the process at the factory and you may spot the harvesters at work along the foreshore near Currie.
(03) 6462 1340; www.kelpind.com.au

Walking

There are plenty of great walks on King Island. One of the best places to start is around the 7000-year-old calcified forest south of Currie. Just near there is the high cliff boardwalk to Seal Rocks Lookout. In the north-east of the island, the Lavinia Nature Reserve contains wetlands of international importance, and is a great spot for birdwatching.

Kelp hanging from drying racks at a King Island processing plant

Wildlife tours

See little penguins and some of the other great birds on this island with King Island Discovery Tours.
(03) 6462 1118 or 0429 621 118; anna@kingisland.net.au

The best known of the Bass Strait islands, King is set apart from most of the others, in the west of Bass Strait. A paradise for gourmands, it has a few ecotourism options as well. Accommodation is generally a mix of B&Bs, cottages and apartments.
1800 645 014; www.kingisland.org.au

King Island: southern bull kelp (Durvillea potatorum) growing just under the low-tide level (left); and fastened stumps of kelp ready for hauling (right)

Far-flung Adventures

Australian ecotourists have the opportunity to travel to some extraordinary, wild places within our national borders, and beyond them to places such as Antarctica. There are companies and small operators dedicated to preserving and promoting their patch of paradise, with eco-friendly activities focusing on ways for ecotravellers to be revitalised by the natural world.

However, such far-flung adventures increase the need to mitigate your carbon footprint, and maximise your environmental considerations when you reach your destination. Unfortunately, in these remote regions, none of the accommodation providers stand out yet as being substantially greener than any other, but it is worth checking with the tourist information services for any new environmental developments before booking your trip.

CHRISTMAS ISLAND, 1700 kilometres north-west of Western Australia, is a birdwatching and diving mecca, and offers nature lovers some unique experiences.

NORFOLK ISLAND, some 1500 kilometres off Australia's east coast, has a dark history as a colonial penal settlement, but a bright future as an ecotourist destination.

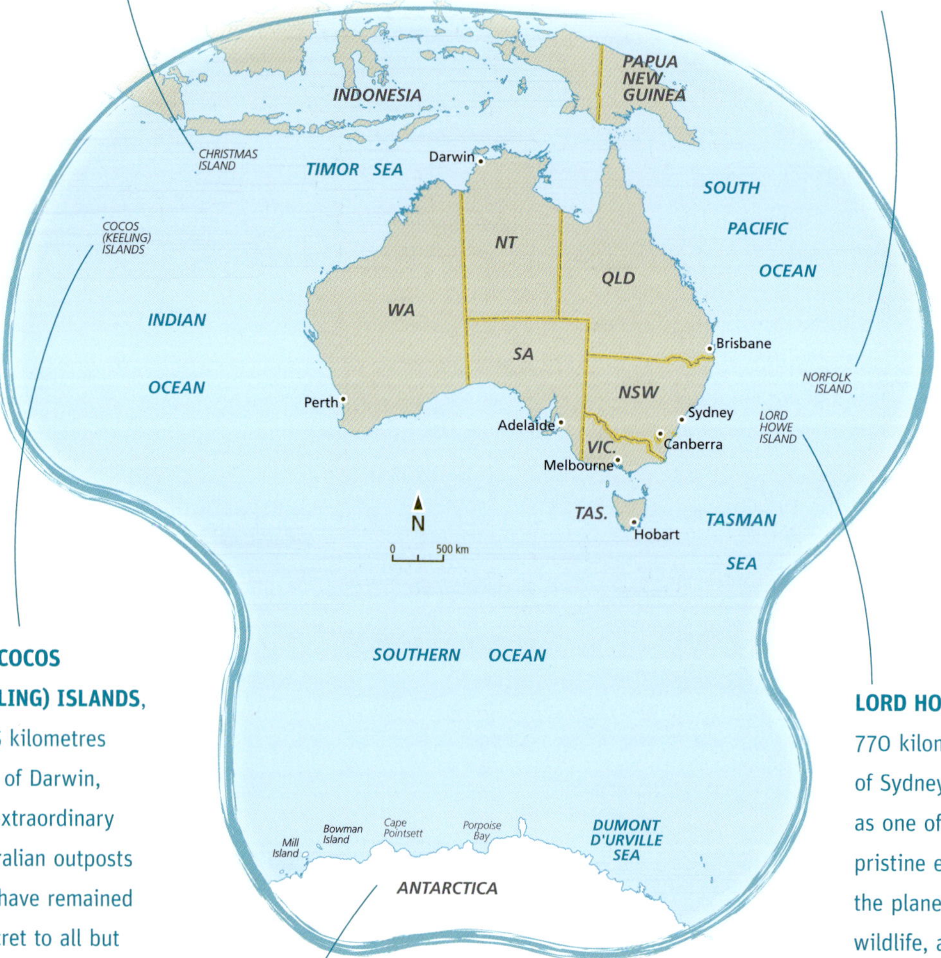

THE COCOS (KEELING) ISLANDS, 3685 kilometres west of Darwin, are extraordinary Australian outposts that have remained a secret to all but a few ecotourists.

LORD HOWE ISLAND, 770 kilometres north-east of Sydney, is renowned as one of the most pristine environments on the planet, with myriad wildlife, and is justifiably World Heritage–listed.

ANTARCTICA is perhaps the ultimate ecotourism destination, and Australians are flocking there in greater numbers than ever before.

Department of the Environment, Water, Heritage and the Arts: (02) 6274 1111; www.environment.gov.au/parks/national-parks

TOP TEN

1 Sit and rest on Petermann Island, on the Antarctic Peninsula, while a parade of penguins struts around you

2 Go sea-kayaking off Norfolk Island, surrounded by marine turtles in the waters below, and seabirds in the skies above and nesting on the rock stacks offshore

3 See the breathtaking view after climbing the 875-metre Mount Gower on Lord Howe Island

4 Join Bird Week on Christmas Island, aiding ornithologists and naturalists in their research into the habits of the island's birdlife

5 Dive off the Cocos (Keeling) Islands, amid coral gardens, tropical fish, turtles and reef sharks

6 Watch the annual red-crab migration on Christmas Island, almost a scene from a prehistoric era

7 See a leopard seal stalk and play with its prey

8 Contribute to the management of Lord Howe Island with a bush-regeneration ecotour

9 Hike on the World Heritage–listed, sub-Antarctic Macquarie Island, which lies in the Southern Ocean some 1500 kilometres south-east of Tasmania

10 Explore a remote tropical paradise in the Cocos (Keeling) Islands group to see the trees laden with hundreds of red-footed boobies

GREEN TRAVEL TIP When camping in wilderness areas, use non-fluoride toothpaste (most children's toothpaste satisfies this requirement). You should still use minimal toothpaste and bury your waste, but the non-fluoride product will be potentially less damaging to the immediate microenvironment.

Lord Howe Island with Mount Lidgbird (left) and Mount Gower

Lord Howe Island

ACTIVITIES

Bush-regeneration ecotour

Here is a great opportunity to give something back to this beautiful place, while enjoying its natural treasures. Join a bush-regeneration ecotour with Lord Howe Island Nature Tours and you will spend mornings removing some noxious weeds from parts of the island and afternoons exploring and enjoying it. The guide on these trips is the naturalist, photographer and author Ian Hutton, whose knowledge of the island's plants and animals is extraordinary. Ian also runs other nature tours, particularly for those with an interest in birds or plants.

1800 671 546; www.lordhowe-tours.com.au

Bushwalking

Lord Howe is blessed with some brilliant medium-length walks and one of the best day walks in the country, the climb to the summit of 875-metre Mount Gower. There are walking tracks through lime-green kentia palm forests, and coastal walks among nesting colonies of seabirds, with stunning views over the island from various vantage points. Do not miss the views from Malabar Hill and Kims Lookout (7 kilometres return).

You will need a guide to tackle the summit of Mount Gower. The exciting 14-kilometre walk includes some exposed sections, with fixed ropes to aid hikers, but the experience is definitely worth it. The rewards include seeing the full range of forest types on the island, including the misty forest at the top, and the Lord Howe Island woodhen. Sea to Summit Expeditions has the main guide to the top, a trusty fifth-generation islander who has done the trip more than 1100 times. (Note that because of the altitude reached, any diving enthusiasts who wish to do the walk will need to remember to finish diving a day or so before the climb.)

Sea to Summit Expeditions: (02) 6563 2218

This special, special place should be high on the wish list of ecotourists everywhere. Situated 550 kilometres east of Port Macquarie on the New South Wales coast, Lord Howe is rightfully World Heritage-listed. It has two dominant, towering mountains – Mount Lidgbird and Mount Gower – with a dark tangle of mist-attracting forest on their summits, stunning coral reefs with some 500 fish species, and abundant wildlife, including one of the world's rarest birds and tens of thousands of nesting seabirds that are generally unafraid of humans. There are 11 beaches, and brilliant snorkelling with sea turtles and metre-long kingfish straight off the shore. Less than 15 per cent of the island has been cleared for settlement, there is a cap of 393 visitors at any one time, and the islanders have established solid environmental policies. These include an innovative vertical composting unit that processes the entire island's organic waste, a bulk food cooperative to reduce waste, and a policy of active discouragement of plastic-bag use for more than a decade. As a result, Lord Howe is known as one of the best ecologically sustainable tourism destinations in the world.

Visitor information: (02) 6563 2114 or 1800 240 937; www.lordhoweisland.info

Cycling

The roads on Lord Howe are great for bike-riding, and by either cycling or walking you can get pretty much everywhere within a few hours. Some of the accommodation places hire bikes, or you can pick them up from Wilson's Hire Service.

Wilson's Hire Service: (02) 6563 2045

Diving and snorkelling

Superb snorkelling can be found right around the island, and the lagoon and Neds Beach in particular are very popular, with 90 species of coral, sea turtles and masses of fish. You can either hire snorkelling gear from the dive shops or take advantage of the gear supplied at Neds Beach, where there are stored masks, fins and snorkels available with a contribution to the honesty box.

If you want some company and guidance in the water – and some knowledge about what you are seeing – Islander Cruises is one of several operators that offers a two-hour guided snorkelling tour, including all gear.

There are more than 50 dive sites, but most are boat dives rather than from the shore. When the snorkelling is this good and this easy, it can be hard to convince yourself to strap on air tanks and the rest of the gear.

Islander Cruises: (02) 6563 2021

Howea Divers: (02) 6563 2290; www.howeadivers.com.au

Pro Dive: (02) 6563 2253; www.prodivelordhowe.com

Kayaking

For a gentle, guided paddle on the lagoon, or something more adventurous – such as kayaking to the sea caves around the northern coastline – try Lord Howe Environmental Tours run by the former ranger of the island. You can also hire glass-bottom kayaks from Pro Dive (*see* details above) and other kayaks from Wilson's Hire Service (*see* details above).

Lord Howe Environmental Tours: (02) 6563 2214; www.lordhoweislandtours.com

*Yellowtail kingfish (*Seriola lalandi*) in a channel at Neds Beach*

Norfolk Island

Rugged and clad in magnificent pines and palms, Norfolk Island sits alone 1500 kilometres east of Brisbane. Much of it has been cleared for settlement and agriculture, but about one-third of the island is taken up by Norfolk Island National Park. The wildlife here is not as prolific as on some islands – there are no amphibians, for example – but bird species include elegant white terns, red-tailed tropicbirds and the extremely rare Norfolk Island green parrot. Ecotourism activities include diving, snorkelling, swimming and cycling.

Norfolk Island Tourism: (672) 32 2147 or (from Australia) 1800 214 603; www.norfolkisland.com.au

ACTIVITIES

Birdwatching

Take a trip out to Phillip Island, just offshore, with Charter Marine for some trekking and great birdwatching. Phillip Island is a major breeding ground for seabirds such as masked boobies, Australasian gannets, terns, tropicbirds and petrels. The main breeding season is from September to April. The morning trip includes a circumnavigation of the island, passing sea caves, cliffs and wildlife.

Charter Marine: (672) 32 3514; www.trekking.nf

Diving and snorkelling

The spectacular volcanic terrain of Norfolk continues under the surface, with caves, tunnels, chasms and chimneys to explore, as well as a wide variety of fish and marine algae. Snorkelling on a colourful coral reef at Emily Bay is particularly recommended. The main dive operator on the island is Bounty Divers, who will help get you in or under the water.

Bounty Divers: (672) 32 4375; www.bountydivers.com

Sea-kayaking

Basalt sea stacks and arches, small islands and towering cliffs make Norfolk one of the most interesting places to sea-kayak in Australia. On a sensational morning tour with Tropical Sea Kayaks you will experience all these geological formations then finish by snorkelling in a crystal-clear, enclosed lagoon. Turtles are a common sight as well as many seabirds, and the kayaks are the stable sit-on-top models that are easy to climb in and out of for snorkelling

Anson Bay beachscape, rimmed by Norfolk Island pines

*Polyps of anchor coral (*Euphyllia ancora*), with long sweeper tentacles, Norfolk Island*

and swimming. Once you have done the tour, you can also hire kayaks and go for a paddle on your own.

Tropical Sea Kayaks: (672) 32 3208;
www.seakayaking.nf

Mountain-biking

Getting around the island on a bike is recommended only for the fit as Norfolk's 34 square kilometres are undulating at best. Although the highest point is only 319 metres above sea level, some of the hills are quite steep. However, if you are up for it, this is a great way to experience the island. You can also ride on some of the tracks in the national park. Bikes can be hired from Land and Sea.

Land and Sea: (672) 32 3418

Walking

There are nine signposted walking tracks in the national park through lush palm forests and stands of Norfolk Island pines. The duration of walks ranges from around 20 to 90 minutes. One of the most recommended walks is to the Captain Cook Monument, which includes walking through rainforest and great coastal views.

Christmas Island

Tours

There is a range of tours on Christmas Island and because of the small numbers of tourists who come here most trips can be adjusted to suit individual interests.

Based on the island, Wet'n'Dry Adventures conducts birdwatching and jungle tours. Based in Singapore, Eco Adventures Worldwide has eco-tour packages to Christmas Island from Kuala Lumpur, which – depending where you live – may be as efficient as flying from Perth. The company has a strong environmental focus and places considerable emphasis on sustainable tourism.

Wet'n'Dry Adventures: (08) 9164 8028 or 0439 215 290;
www.divingchristmas.com
Eco Adventures Worldwide (Singapore):
(65) 6538 4441; www.adventures.com.sg/CI/

Phillip Island, just off the Norfolk Island coast

*The very rare Abbott's booby (*Papasula abbotti*) on Christmas Island*

*The Christmas Island imperial pigeon (*Ducula whartoni*)*

This nature-lovers' paradise, some 2600 kilometres north-west of Perth, is the site of the most spectacular animal migration in Australia – when 100 million red crabs leave their burrows in the forest to go down to the sea to breed. The island is also home to the very rare Abbott's booby, some amazing other birdlife, massive robber crabs up to 60 years old, and brilliant snorkelling and diving. More than 60 per cent of the island is protected within Christmas Island National Park.

Christmas Island Tourist Association: (08) 9164 8382; www.christmas.net.au

WHERE TO STAY

You can camp at Dolly Beach and the Pink House Research Station, with few facilities, but you will need a permit from Parks Australia. The island has a range of other accommodation options (*see* tourist association details above).

Parks Australia Christmas Island: (08) 9164 8700; www.environment.gov.au/parks

ACTIVITIES

Birdwatching

Christmas Island is a birdwatcher's wonderland, with frigatebirds, tropicbirds and boobies, and some endemic species, such as the Christmas Island imperial pigeon. There are an estimated 80 000 seabirds that nest on the island. In September each year, a major event, Bird Week, is organised, with opportunities to be involved in banding, mapping and other research, alongside some talented and well-respected ornithologists and naturalists.

Red-crab migration

The spectacular red-crab migration occurs when the wet-season rains have set in, and exact dates can never be given. However, tourists wishing to see this phenomenon are advised to come in the last quarter of the moon in November or December.

*Pennant coralfish or longfin bannerfish (*Heniochus acuminatus*), Christmas Island*

*Christmas Island red crabs (*Gecarcoidea natalis*) during the annual downward migration*

Direction Island beach on the Cocos (Keeling) Islands

Snorkelling and diving

The diving off Christmas Island is simply extraordinary, and there are some great snorkelling spots straight off the shore – Flying Fish Cove is particularly recommended. The sharp drop-off to the ocean floor is only about 20 metres from the shoreline, providing divers with easy access to beautiful coral-covered walls, and habitat for sharks, tuna, wahoo, barracuda and a kaleidoscope of tropical fish. You are also likely to spot green and hawksbill turtles and, between November and April, there is a reasonable chance of seeing whale sharks and manta rays. The waters are generally very calm from April to October, but can get choppy in the wet season although visibility usually remains at about 20 metres.

Wet'n'Dry Adventures: (08) 9164 8028 or 0439 215 290; www.divingchristmas.com

Christmas Island Divers: 0419 759 617; www.christmasislanddivers.net

Walking

There are plenty of short nature trails and mid-length walks through Christmas Island National Park and to remote beaches. Some lead along boardwalks through the rainforest, and others involve negotiating rugged coastal tracks and some wading. Particularly recommended are walks in the Dales, and at Dolly Beach and the old Railway Station at South Point.

Parks Australia Christmas Island: (08) 9164 8700; www.environment.gov.au/parks

Cocos (Keeling) Islands

ACTIVITIES

Canoeing

Join a guided four-hour, island-hopping, canoeing, snorkelling and fishing tour. You can book at the visitor centre (*see* details next page).

Cultural tour

Around 500 Cocos Malays live on Home Island, following a Muslim lifestyle and generally isolated from the rest of the world. To gain an

A further 900 kilometres west of Christmas Island is the Australian outpost of Cocos (Keeling) Islands, one of the most extraordinary places. There are 26 islands in the group, and only two are inhabited. The water is the same unbelievable turquoise you see in the brochures, the birdlife is incredible and the snorkelling and diving is certainly some of the best anywhere. Tourism is not big here so there are few visitors around, except in the July–September peak period. To take into account your carbon footprint in flying here, it may be worth visiting Christmas Island as well, which is on the same flight from Perth.

Visitor centre: (08) 9162 6790; www.cocos-tourism.cc

*Christmas frigatebirds (*Fregata andrewsi*) and red-footed boobies (*Sula sula*) in Pulu Keeling National Park*

insight into the lives of these people you can take a three-hour cultural tour that explores the island's unique history and traditions. Bookings can be made at the visitor centre (*see* details above).

Cycling

With its highest point only 9 metres above sea level, West Island is ideal to explore by bike as the roads are flat all the way. You can hire bikes on the island from Cocos Bike and Scooter Hire.

Cocos Bike and Scooter Hire: (08) 9162 6768

Island-hopping

If you are fit and watch the tides carefully, you can walk and wade the 15 kilometres of reefs and islands between Home and West islands, enjoying tiny island after island covered in coconuts, birds, crabs and little else. A new, guided trip of this route led by a Cocos Malay resident includes camping overnight on one of the islands, and the supply of all your food and camping gear. Contact the visitor centre (*see* details above) for more information.

Snorkelling over coral in the Cocos Islands

Pulu Keeling National Park

A trip out to this remote, uninhabited island, 24 kilometres north of the main group of islands, with a Parks Australia ranger will be one of the most extraordinary wildlife experiences of your life. Dense masses of frigatebirds and red-footed boobies fill the pisonia trees and large red hermit crabs swarm the shores. The park has the largest breeding colony of red-footed boobies in the Indian Ocean. The birds are generally quite unafraid of humans so at times you can get quite close to fluffy chicks in their nest.

The number of visitors allowed into the park is very strictly limited in order to minimise the impact on the birds, with trips currently held about once a month only. Bookings can be made through the visitor centre (*see* details on page 298).

Snorkelling and diving

A coral atoll, Cocos has superb snorkelling and diving, with sheltered sites and a dramatic drop-off into the abyss on the ocean floor. The water is crystal clear and filled with beautiful coral gardens, sharks, turtles, pelagic species and thousands of tropical fish. The friendly dive operators at Cocos Dive are passionate about the place and have a great story to tell. They can help you get started with snorkelling or diving and know of some great locations for those who are more experienced.

Although there are bountiful sites to choose from, one of the premier spots is Direction Island (pictured on page 297). This stunning place has exquisite white sandy beaches and a snorkelling spot called the Rip, which has corals, reef sharks, huge wrasse and parrotfish. One of the tour operators, Geoff Christie, can take you there in a glass-bottom boat.

Cocos Dive: (08) 9162 6515; www.cocosdive.com

Geoff Christie: (08) 9162 7646

*King penguins (*Aptenodytes patagonicus*) and cruise ship*

Antarctica

Cruises

The most important thing when choosing a cruise to Antarctica is to make sure the operator is an active member of the International Association of Antarctic Tour Operators (IAATO), which has set in place site-management plans for 20 of the most visited sites, including restrictions on how many people can be on shore at a time, and the number of vessels that can be there.

There is no difficulty in convincing most Australian wildlife lovers of the wonders awaiting them in Antarctica – dense colonies of penguins, blue icebergs the size of apartment blocks, lolling seals, whales jumping out of the water everywhere, Antarctic terns and legendary albatrosses. It will leave you breathless. Australians make up the fourth-highest visitor numbers to the frozen continent. But the hardest thing about being an ecotraveller to this most precious and beautiful continent is trying to justify the environmental cost of getting there. The carbon footprint alone is daunting – a moderate-sized vessel uses 16–18 tonnes of fuel a day when on the move, leaving each passenger with an estimated carbon debt of 5–8 tonnes. On top of that, most Australian Antarctic visitors travel via South America, so have long flights with another 8 tonnes of carbon emissions to take into account.

The number of cruises where passengers do not step off the ship at all is increasing – but if you have gone all that way it makes sense to have a look around onshore in controlled landings or in excursions in the zodiac inflatable boats. The impact on the wildlife has generally been shown to be negligible if people follow the IAATO guidelines, and is also reduced when tourists travel in smaller groups.

The other choice Australians have is either to go due south to sub-Antarctic islands such as Macquarie then on to the Australian Antarctic Territory – which involves a long and often rough sea voyage – or to join 90 per cent of Antarctica's tourists in flying to the southern tip of South America, and heading for the more accessible wildlife-dense Antarctic Peninsula, just two days sailing away. It is expensive whichever way you go, although if you are prepared to get to Ushuaia, in southern Argentina, and wait, you may be able to pick up a half-price, last-minute cruise ticket from one of the travel agents there.

Most of the quality tour operators have expert naturalists, historians and others

Exploring the icy environment of Petermann Island with Peregrine

*Blue-eyed shag (*Phalacrocorax atriceps*) on Petermann Island*

on board who not only help guide, but also provide informative and fascinating lectures during the long sea crossings. Peregrine runs an outstanding Antarctic program, which includes options for sea-kayaking (an incredible experience, but limited to the first people to book) and, if the weather cooperates, camping overnight on the continent. The company has excellent guides and lecturers, and supports and raises money for environmental projects such as albatross conservation.

The well-known Australian company Aurora Expeditions, with its very strong environmental ethos and credentials, has an outstanding record in conducting tourism in Antarctica and other remote areas. Trips can include climbing virgin peaks, sea-kayaking or more conventional Antarctic exploration. As well as the Antarctic Peninsula there are expeditions taking in Macquarie Island and the Ross Sea.

Heritage Expeditions, a New Zealand company, specialises in sub-Antarctic islands of the Ross Sea and East Antarctica, and stresses conservation and responsible travel on its expeditions south. It runs an annual Cruise For Conservation, contributing 5 per cent of the advertised fare to an environmental cause. This operator also owns a covenanted area of native forest in New Zealand.

There are various other operators, including some (particularly for seafarers after a hard-core adventure) who sail to and from Antarctica. The *Spirit of Sydney* is one such IAATO-accredited operator that offers sailing trips to just a handful of people.

Peregrine: 1300 791 485; www.peregrine.net.au
Aurora Expeditions: (02) 9252 1033 or 1800 637 688; www.auroraexpeditions.com.au
Heritage Expeditions (NZ): 0011 64 3 365 3500; www.heritage-expeditions.com
Spirit of Sydney: (07) 3395 5734; www.spiritofsydney.net

Research opportunities

One way to justify going to Antarctica is to take part in important research by joining a team at an Australian base. The Australian Antarctic Division (AAD) does not just require scientists; it needs chefs, engineers, doctors, plumbers and others. There are summer stints available as well as longer over-winter opportunities but competition for spots is fierce. Find out about current positions at the AAD website.

www.aad.gov.au

An excursion in a zodiac inflatable boat

Index

ACCOMMODATION, FOOD AND WINE

accommodation

camping

ACTIVITIES

NATURAL ATTRACTIONS

PLACES

Publications manager
Astrid Browne

Project manager and editor
Helen Duffy

Editorial assistance
Melissa Krafchek

Design
desertpony

Cartographers
Bruce McGurty, Paul de Leur, Emily Maffei

Indexer
Fay Donlevy

Photo selection
Helen Duffy

Pre-press
PageSet Digital Print & Pre-press

Explore Australia Publishing Pty Ltd
85 High Street
Prahran 3181

ISBN 13 978 1 74117 269 0

10 9 8 7 6 5 4 3 2 1

Printed and bound in China by C & C Offset Printing Co. Ltd

The author, Ken Eastwood, gratefully acknowledges the assistance of the tourism bodies in New South Wales, South Australia, Tasmania and Queensland, and thanks those operators in this book that allowed him to experience many of the tours and accommodation.

Photo credits

Abbreviations

AEL Aquila Eco Lodges
AG Australian Geographic
AL Australian Arid Lands Botanic Gardens
AN Adventure North
APT APT Wilderness Adventures
AR Amarant Retreat
AS Australian Scenics
ASDP Alice Springs Desert Park
AT Anthology Travel
AUS Auscape International
AW Auswalk
AWC Aurukun Wetland Charters
BAM Bamurru Plains
BB Burnside Bungalows
BBS Batemans Bay Sailing Charters
BD Brett Dennis
BIC Bruny Island Charters
BJ Busselton Jetty & Underwater Observatory
BOM Bombah Point
BP Bruce Postle
CA Craig Abraham
CC Chris Crerar
CCM Crystal Creek Meadows
CS Cloud Song
CV Crocodylus Village
CW Cullen Wines
DCH Darwin Central Hotel
DF Don Fuchs
DHG Dennis Harding
DIR Dunk Island Resort
DJ Darren Jew
DMR Daylesford and Macedon Ranges
DWC Dolphin Watch Cruises – Jervis Bay
DWL Daintree Wilderness Lodge
DZP Daniel Zupanc
EAP Explore Australia Publishing
EI Evolving Images
FAP Frances Andrijich Photography
FB Faraway Bay
FP Freeman Productions
GD Grant Dixon
GEL Geoffrey Lea
GL Gary Lewis
GM Grahame McConnell
GP Gecko Photographics
GRB Graham Robertson
GU Guurrbi Tours
GUL Amy Gulick
HBR Huon Bush retreats
HH Hahndorf Hill Winery
ICT Island Cycle Tours
JA Jon Armstrong
JB John Baker
JC Jurien Charters
JD Jamie Durant
JFH John Fairhall
JK John Krutop
JL John Landy
JLE John Lewis
JLO Jiri Lochman
JM Jon Miller
JPF Jean-Paul Ferrero
JS Jay Sarson
KAT Kathie Atkinson
KAW Kosciuszko Alpine Walks
KCL Kooljaman at Cape Leveque
KE Ken Eastwood
KQ Kimberley Quest II (Pearl Sea Coastal Cruises)
KV Courtesy of Krinklewood Vineyard
LAN Mike Langford
LGS Lets Go Surfing
LS Len Stewart
LT Lochman Transparencies
MA Michael Anlezark
MAN Mangrove Route
ME Melanie Erler/McLeod EcoFarm
ML Marie Lochman
MM Monkey Mia Dolphin Resort
MR Michael Rayner
MS Mark Spencer
MT Masons Tours
NR Nick Rains
NEG Noosa Enterprise Group
NM Nina McDougall
NRR Ningaloo Reef Resort
NTTC Northern Territory Tourist Commission
OCS Outback Coast Safaris
OF The Odd Frog
OO Ossies Outback
OOST Out Of Sight! Tours
OSF Oxford Scientific Films/Karen Gowlett-Holmes
OTS Odyssey Tours and Safaris
PC Paperbark Camp
PE Peter Eve
PF Paul Foley
PPC D. Parer & E. Parer-Cook
PT Pure Tasmania
PV Parks Victoria
QS Red Bluff/Quobba Station
RS Rachel Steadman
RW Rob Walls
SA Sailaway
SAF Saffron
SATC South Australian Tourism Commission
SDM Steven David Miller
SL Suzanne Long
SND Becca Saunders
SOL Southern Ocean Lodge
SS Sal Salis
SW Susan Wright
TB The Buckland
TEC Tanonga Eco Lodges
TIC Tasman Island Cruises
TNSW Tourism New South Wales
TQ Tourism Queensland
TT Tourism Tasmania
TV Tourism Victoria
UE Undersea Explorer
UT Uptuyu Tours
VEK Michael Van Ewijk
WFT Walker Family Tours
WIC S. Wilby & C. Ciantar
WOB Way Out Back
WOC Wadlata Outback Centre
WZ Werribee Open Range Zoo

Except when images on a page are all from the one source, photographic credits are listed from top (left to right) then bottom (left to right).

Front cover
(a) BAM (b) DIR (c) FB (d) AW (e) PC (f) AS

Back cover
(a) FP/AWC (b) NTTC (c) LT/LS; author photo: Melissa Spry

Title page
Pure Tasmania

Contents pages
iv–v (a) SATC (b) KAW (c) BAM; vi–vii (a) SATC (b) TQ (c) MM (d) LT/JL; viii–ix (a) TV (b) WZ (c) AT (d) KE; x (a) JC (b) Courtesy of Voyages Hotels & Resorts

Design elements
Green tag: ©iStockphoto.com/emily2k
Postcard: ©iStockphoto.com/Effinity Stock Photography
Parchment paper: ©iStockphoto.com/Nic Taylor
Endpapers and contents pages (background): ©iStockphoto.com/Nic Taylor

Other pages
8–9 ©iStockphoto.com/kertlis; 11 TNSW; 12 KE; 13 AG; 14 LGS; 15 TNSW; 16 PC; 17 (a) KAW (b) PC; 18–19 PC; 20 DWC; 21 (a) CCM (b) CS; 22 TNSW; 23 BBS; 24 BP; 25 KE; 26 (a) KE (b) TNSW/SW; 27 TNSW; 28 KAW; 29 (a/b) KAW (c) TNSW/JA; 30–2 TNSW; 35–7 KE; 38 TNSW/NR; 41 KV; 42 (a/c) BOM (b) TNSW; 43–4 TNSW; 45 KE; 46 TNSW/DF; 47 (a) KE (b) TNSW/GM; 48 (a) KE (b) TNSW/PF; 49–50 KE; 51 (a) AUS/VEK (b) KE; 53 KE; 54 TNSW/DF; 56 TNSW; 57 TNSW/GP; 58 (a) TNSW/SW (b) TNSW; 59 TNSW; 61 TNSW/EI; 62–3 BP; 65 (a/c) OTS (b) MAN; 66 (a) DCH (b) SAF; 67 MAN; 68 NTTC; 70 BAM/PE; 71 OTS; 72–3 NTTC; 74 WOB; 76 (a) OTS (b) ASDP; 77 NTTC; 78 EAP/NR; 79 NTTC; 80 (a) OTS (b) Courtesy of Voyages Hotels & Resorts (c) EAP/NR; 81 OTS; 82–3 Courtesy of Tourism Queensland; 85–90 TQ; 91 (a) TQ (b) BP; 92 TQ/DJ; 94 MR; 95 TQ; 96–8 KE; 99 (a) BP (b) NEG; 100–1 BP; 102 TQ/DJ; 103 NEG; 104–5 TQ; 106 KE; 108–10 TQ; 111 (a) TQ (b) DIR; 112 SA; 113 (a/c) KE (b) TQ; 114 BP; 115 (a/c) KE (b) TQ; 116–17 KE; 118 (a) TQ (b) KE; 119 KE; 120–2 TQ; 123 BP; 124 (a) MT (b) DWL (c) KE; 125 AN; 126 FP/WFT; 127 (a) UE (b) SA; 128 (a) CV (b) BP; 129 FP/AWC; 130 (a/c) FP/AWC (b) AN; 131 (a) GU (b) FP/AWC; 132–8 TQ; 139 (a) BP (b) TQ; 140–1 BP; 143 (a) BP (b) OO; 145 LT/JS; 147 AS; 148 (a) EAP (b) AUS/SL; 149 LT/JLO; 150 BB; 151 (a) BB (b) AUS/SDM; 152 (a) LT/BD (b) AUS/LAN; 153 BJ; 154 (a) BJ (b) CW/FAP; 156 OOST; 157 LT/JLO; 158 AUS/DZP; 159–61 LT/JLO; 162 MM; 164 EAP/JB; 165–7 MM; 168 SS; 169 QS/RS; 170 OCS; 171 NRR; 172 KQ; 173 UT; 174 (a) FB (b) KQ; 175 (a) APT (b) KQ; 176 (a) BP (b) KCL; 177 LT/ML; 178–9 FB; 180–1, 183 BP; 184–7 TV; 189 BP; 190 AG; 191 TV; 192 (a/c) BP (b) EAP/JB; 193 BP; 195 ME; 196 (a/b) EAP/GL (c) BP; 198 AW; 199 (a) TV (b/c) JL (d) BP; 200 (a) TV (b) BP; 201–2 BP; 203 (a) AR (b) BP; 204 (a) BP (b) JM; 205–6 TV; 207 (a) AG (b) OF/NM (c) TB/JD; 208 (a) TV (b) PV; 209 TV; 210 (a/c) TV (b) PV; 211 TV; 212 (a) PV (b) JM; 213 TV; 214 AW; 215 EAP/JK; 216 TV/DMR; 217 AEL; 218 TV; 219 BP; 220–1, 223 BP; 224 SATC; 225 BP; 226–7 SATC; 228 BP; 230 (a) SATC (b) KE; 231–3 SATC; 234 HH; 235 SATC; 236 BP; 237 SATC; 238 BP; 239–42 SATC; 243 BP; 244 SOL; 246 (a) SATC (b) BP; 247 KE; 248 SATC; 250 (a) TEC (b) AL/MA; 251–2 SATC; 253 WOC; 254 AG; 255 (a) SATC (b) AUS/WIC; 256–7 ©iStockphoto.com/abzee; 258 KE; 260 AUS/DHG; 261 (a) AUS/GEL (b) KE (c) ICT/CC; 262 TIC; 263 AUS/OSF–KG-H/; 264 (a) HBR (b) KE; 265 KE; 266 TT; 267 (a) KE (b/c) AG; 268 KE; 269 BIC; 270 (a) EAP/NR (b) AUS/WIC; 271–2 PT; 273 KE; 274 (a) AUS/JFH (b) AUS/JLE (c) AT; 275 PT; 276 AUS/JFH; 277 (a) AG (b) AUS/PPC; 278 AUS/KAT; 279 Courtesy of Voyages Hotels & Resorts; 280 (a/c) AT (b) AG; 281 GD; 283 (a) KE (b) AG (c) AS; 284–5 AS; 286 AG; 287 (a/c) AUS/RW (b) AUS/MS; 288–9 ©iStockphoto.com/Tammy616; 291 CA; 292 AG; 293 AUS/SDM; 294 BP; 295 (a) AUS/SND (b) BP (c) AUS/GRB; 296 (a/c) AUS/JPF (b) AUS/GUL; 297–8 AG; 299 CA; 300–1 KE